Bastards *and* Foundlings

Bastards and Foundlings

Illegitimacy in Eighteenth-Century England

Lisa Zunshine

THE OHIO STATE UNIVERSITY PRESS
Columbus

Copyright © 2005 by The Ohio State University.
All rights reserved.

Library of Congress Cataloging-in-Publication Data

Zunshine, Lisa.
Bastards and foundlings : illegitimacy in eighteenth-century England / Lisa Zunshine.
    p. cm.
Includes bibliographical references and index.
ISBN 0–8142–0995–5 (alk. paper)—ISBN 0–8142–9073–6 (cd-rom) 1. English literature—18th century—History and criticism. 2. Illegitimacy in literature. 3. Illegitimate children—Great Britain—History—18th century. 4. Illegitimacy—Great Britain—History—18th century. 5. Illegitimate children in literature. 6. Parent and child in literature. 7. Foundlings in literature. 8. Adultery in literature. I. Title.
PR448.I49Z86 2005
820.9'3552—dc22
                    2004026571

Paper (ISBN: 978-0-8142-5455-4)
Cover design by Dan O'Dair.
Text design by Jennifer Forsythe.
Type set in Baskerville.

The paper used in this publication meets the minimum requirements of the American National Standard for Information Sciences—Permanence of Paper for Printed Library Materials. ANSI Z39.48-1992.

9 8 7 6 5 4 3 2

—Bon jour!—good-mororow!—so you have got your cloak on betimes—but 'tis a cold morning, and you judge the matter rightly—'tis better to be well mounted, than go o'foot—and obstructions in the glands are dangerous—And how goes it with thy concubine—thy wife—and thy little ones o'both sides?

—Laurence Sterne,
The Life and Opinions of Tristam Shandy, Gentleman, 1759–1767

Contents

List of Illustrations		ix
Acknowledgments		xi
INTRODUCTION	Cultural Narratives of Illegitimacy	1
CHAPTER 1	Bastard Daughters and Foundling Heroines: *Rewriting Illegitimacy in* The Conscious Lovers	23
CHAPTER 2	Moll Flanders *and the English "Shelter for Bastards"*	40
CHAPTER 3	Kicking Out the Cubs: *The Wrong Heirs in Richardson's* Clarissa	64
CHAPTER 4	Tom Jones: *Resisting the Mythologization of Bastardy*	86
CHAPTER 5	Female Philanthropy, the London Foundling Hospital, and Richardson's *The History of Sir Charles Grandison*	101
CHAPTER 6	The Children "Owned By None": *Divided Bastardy in Frances Burney's* Evelina	127
CHAPTER 7	Harriet Smith in Brunswick Square: *"Common Sense" Bastardy in Austen's* Emma	152
POSTSCRIPT	BBC Rewrites Tom Jones's Illegitimacy	169
Notes		173
Bibliography		200
Index		219

Illustrations

FIGURE 1
    Study for the Foundlings by William Hogarth (1697–1764); pen, ink, and wash; 4³⁄₈ by 8³⁄₈ in. (11.1 by 21.3 cm). Reproduced with permission of the Yale Center for British Art, Paul Mellon Collection.   44

FIGURE 2
    CF 1852 *March of the Guards to Finchley.* 1750 by William Hogarth (1697–1764). Coram Foundation. Foundling Museum. London. UK/Bridgeman Art Library.   102

FIGURE 3
    CF 71802 *The Finding of the Infant Moses in the Bullrushes.* 1746 (oil on canvas) by Francis Hayman (1708–1776). Coram Foundation. Foundling Museum. London. UK/Bridgeman Art Library.   107

Acknowledgments

For their patient reading of different versions of the manuscript and most valuable suggestions, I am deeply grateful to the late Everett Zimmerman, to Elizabeth Heckendorn Cook, Robert A. Erickson, Anita Guerrini, Christopher Hair, Robert Markley, Judith Prats, Judith Schiffbauer, Kristina Straub, and William B. Warner. The NEH Summer Stipend FT-46616-02 and generous travel and research grants by the College of Arts and Sciences at the University of Kentucky, Lexington, made the revision process possible and enjoyable. The readers commissioned by The Ohio State University Press offered crucial feedback; the Press's director, Malcolm Litchfield, the acquisitions editor, Heather Lee Miller, and the copyeditor, Maggie Diehl, deserve the highest praise for their professionalism.

Chapter 5 of this study appeared in *Writing English Infanticide: Child-Murder, Gender, and Print, 1722–1859*, ed. Jennifer Thorn (The University of Delaware Press, 2003); parts of the introduction and chapter 1 appeared in *Modern Philology* 102:4. I wish to thank Jennifer Thorn and the editorial boards of The University of Delaware Press and *Modern Philology* for their permissions to reprint these materials here. I am also grateful to the Yale Center for British Art, Paul Mellon Collection, for their permission to reproduce William Hogarth's *Study for the Foundlings*, and to Coram Foundation, Foundling Museum, London, and UK/Bridgeman Art Library for their permission to reprint Hogarth's *March of the Guards to Finchley* and Francis Hayman's *The Finding of the Infant Moses in the Bullrushes*. Finally, I want to thank the College of Arts and Sciences at the University of Kentucky, Lexington, whose timely and generous financial support has made the reproduction of these illustrations possible.

Introduction

CULTURAL NARRATIVES OF ILLEGITIMACY

Demographers and historians refer to the eighteenth century as the "century of illegitimacy,"[1] pointing out that "in every city in England and the continent for which data are available, the upsurge of illegitimacy commenced around 1750 or before."[2] While they offer a variety of reasons to explain this increase, which remains "unprecedented in the known history of the British population,"[3] they all agree that this phenomenon must have touched everyone who lived at that time and played a crucial role in the economic, social, and cultural life of the Enlightenment.

But if so many families had to deal with the presence of illegitimate daughters, sons, sisters, brothers, and stepchildren, how did it influence the fictional stories that these families wanted, or pointedly did *not* want, to read? When contemporary writers portrayed bastard children and their parents—or when they carefully edited direct references to bastardy out of their narratives—whose perspective did they espouse, and why? And can we say that the fictional reimaginings of the social practices surrounding illegitimacy had any effect on these practices? For example, did the endless succession of plays and novels featuring lost and found children—the "foundlings"—impact the period's view of the real-life foundlings, that is, the illegitimate children of serving women liable to be abandoned or even murdered by their mothers? Or, turning to another representational tradition, did the stories portraying sympathetically the "little ones o'both sides" (to adopt Laurence Sterne's euphemistic phrasing) contribute to the gradual erosion of the official view of the bastard as a social and economic pariah?

To begin to answer these questions, this study brings together research from several different disciplines, such as law, history, and cultural and literary studies. It pits the official legal views on illegitimacy against the actual everyday practices that frequently circumvented the law. It reconstructs the history of social institutions called upon to regulate illegitimacy, such as the London Foundling Hospital, and it examines a series of foundling narratives written, arguably, in response to the same concerns that underlay the emergence and functioning of such institutions. And throughout, it emphasizes the multiplicity of cultural meanings of bastardy, striving to redefine the "century of illegitimacy" as the "century of illegitimac*ies*."

Eighteenth-Century Bastardy: Definition and Categories

What constituted the eighteenth-century category of bastard? The official view can be summed up by referencing two contemporary authorities. Samuel Johnson's *Dictionary of the English Language* viewed a bastard as a child "begotten out of wedlock"; William Blackstone's *Commentaries on the Laws of England* asserted that an illegitimate child could "inherit nothing, being looked upon as the son of nobody . . . incapable even of a gift from [his] parents" (I:434). In practice, Johnson's and Blackstone's definitions were belied by the bewildering variety of legal and informal unions comprising the fabric of eighteenth-century family life[4] as well as by the broad range of attitudes toward bastard children held by people belonging to different social classes and geographic regions. To begin to make sense of this multitude of perspectives, I have grouped the eighteenth-century views of bastardy into the four categories, with a brief note on the relative prominence of each category in the works of fiction:

❖ The bastard could be viewed as the threatening pretender to the legal family's property, bearing out William Wycherley's 1676 observation that even though there is a "Law . . . against Bastards, . . . the Custom is against it, and more people get estates by being so, that lose 'em."[5] In 1735, the *Universal Spectator* published an anguished letter from an illegitimate man who complained that his "liberal education," charity, and good principles notwithstanding, his relatives viewed him as a pariah, and particularly those on his father's side considered him as "a Robber who . . . unjustly deprived them of a small Estate [his father] settled upon [him]."[6] Although the relationship between the legitimate and illegitimate siblings could

Cultural Narratives of Illegitimacy

develop in many different directions, not always following the trajectory of enmity, the middle-class perspective on a bastard frequently centered on his capacity to disrupt the smooth transfer of property and to poison the emotional well-being of the legal family. Even though I am generally reluctant to use the word *middle-class* as an umbrella term for the complex internal hierarchies of that elusive and much debated social entity, the term is quite useful for the discussion of illegitimacy because it denotes the middle ground between the extreme "haves" and "have-nots" of the English population. Moreover, the overwhelming majority of eighteenth-century fictional bastards either came from this sprawling social stratum, or, importantly, *expressed its views*. That is, a character could be presented as a daughter of a baronet, but her own and her family's perspective of her (presumable) bastardy would unmistakably reflect the concerns of middle-class readers, whose experience of illegitimacy was very different from that of aristocracy (as discussed in detail in the chapter on Burney's *Evelina*).

❖ Illegitimacy had no discernible economic consequences and carried relatively little social stigma for children born to common-law unions among the rural poor of the south and east, especially toward the end of the century.[7] The incidence of such unions increased in times of high prices of food and housing and resulted in a variety of domestic living arrangements. The offspring of common-law marriages were still recorded in parish registers as "bastards," but because their parents "had no inheritance to pass on"[8] and expected the children to enter the labor market as early as possible, their illegitimate status did not put them at any manifest disadvantage compared to the children born to officially married couples.[9] The practice of cohabitation among agricultural laborers thus effectively demystified the cultural category of "bastard" by demonstrating vividly its dependence on the presence or absence of heritable property. Not surprisingly, there is hardly a mention of this particular type of bastard in the period's fiction.

❖ The upper-class attitude toward illegitimacy was also tolerant because, as Ruth McClure has argued, aristocrats were protected by their "great wealth" from any "economic threat, including that posed by bastards."[10] If the father and the mother both belonged to nobility, their illegitimate offspring could marry well and (if male) could be advanced to high office.[11] We learn from John Habakkuk that where "the father had legitimate issue, even if it was only female, illegitimate children posed no problem for the succession to the family estate. They were, however, sometimes generously treated, as a sort of younger children."[12] So when a "virtuous and brave fellow" from Fielding's *Jonathan Wild* (1743) complains that after serving for twenty-five years as "the eldest lieutenant [of] the ship," he was not able to obtain a ship of his own, all the while seeing "several boys, the *bastards of noblemen*, put over his head" (185; emphasis added), we may remember the fate of the illegitimate son of the tenth Earl of Pembroke, who was "brought up in the family and in due course became an admiral."[13] Similarly, Habakkuk tells us that "one of the illegitimate daughters of Sir Edward Walpole married successively the second Earl of Waldergrave and the Duke of Gloucester. It was when a landowner had illegitimate male issue and no other children that a problem arose of succession to the estates, as it did in the families of the Duke of Bolton, the Earl of Nottingham, and the last Sheffield Duke of Buckingham."[14] Although occasionally referred to in eighteenth-century fiction, well-to-do aristocratic bastards did not figure prominently in it. With its relative lack of conflict, the upper-class legitimacy had as little dramatic potential for writers as did the everyday illegitimacy among rural laborers.

❖   Illegitimate children of unwed serving women abandoned by their sexual partners (who, as Randolph Trumbach has persuasively demonstrated, mostly came from the same social stratum[15]) fared worst of all. Their mothers were known to attempt to conceal their pregnancies and get rid of their infants to avoid shame, the certain loss of employment (prostitution was often the only remaining option), and, frequently, punishment for burdening their parishes with fatherless charges. Those able to afford a nominal fee could turn to wet nurses, grimly nicknamed "killer-nurses,"[16] who were willing to quietly starve bastard infants left in their custody. (The cost of a nurse who would really take care of the child was "often equivalent to the [woman's] entire annual wage"[17]). Writing in 1727, Tomas Coram, one of the champions of the English infanticide prevention campaign, complained about the "daily sight of infant corpses thrown on the dust heaps of London."[18] He was seconded by Thomas Bray, who compared the illegitimate victims of infanticide to "Warts and Wens, and other filthy Excrescencies . . . defacing and weakening . . . the Body Politic" (16), and Bernard Mandeville, who observed that the abandonment of illegitimate children by their indigent mothers was an outrage that should not be tolerated by a "civiliz'd Nation" (65). Established in 1739, the London Foundling Hospital explicitly targeted female servants who had no means of supporting illegitimate children on their own and thus could be prevented from committing the crime of child-murder and reclaimed to virtue only through the opportune intervention of a public charity. Serving-class bastardy was routinely depicted in fiction, frequently (though not exclusively) as a correlative to the middle-class family anxiety about the encroaching illegitimate children of its philandering patriarch.

Students of eighteenth-century literature wishing to understand the role of fiction in the reimagining of bastardy in the Enlightenment may well find themselves doubting the usefulness of the blanket concept of illegitimacy when applied across social classes and geographic regions. Being recorded in the parish register as "bastard" must have meant one thing to an agricultural laborer from Culcheth in South Lancashire, whose cohabiting parents—like the parents of the majority of his peers—could not afford to marry, and quite another to Richard Savage, an ambitious nobody who spent years demanding that the Countess of Macclesfield acknowledge him as her long-lost "natural" son and bestow upon him the proper accoutrements of aristocratic wealth and prestige (she refused). It must have meant yet something else to a young charge of the London Foundling Hospital, whose early awareness of her humble station in life was to be fostered, among other things, through learning by heart and singing during public performances the following hymn:

> Wash off my foul offence,
> And cleanse me from my Sin;
> For I confess my crime, and see
> How great my Guilt has been.
>
> In Guilt each part was form'd
> Of all this sinful frame;
> In Guilt I was conceiv'd and born
> The Heir of Sin and Shame.[19]

But if we accept that eighteenth-century writers lived in a world where the concept of bastardy was anything but monolithic and where the lack of the parents' marriage license hardly established any meaningful common denominator between an illegitimate son of a duke brought up to inherit a portion of his father's estate and an inmate of the Foundling Hospital, we begin to realize that the period's fictional treatment of illegitimacy was fitful and selective. Some experiences of illegitimacy were completely obliterated from the literary discourse; others were rewritten so thoroughly that they have so far remained unrecognized as such by students of eighteenth-century culture; still others were presented as normative or universal, masking the remarkable diversity of personal and cultural readings of the phenomenon of "dishonourable birth."[20]

The project of reconstructing the cultural history of eighteenth-century illegitimacy thus necessarily involves probing textual omissions and strategic silences. This approach is similar to that used by John Boswell, whose seminal study of representations of abandoned children from antiquity to Renaissance was an inspiration for this book. Boswell observed that literature tends to provide "essential information almost in spite of itself—like a witness whose nervousness is more revealing than his testimony—and is a kind of evidence which would rarely if ever occur in purely historical sources."[21] The eighteenth-century fictional treatment of bastardy was increasingly subject to a system of unspoken cultural conventions, bound up with deeply felt familial concerns of readers and writers; to detect those conventions, however, one has to look not only at the texts openly obsessed with bastardy, such as Laurence Sterne's *Tristram Shandy*, Henry Fielding's *Tom Jones*, and Mary Robinson's *The Natural Daughter*, but also at those that testify "in spite of themselves" by either appearing to have nothing to do with illegitimacy, such as Richard Steele's *The Conscious Lovers*, or by treating it only marginally, such as Samuel Richardson's *Clarissa* and *Sir Charles Grandison*.

Male Bastards and Female Foundlings

To understand how some bastards managed to enter the polite discourse while others were barred from it, we need to rediscover the complex literary innuendoes of the eighteenth-century term *foundling*. Although in some contexts this word was used interchangeably with *bastard* (e.g., people could refer to any abandoned child as a foundling, and it was widely, though not always correctly, assumed that *all* abandoned children were born outside of marriage), this was rarely so in fiction. Authors aiming at fostering "good breeding"[22] in their audience were extremely careful about specifying whether the parents of their lost and found protagonists had been married at the time of their conception, and, as it turns out, the overwhelming majority of temporarily displaced children of the Enlightenment's belles lettres were conceived within lawful if ill-starred wedlock, as were, for instance, Indiana from Richard Steele's *The Conscious Lovers,* Fidelia from Edward Moore's *The Foundling,* Amelia from George Colman's *The English Merchant,* Evelina from Frances Burney's eponymous novel, Emmeline from Charlotte Smith's *Emmeline,* Joanna from Thomas Holcroft's *The Deserted Daughter,* Rosa and Elinor from Agnes Maria Bennett's *The Beggar Girl and Her Benefactors,* Virginia from Maria Edgeworth's *Belinda,* Fanny from the anonymous *Fatherless Fanny,* and others. A typical "foundling" would be raised by strangers, leave her adopted family upon reaching marriageable age, go through numerous ordeals (during which she acquired an eligible suitor while retaining her chastity), and finally discover her true kin, reassert her legitimate status, and reestablish herself as part of her biological family.

Though structurally similar to the real-life bastard as an outsider forcefully inserting herself into the family and social order, the fictional foundling differed in important ways from her money- and status-hungry illegitimate counterpart. Her quest was for moral excellence and true identity,[23] and if the revelation of that identity was accompanied by a shower of tears, titles, and estates, this bounty was bestowed by the parent who frequently did not have any other children and was therefore delighted with the reappearance of the long-lost legitimate offspring. One can speak, in other words, about the culturally recognizable literary category of *legally born* foundlings (henceforth referred to simply as "foundlings") carefully conceptualized as having nothing in common with such people as the illegitimate correspondent of the *Universal Spectator,* perceived as a "robber" by his disgruntled legitimate siblings. As I will argue, however, it is precisely the insistence that the fictional foundling represents no threat to the economic and emotional well-being of her biological family that makes such a character embody most trenchantly the eighteenth-century anxiety about illegitimacy.

But once we place the eighteenth-century fictional foundling into a separate cultural category suggestively related to and yet recognizably different from the category of "bastard," we are confronted with *The History of Tom Jones, a Foundling.* The most famous eighteenth-century "foundling" clearly does not fit the paradigm of rediscovered legitimacy. Tom's bastardy alerts us to a curious pattern in the period's literary treatment of children born outside or "almost" outside of wedlock. When eighteenth-century fictional narrative featured an abandoned child, his or her gender served as a largely reliable predictor of whether at the end of the story, he/she would turn out to be a legitimately born foundling or a bastard. Lost male children, such as Tom Jones and Humphrey Clinker, were allowed to stay illegitimate. The majority of their female counterparts, on the other hand, suffered the threat of illegitimacy throughout the story, only to discover at the end that their parents had been married at the time of their conception. If the bastardy of male foundlings could be decried by readers (e.g., Fielding was widely criticized for refusing to "reveal" at the end of his novel that Tom's parents had been secretly married), the bastardy of female foundlings was not even considered a controversial issue: it barely existed.

A closer look reveals that it is not just the fictional *lost and found* children who were coded as legitimate or illegitimate depending on their gender. If the work of eighteenth-century literature featured a pregnant woman who was not married at all or married to a man other than the father of her child, in the majority of cases, her newborn child would turn out to be a boy. Examples include not only Daniel Defoe's Colonel Jack, Fielding's Tom Jones, Tobias Smollett's Humphrey Clinker, and, possibly, Sterne's Tristram Shandy, but also several boys born to Defoe's Moll and Roxana; the son of the younger daughter of Monsieur Douxmourie from Eliza Haywood's *Lasselia;* William Godolphin Jr. from Smith's *Emmeline;* Peregrine Pickle from Smollett's eponymous novel; Mr. Macartney from Burney's *Evelina;* the son of Theodosia Snap from Fielding's *Jonathan Wild;* the sons of Sir Thomas Grandison and Mrs. Oldham from Samuel Richardson's *Sir Charles Grandison;* the sons of "Thomasine" and Tom Belton from *Clarissa;* the son of Lovelace and Miss Betterton; the imaginary twins that Lovelace envisions suckling at Clarissa's breast;[24] the son of Miss Burchell in Frances Sheridan's *The Memoirs of Miss Sidney Bidulph;* the son of Kattie Buhanun and Lord Denningcourt from Bennett's *The Beggar Girl and Her Benefactors;* Mr. Milford from Holcroft's *The Road to Ruin* and the son of Mr. Elford's servant, Mary, from Holcroft's *Hugh Trevor;* Gregory Glen from Robert Bage's *Hermsprong; or, Man As He Is Not;* the son of William and Hannah from Elizabeth Inchbald's *Nature and Art;* Frederick, the son of Baron Wildenhaim and Agatha Friburg from August von Kotzebue's *Love Child,* known to the English audiences as *Lovers' Vows,* adapted by Inchbald (and *almost* performed at Mansfield Park); the anonymous victim of infanticide from Mary Hays's *Memoirs* of *Emma Courtney;* two anonymous boys from Amelia Opie's *Adeline Mowbray;* and many others.

This list may seem overlong, but its length underscores the casual ubiquity of male bastards in the works of fiction. The comparable list of female bastards would be much shorter, including the daughter of Mr. B and Sally Godfrey from Richardson's *Pamela,* a daughter of Mr. Bilson from Sarah Fielding's *The History of the Countess of Dellwyn,* the daughters of Solomon Mushroom from Bennett's *The Beggar Girl and Her Benefactors,* Louisa from Haywood's *The Fortunate Foundlings,* and Eliza and Harriet from Austen's *Sense and Sensibility* and *Emma,* respectively. In other words, the eighteenth-century tendency to allow fictional male foundlings—but not their female counterparts—to remain illegitimate seems to be part of a larger literary tradition of conceptualizing bastardy as a fate reserved predominantly for male characters.

John Shebbeare's *The Marriage Act* (1754) is paradigmatic in this respect. A veritable catalogue of illicit couplings, it was written to condemn Lord Hardwicke's 1753 "An Act for the Better Preventing of Clandestine Marriages" (26 George II, c.33), which introduced mandatory parental consent for marriages of children under the age of twenty-one.[25] The new bill was aimed at deterring penniless opportunists of both sexes from eloping with underage heirs and heiresses by postulating that a priest who weds such a couple without parental permission would be tried and transported, and that the children born to this faux marriage would be considered illegitimate. Those objecting to the Act pointed out that it would serve mainly the interests of aristocrats who could further consolidate their power by arranging marriages within their own class or with the richest segment of population, that it would force young people into marriages of convenience aimed at pleasing their avaricious parents rather than at following their own hearts, and that it would enable unscrupulous men to seduce and abandon naive young women after having allegedly "married" them. Shebbeare's novel is a passionate two-volume harangue against the Act, which "has given designing people the power of . . . bastardizing whole families to their utter destruction" (2:181). The author presents one fictional case study after another in which a daughter perishes after being married off to a man chosen by her greedy parents or is ruined by a rake who tricks her into a secret marriage not considered legal under the new law. The novel fleshed out a widely held prediction that the bill would dramatically increase the incidence of bastardy, a prediction that apparently never materialized because although bastardy rates continued to rise, historians do not see it as a consequence of the Marriage Act.[26] Also, significantly for the present argument, Shebbeare's concept of illegitimacy is unequivocally gendered.

Thus when one of the least sympathetic victims of the new law, Lady Sapplin, runs off to Paris with her lover, leaving behind her aristocratic husband whom she married on the instigation of her nouveau riche parents hankering after a title, she is treated to the following explanation of how extramarital affairs are looked upon in France: "There is so much suspicion in all husbands that the children are not their own, [one] seldom [sees] any tenderness between the father and son; the first finding no inclination for a child which he suspects is not of his begetting, and the child having but little reverence for a man who very probably is not his father" (2:154).[27] Note the automatic assumption of the gender of the child born to an adulterous French mother, France functioning here and throughout the novel as a sad example that England, newly wrecked by Lord Hardwicke's Act, is sure to follow soon. Meanwhile, back in England, all bastard children born as a consequence of the Act are also male, as is the son of Lady Sapplin and her hairdresser, Mr. Samuel Waitwell; the son of Lord Sapplin and Lucy Shelton; the son of Miss Standish and Mr. Wright; and the son of Mrs. Lulworth and Mr. Thomas. The uniform gendering of these "true" bastards appears even more striking when we hear the story of one Mr. Sterlin and his three legitimate children, who are retroactively bastardized after the death of their parents by their evil uncle, who wishes to steal their estate and is abetted in his criminal designs by the new law. One of these three children is a girl, "called Patty after her [late] Mamma" (2:222), who was a paragon of virtue and elegance. The little Patty's gender thus underscores the profound falsity of the uncle's insinuations that these children are "all bastards" and as such "don't inherit any estates," and it reinforces the unspoken convention rendering a bastard heroine a conceptual monstrosity (2:225).

Further eloquent testimony to the force of this convention comes from a novel that all but advertised itself as the story of the female bastard: Mary Robinson's *The Natural Daughter* (1799). Midway into the narrative, we learn that its *nominal* title character, the little Fanny, was conceived in circumstances that drastically palliate her illegitimacy (I emphasize the word nominal because Robinson cultivates her readers' confusion about who exactly the "natural daughter" of the title is). Traveling through revolutionary France, an English gentlewoman is arrested on the orders of Marat and thrown in prison. She is told that an English gentleman of her acquaintance can procure her freedom if she agrees to marry him. Faced with the imminent execution, she accepts his offer only to learn, after the marriage is consummated, that her new husband (who swiftly departs for England) deceived her and that the "pretended priest who . . . united [them] was nothing more than the *valet de chambre* of the infamous Marat" (166). When she does manage to escape the French reign of terror and return to her native country, she first abandons the newborn Fanny but then recovers her and retires to rural Switzerland to raise her. The rhetoric describing the marital status of the woman who sincerely believes herself to be married at the time when her child is conceived is purposively ambiguous. On the one hand, Robinson gets much ideological mileage from condemning heartless self-righteous people who censure unwed but virtuous motherhood. On the other hand, rendering the issue of Fanny's bastardy and her parents' unwed state moot, her mother is characterized as "*married* and deserted," and mourning "the falsehood of an ungrateful *husband*" (282; emphasis added).

Moreover, Robinson's readers cannot help applying the novel's title not just to Fanny, a secondary character, but also to its main protagonist, the unquestionably legitimate Martha Morley. Martha's kindness and attention to her family members render her the true—that is, "natural"—daughter, as opposed to her clearly "unnatural" sister, spoiled, sensual, and deceitful Julia, whose acts of selfishness include ostracizing the upright and suffering Martha and locking her own mother in a madhouse. Robinson's editor, Sharon Setzer, sees the contrast between Martha and Julia as complicating "the easy equation between 'natural' and 'illegitimate.'"[28] One effect of such complication is further attenuation of our perception of Fanny as bastard and thus "the" natural child of the novel.

Predictably, the indisputably illegitimate child figuring in *The Natural Daughter* is a boy, the infant son of the hypocritical Mr. Morley and Julia, who augments "her catalogue of crimes" (281) by neglecting and destroying her newborn. Robinson's fancy footwork around the issue of female but not male illegitimacy—the story of Fanny's "revolutionary" conception presents a striking contrast to the chronicle of shameless fornication leading to the birth of the male bastard—is particularly remarkable given what we know about the possible origins of her novel. Setzer considers the earlier critical tradition of tracing *The Natural Daughter* to Robinson's plan to write "a fictional expose of Susan Priscilla Bertie, the natural daughter of the Duke of Ancaster and the recent bride" of Robinson's lover, Banastre Tarleton, and she counters it with a different explanation, pointing to Robinson's "sympathetic identification with women like Mary Wollstonecraft, the mother of another illegitimate Frances conceived in revolutionary France."[29] That the textual genesis of *The Natural Daughter* can be traced not to just one but two different female bastards makes even more poignant the novel's endeavor to represent Fanny as not *really* illegitimate or, in any case, *less* illegitimate than her male counterpart.

How far back can we trace the literary genealogy of the eighteenth-century correlation of legitimacy with gender? In her study of illegitimacy in Renaissance drama, Alison Findlay observes that the overwhelming majority of the period's fictional bastards were male. To explain such demographic uniformity, she suggests that female bastardy simply did not present the playwright with much dramatic potential: "legal illegitimacy affected one's rights to inheritance, succession, and the exercise of authority, advantages usually enjoyed by men. [As] under patriarchal law, women were normally excluded from the inheritance of estate, position, or power . . . bastardy merely reinforced their already marginal status."[30] Since Findlay does not make a distinction between foundlings and bastards, referring to *all* abandoned children as bastards, she does not acknowledge that in the rare cases in which Renaissance writers *did* portray abandoned female children (e.g., Shakespeare's Perdita and Marina), they were born to married parents. The legitimate status of such heroines makes a crucial difference, however, for the present argument because the figure of the abandoned female child, relatively rare in Renaissance drama, becomes so omnipresent in eighteenth-century belles lettres.

The sharp increase in the general number of female protagonists in the fiction of the Enlightenment is a well-discussed phenomenon in eighteenth-century studies. So it would be only logical to suggest that the Enlightenment's tendency to use a woman as the "vehicle for testing the possibilities of an individualist ethic"[31] manifested itself in the growing numbers of female foundlings. We can argue, furthermore, that whereas *both* Renaissance and eighteenth-century writers were extremely reluctant to leave their foundling heroines illegitimate, the shifting gender ratio of the protagonists in the latter period finally allows us to recognize the obligatory legitimacy of the female foundling as a significant literary phenomenon.

To take this argument further, one may suggest that the tendency to monitor the legitimacy of the female protagonist more vigilantly than that of her male counterpart could be traced to the novel of antiquity (e.g., Heliodorus is careful to show that his Charicleia was born within a legal union) and to the Old Testament precept that prohibited priests from marrying women whose mothers had been born out of wedlock. If we consider that a patriarchal culture would tend to seize on any correlation that seems to render female sexual behavior less threateningly unpredictable to the surrounding males, the tradition of predicting the young woman's sexual virtue through the known chastity of her female ancestor(s), could account, at least in part, for the vitality of the literary trope of the *legitimate* female protagonist, including the female foundling.

Readers thus must not have been too surprised to learn that the illegitimate daughters of Sir Solomon Mushroom from Bennett's *The Beggar Girl and Her Benefactors* (1797), though brought up as heiresses of a rich Member of Parliament with no knowledge of their bastardy, still possess "innate vulgarity" (4:28), which renders their style of clothing a "satire on decency" (4:2) and their conduct lacking in either "sense [or] principles" (4:37). Predictably, these fruits of cohabitation later distinguish themselves by their own sexual misdemeanors: the elder cheats her husband with the uncouth Jacob Lowder; the younger sleeps with her fiancé before marriage and impudently defends her actions with a speech that glibly mixes the rhetoric of "honour" and "keeping" (the term often used to refer to the practice of keeping mistresses): "Lord Delworth and I have been as good as man and wife ever since I have been in the country.... My honour and my heart are in my own keeping; I have pledged the one, and yielded the other, [and] I shall keep to my engagement" (5:236–37). To emphasize that whereas the sisters' vulgarity could be explained by the modest origins of their parents, their lack of chastity is the direct consequence of their illegitimacy, Bennett contrasts their behavior with that of Elinor Bawsky, one of the novel's numerous foundlings. The legitimate child of a serving-class couple, Elinor is mistakenly thought to be the daughter of a countess and taken into her presumed mother's mansion, from which she later elopes with the low-born Jackie Croak. Whereas her embarrassing infatuation with Jackie, who at one point hires himself out as a footman, betrays her own inconspicuous origins, her legitimacy guarantees that she will not "yield" her "heart" in the manner of Charlotte Mushroom before officially marrying her "dearest love" (5:203). In other words, blood (class) will out, but *female* bastardy will out even surer.

But, apart from the old literary convention of "guaranteeing" the chastity of fictional heroines via the chastity of their mothers, can the requisite legitimacy of the female protagonist be traced to certain real-life social practices? Did female bastards indeed fare worse in the eighteenth-century marriage market than their male counterparts? I have found no consistent evidence of such discrimination and have to conclude that the money and social connections, or lack thereof, of the bastard typically trumped the consideration of gender. In the cases where bastardy of a prospective bride had indeed been used as a pretext for rejecting her, financial problems had also been conspicuously present. Thus, as I show in the next chapter, the lack of adequate funds might have played a key role in the rejection of Steele's own natural daughter by Richard Savage, even though her illegitimacy was used as an excuse (illegitimacy, one should add, that did not prevent her from soon marrying another man, and one who must have made a much better husband than the unstable Savage ever could). In other words, the emphasis on the legitimacy of the fictional female protagonist emerges as a complex compensatory fantasy that responded to a gamut of readers' personal anxieties, ranging from the desire to control and predict young women's reproductive behavior to the acute awareness of the particularly weak bargaining position of that female bastard who could command no financial and social support from her family.

Resisting Symbolism: Property, Social Personality, and the Foundling Narrative

As a persistent feature of the eighteenth-century literary endeavor, the foundling motif has generated a fair share of critical discussions in the last thirty years. These discussions, however, focus primarily on the rich symbolic potential of the foundling trope and, to a lesser degree, on its indebtedness to the literature of antiquity, and as such they do not require any principled differentiation between bastards and legitimately born foundlings. The bastard, the foundling, and the orphan all merge into one fuzzy category, and it is the fascinating literary genealogy of such a character, on the one hand, and her titillatingly fluid kin and class affiliation, on the other, that pique scholars' interest.

A paradigmatic example of the "genealogical" perspective is Margaret Anne Doody's analysis of the relationship between the eighteenth-century foundling and the protagonist of such ancient novels as Heliodorus's *An Ethiopian Romance* (c. 250–380 A.D.). Drawing in particular on the striking similarities between the journeys of self-discovery of Heliodorus's Charicleia and Burney's Evelina, Doody develops her argument about the "community of literature," that is, the strong tradition of continuity between the ancient romance and the early modern novel.[32]

Using a different approach, scholars such as Lynn Hunt and Michael McKeon explore the ontological uncertainty central to the image of the foundling, which renders her a fit symbol of broader social changes. Commenting on the popularity of representations of abandoned children around the time of the French Revolution, Hunt demonstrates that such representations were co-opted to serve a wide variety of political agendas; what remained invariable, however (and connected the French foundling novel to its English counterpart), was the tendency to use the figure of a seemingly free-floating child as a symbol of the "shifting world." McKeon sees the eighteenth-century fictional bastard as a hero used to convey an "implicit criticism of aristocratic ideology . . . within the context of progressive ideology."[33] Illegitimate characters, in this view, are representative of the larger class of "progressive protagonists who possess 'true' as distinct from inherited, gentility, especially in narratives that progressively insist . . . that their heroes are capable 'of acquiring Honour' even in the total absence of ancestry."[34] It is significant that neither Hunt nor McKeon differentiates explicitly between fictional bastards and foundlings. Hunt, in fact, refers instead to a broad category of "children . . . almost always without fathers . . . illegitimate, foundlings, orphans, or . . . virtually so."[35] The illegitimacy of characters thus matters only so far as it frees them from an allegiance to a specific family or social class and allows them to embody the promise of expanded social and economic possibilities of the Age of Enlightenment.

Two recent rearticulations of this view are offered by Wolfram Schmidgen and Ala A. Alryyes. Schmidgen argues that as "a creature of the threshold," existing "both inside and outside society," the bastard can "cross hierarchical divisions and . . . enact a radicalized social mobility," even though his or her mobility remains compromised: "curiously disembodied, simultaneously traversing and leaving inviolate the boundaries of an uneven social space."[36] Note that in his compelling analysis of the illegitimate protagonist's "placelessness,"[37] Schmidgen does not differentiate between bastards and foundlings either, calling both Fidelia from Moore's *The Foundling* and Evelina from Burney's eponymous novel "bastards,"[38] even though both Moore and Burney went to some lengths to present their heroines as *legitimate* foundlings.

Alryyes takes as his starting point Lauren Berlant's "theory of infantile citizenship," with its focus on "a young person" as a "*stand-in* for a complicated and contradictory set of anxieties about national

INTRODUCTION

identity,"[39] to argue that the "sufferings of the homeless child" become "a central element in nationalist narratives" of eighteenth-century England.[40] Alryyes does touch on the differences in the status of children who "leave home, such as Robinson Crusoe, or children who have no homes, such as the *bastard* Colonel Jacque, the *kidnapped* Captain Singleton, or the *abandoned* Moll Flanders."[41] On the whole, however, his study is dedicated to investigating the possible "nationalist" meaning of the fictional protagonists' "natural" or self-imposed *orphan* state, and as such is not invested in differentiating between legitimate and illegitimate characters. Tellingly, he observes that "central" as "the *orphan's* story" has been to the nineteenth-century British novel, its origins can be found in *Tom Jones,* for "like the *orphans* of the nineteenth-century novel, Fielding's foundling's loose parentage allows him a freedom not granted the other child heroes."[42]

Among the scholars who did comment on the difference between bastards and foundlings, Marthe Robert and Christine van Boheemen offer a Freudian interpretation of this difference that pointedly transcends specific historical circumstances. Having argued that the classical romance was at times instantiated as a story of the murderous Bastard—thus reflecting the complex Freudian dynamics of the child's fantasy about his family—Robert has read the "bastardy" of such a protagonist as a reflection of his dark impulses rather than his actual illegitimacy. Consequently, she refers to Oedipus, who was actually legitimate, as a "Bastard . . . never done with killing his father in order to take his place, imitate him or surpass him."[43] Similarly, van Boheemen locates the bastardy of Tom Jones in the context of "Lacan's revision of Freudian psychoanalysis," suggesting that Tom's illegitimacy transforms the search for an "actual father . . . into the quest for the name-of-the-father, for a symbol in language representing the law of patriarchal transmission of power, property, and identity."[44]

The explorations of the symbolic potential of the foundling figure as well as of the "genetic inheritance" of the eighteenth-century foundling narrative constitute an important background for this study, even though my approach differs significantly from those outlined above. I assume that illegitimacy profoundly impacted the production and the reception of the eighteenth-century foundling narrative.[45] Moreover, I consider the British Enlightenment as invested in downplaying a connection between its fictional foundlings and its real-life bastards, an investment that still haunts eighteenth-century studies today as scholars continue to treat their period's obsession with the foundling motif as separate from the vexed issue of illegitimacy.

Cultural Narratives of Illegitimacy

Although it may not always be possible or even necessary to resist a symbolic interpretation of eighteenth-century foundling stories, we ought to remember that for the readers of that time any possible symbolic meaning of such stories was impacted by their everyday dealing with practical repercussions of illegitimacy.

The claim that a personal involvement with the issue of illegitimacy affected both the authors and the readers of the eighteenth-century foundling narrative can be easily interpreted as an invitation to inquire into the private circumstances of the authors of foundling fictions. This approach is neither new (Richardson, after all, insisted that Tom Jones was "made a natural child" because Fielding's first wife, Charlotte Cradock, "was such") nor, by itself, particularly illuminating. The acknowledgment that the writer could indeed use the foundling motif with all its traditional classical trappings to express in a sublimated form his worries about the fate of his own bastard child is simply a first step in historicizing the eighteenth-century foundling narrative. The next step is to ask what factors set eighteenth-century England apart from other societies practicing illegitimacy,[46] thus lending a recognizable common meaning to the various fictional expressions of private anxieties about "natural" children. One crucial factor to consider here is the eighteenth-century view of property as the catalyst of social personality.

The notion that property functions as "both an extension and a prerequisite of personality" and that "different modes of property [generate] different modes of personality"[47] constituted an important tenet of Western tradition inherited by the English Enlightenment. Whereas the seminal study that follows the crisis of this view in late seventeenth- and eighteenth-century England, J. G. A. Pocock's *Virtue, Commerce, and History*, is *not* concerned with the epistemologies of illegitimacy, it provides a useful starting point for our discussion of eighteenth-century representations of bastardy. Pocock posits the "fascinating and elusive relationship between the notions of right and ownership, and . . . that world of language in which 'property'—that which you owned—and 'propriety'—that which pertained or was proper to a person or situation—were interchangeable terms."[48] The evolution of the early modern views of bastardy could then be understood within the context of the broader crisis of the ideological system engendered by the old feudal mode of production, according to which property and propriety were indeed interchangeable terms.

Thus, as long as the heritable, preferably landed, property remained the only source of livelihood and a guarantee of what Pocock calls the "moral personality . . . and the opportunity of virtue,"[49] the illegitimate offspring could be viewed as "improper" because "unpropertied"—that is, threatening, socially subversive, and amoral. Hence the emphasis was on representing illegitimate characters as outsiders in the Renaissance. Bastards figured largely in sixteenth- and seventeenth-century literature, mostly as villains associated with treachery, promiscuity, atheism, disintegration of community, and death (e.g., Shakespeare's Edmund, Caliban, and Don John; John Kirke's Suckabus; Gervase Markham and William Sampson's Antipater), or—in rare cases—as benevolent if zany aliens, often endowed with a poetic or prophetic gift (e.g., Springlove from Richard Brome's 1641 *A Jovial Crew*). Sometimes historical figures were retroactively bastardized in order to provide a psychosocial legitimation for inauspicious turns in a community's political past. The 1591 anonymous *The Life and Death of Jack Straw*, for example, depicted the peasant revolt of 1381, headed by a character whose bastardy was invented by the author of the play. The 1607 anonymous *Claudius Tiberius Nero* featured an emperor whose illegitimacy was also an invention, a fitting symbol of the "illegitimate nature" of his political regime.[50]

Pocock argues that England's financial revolution of the 1690s strengthened the developing moral opposition between the "landed interests" and "monied interests" and thus precipitated a crisis in the traditional association of landed property with propriety: "property moved from being the object of ownership and right to being the subject of production and exchange, and . . . the effect of this on the proposition that property was the basis of social personality was to make personality itself explicable in terms of a material and historical process of diversification, refinement and perhaps ultimate decay and renewal."[51] The challenge of defining—and accepting—social personality in relation to *volatile* property demanded a new conceptual flexibility and could allow, among other things, for a more "enlightened" perspective on the social position of bastards, whose relationship to property had been paradigmatically troubling.

The relationship between the socioeconomic history of England and the cultural view of bastards could be thus described as follows: The further along we are in the "long, slow, cumulative process culminating in the industrial revolution,"[52] the more ambiguous the fictional representations of bastards seem to become. The reason for this representational adjustment is the slowly developing awareness on the part of the middle-class population (i.e., the population most sensitive to the economic threat represented by bastardy) that, at least up to a point, inheritance did not define in absolute terms the person's financial destiny, and that the loss of some part of one's heritable property to an illegitimate sibling could in principle be recouped by future economic entrepreneurship. To put it starkly, the Enlightenment could in principle afford a slightly more enlightened attitude toward "sons of nobody" because their legitimate brothers felt increasingly empowered by the economic possibilities of venture capitalism.

This new feeling of empowerment by no means translated into the legally sponsored embrace of bastards as fully enfranchised members of the economic order. (In fact, the British laws postulating the socioeconomic exclusion of illegitimate children had been remarkably resilient; as late as 1978, the House of Commons rejected "A Bill to remove the legal disabilities of children born out of wedlock."[53]) A tentative development of a relatively more tolerant attitude toward bastards manifested itself rather in the increasingly vocal articulation of the view that the "unhappy innocents" (Richardson, *Sir Charles Grandison*, I:366) should not be made to pay for their parents' sins. The opening of the London Foundling Hospital in 1739, dedicated to saving the lives of illegitimate children of the poor, was one palpable manifestation of that view, a manifestation by no means unambiguous, however, since this public charity was sometimes described as shouldering the burden that might have otherwise been borne by the legitimate children of the father of the bastard.

When it came to fictional representations of illegitimacy, the situation was equally complicated. To begin with, the figure of the dripping-with-venom bastard—venomous *because of his bastardy*—disappears from eighteenth-century belles lettres or moves so radically to the back of the stage that we hardly notice his skulking presence. This excision of the vile bastard as a nearly ubiquitous literary type is accompanied by the introduction of the similarly ubiquitous virtuous foundling. Furthermore, whereas the overwhelming majority of sixteenth- and early-seventeenth-century literary texts featuring illegitimate characters conclude with the triumphant expulsion of the malevolent bastard from the community,[54] most of the eighteenth-century *supposed bastards* (particularly the females) turn out to be legally born foundlings who wind up reintegrated into the social order. One way of reading this crowding out of one literary type/social destiny by another is to suggest that the ascendance of the benevolent foundling exemplified the Enlightenment's readiness to assume a more humane attitude toward illegitimate children—a belles lettres equivalent of the fact that the charitable public institution designed to shelter *bastards* was called the *Foundling* Hospital.

At the same time, the literary rewriting of bastards as foundlings fit to be claimed by their long-lost families was crucially implicated with the self-perpetuation of the socioeconomic system privileging legitimate children. A cultural potential for a more enlightened perspective on the plight of bastards notwithstanding, the transfer of property to the hands of the *legal* heir remained the key concern of the eighteenth-century foundling narrative.

The emphasis on the psychosocial function of property thus qualifies the current critical view of the eighteenth-century generic foundling/bastard/orphan character as a paradigmatic progressive protagonist embodying "an implicit criticism of aristocratic ideology."[55] On the one hand, there is a certain intuitive appeal to considering such a character representing what John Richetti describes as the eighteenth-century fictional narrative's "progressive, even at times utopian, conviction that things should be different from the way that they have always been and that the new order is full of opportunity for the hard-working and the meritorious."[56] On the other hand, the traditional exegetical model that collapses foundlings, bastards, and orphans into one broad category of "progressive" protagonists seems less persuasive once we notice how many of the Enlightenment's fictional foundlings depend on the acquisition of inherited property (preferably landed property) and how sensitive a subject the correlation between the acquisition of that property and the establishment of the exact marital status of the protagonist's parents is. Our tendency to look for an overarching narrative of progress emerging from the eighteenth-century foundling fictions is thus checked by our realization that those fictions were fueled, to a significant degree, by the very real presence of a large class of people—illegitimate daughters, sons, sisters, brothers, and stepchildren—who were officially denied social personality by being denied the right to inherit property and whose attempts to acquire such personality—via inheriting property—were read with an uneasy mixture of opprobrium and compassion.

A Brief Outline of This Book

Each following chapter focuses on one or two "canonical" plays and novels (such as *The Conscious Lovers, The Foundling, Tom Jones,* and *Emma*) and a constellation of lesser-known works (such as Hays's *The Victim of Prejudice*, Haywood's *The Fortunate Foundlings*, and Bennett's *The Beggar Girl*), considering them in the context of everyday practical dilemmas posed by illegitimacy. The first and second chapters, respectively, analyze Steele's play *The Conscious Lovers* (1722) and Defoe's *Moll Flanders* (also 1722) in relation to the early-eighteenth-century concern about the widespread practice of infanticide and the campaign to establish the English "House of Orphans," a foundling hospital similar to those existing by that time in many European countries. The third chapter offers a bifurcated analysis of Edward Moore's play *The Foundling* (1747) and Samuel Richardson's *Clarissa* (1747–48), highlighting the difference between the representational challenges faced by the playwrights and novelists responding to the eighteenth-century preoccupation with the issue of bastardy. The fourth chapter compares the bastard-foundling hero of Fielding's *Tom Jones* (1749) with other illegitimate heroes of eighteenth-century fiction, such as Savage's "Bastard" (1728), Haywood's Horatio (*The Fortunate Foundlings*, 1744), and Smollett's Peregrine Pickle (1751) and Humphrey Clinker (1771), problematizing the accepted critical view of Tom Jones as a paradigmatic progressive protagonist of eighteenth-century belles lettres.

The fifth chapter returns to the history of the London Foundling Hospital, reading Richardson's last novel, *Sir Charles Grandison* (1753–54), as offering an ambivalent emotional justification for the presumably self-imposed exclusion of women of quality from public participation in the affairs of the Foundling Hospital at mid-century. The sixth chapter uses Charles Burney's attempt, in 1774, to turn the Hospital into the first national public school of music—a project in which he was assisted by Frances Burney—as an important background for the treatment of the theme of illegitimacy in *Evelina* (1778). The concluding chapter focuses on the story of Harriet Smith, the bastard protégé of Emma Woodhouse in Jane Austen's *Emma* (1816), arguing that Austen capitalized on the cultural iconography of the Hospital to offer a corrective to the rule of configuring the legitimacy of the fictional foundling as a function of her gender.

The larger goal of the insistent cross-referencing between the historical and the literary that drives the argument of this book is to put illegitimacy on the map of eighteenth-century studies as a crucial fixture of the period's imaginative landscape. Whereas I cannot claim that the reconstruction of the dialogue between the foundling fictions and the concern about bastardy somehow covers or exhausts the complex topic of the cultural meanings of illegitimacy in the "long" eighteenth century, I am convinced that by listening to the many voices of that hitherto unnoticed dialogue, we come closer to recognizing illegitimacy as an important, far-reaching, and immensely complex sociopolitical institution of the British Enlightenment.

- I -

BASTARD DAUGHTERS AND FOUNDLING HEROINES

Rewriting Illegitimacy in The Conscious Lovers

Richard Steele's play *The Conscious Lovers* (1722) occupies a special place in eighteenth-century literary history. It is considered a paradigmatic "sentimental comedy... associated with the early-eighteenth-century reform movement"[1] and testifying to the theatre's prescient recognition of the rising ("always rising," as one critic has noted[2]) power of the middle-class audience.[3] *The Conscious Lovers* features a young woman named Indiana whose origins remain unknown until the last scene of the play, in which she is revealed to be the long-lost daughter of an affluent London merchant, Mr. Sealand. The happy discovery is followed by a wedding: Indiana's steadfast admirer and protector, Bevil Junior, a scion to an old aristocratic family, can now marry the beauteous foundling with the blessing of his father, Sir Bevil. Where the Dorimants and Harriets of the Restoration stage thrust and parry with witty repartees, Bevil Junior and Indiana vie with each other in their noble and disinterested behavior. To devotees of William Wycherley and George Etherege, *The Conscious Lovers* did not even feel like a comedy (John Dennis thought that Indiana's story was "downright tragical"[4]), but Steele remained convinced that "it must be an improvement of [comedy] to introduce a joy too exquisite for laughter, that can have no spring but in delight, which is the case of this young lady."[5] Steele, as Lisa Freeman argues, billed his "new kind of drama" as offering to the growing middle-class audience "something of more enduring value than the transitory laughter and passions of laughing comedies: an education in polite values, polite behavior, and polite feeling"—a ticket into the "class of the refined."[6]

CHAPTER 1

"Polite" to the point of being characterized as "wooden" by modern critics,[7] *The Conscious Lovers* seems to be the least likely candidate among early-eighteenth-century plays for embodying the period's preoccupation with illegitimacy. The comedies of the preceding decades were, after all, much more outspoken in their references to bastards. At times such references scored political points, alluding to the adulterous virility of the kings,[8] but by and large they simply treated illegitimacy as a fact of life integral to everyday economic, social, and sexual interactions. In Colley Cibber's *Love's Last Shift* (1696), a young woman named Hillaria wonders who the "over-shy" Lady seen at a fashionable outing is. Her cousin, Young Worthy, offhandedly replies: "Hang her, she's a Jest to the whole Town: For tho' she has been the Mother of two By-blows, she endeavors to appear as ignorant in all Company, as if she did not know the Distinction of Sexes" (575). Also, in George Farquhar's *The Recruiting Officer* (1706), Captain Plume advises his friend (also named Worthy), whose courtship has stalled, to mortify his haughty lady's pride by lying "with her Chamber-maid and [hiring] three or four Wenches in the Neighborhood to report that [Worthy] had got them with Child." Plume rounds out his advice with an implicit panegyric to the sexual prowess of the king's army, noting that with "so many Recruiting Officers in Town," the number of "Bastards" has to increase: "I thought 'twas a Maxim among [our Officers] to leave as many Recruits in the Country as they carry'd out." Worthy acknowledges the double entendre with a pun of his own: "No body doubts your Good-will, Noble Captain, in serving your Country with your best Blood—Witness our Friend Molly at the Castle—There have been Tears in Town about that Business, Captain" (697).

It is true that the action of *The Conscious Lovers* is obliquely driven by Sir Bevil's fear of having an illegitimate daughter-in-law or illegitimate grandchildren. The happy ending of the play is a quiet sigh of relief prompted by the public confirmation that, though a child "lost" by her parents, Indiana is no bastard, and that she has never been—contrary to what was suspected—Bevil Junior's kept mistress. That Indiana could have been a bastard is tacitly indicated in Steele's 1720 essay in *The Theatre*, in which, as Freeman observes, Steele "takes great pains to underline the idea that while Sealand may have fallen into the dissipated and spendthrift ways of a Restoration rake in his earlier years, he has subsequently undergone a kind of reformation and is now distinguished by a fastidious sense of industry [and] economy."[9] Indiana, in other words, could have been conceived out of wedlock back in the heady days of the last century, and she seems to have avoided such a destiny by a hair's breadth.[10] Still, *The Conscious Lovers* contains no explicit mention of bastardy, and its author manages to work around that notorious issue in a newly *polite* way, without the coarse references to "by-blows" and "new recruits."

But commendable as the project of sanitizing the language of the stage was in the post-Collier England,[11] it was not just the vernacular of illegitimacy that needed to be reformed or excised. The crucial turns of the play's plot and even its famed "politeness" were informed, at least in part, by Steele's determination to silence a host of public and personal problems bound with bastardy that were forcing their way into his comedy. It is likely, in other words, that the eighteenth-century paradigmatic sentimental comedy owes some of its distinguishing features to the author's commitment to negotiating the scandalous issues of bastardy and child murder through the idiom of the traditional "foundling" romance featuring a serendipitously discovered long-lost child.

In this chapter I begin my argument about the possible "bastard" origin of Steele's "foundling" comedy by turning to the children whose fate provided an important (if largely unmentionable in polite society) point of reference for the fictional reimagining of bastards: the illegitimate offspring of the poor, liable to be abandoned and even murdered by their desperate mothers. I discuss Steele's project of providing a respectable ancient genealogy for his new "improved" comedy and demonstrate that the plays of his chosen literary progenitor—Terence—acquired an eerie topicality in infanticide-infested London because of the Roman playwright's casual references to the exposure of unwanted infants. (Even his admiring translator, Laurence Echard, had to admit that such references make Terence's comedies unsuitable for the English stage.) Somewhere in the process of working on *The Conscious Lovers*, which took almost a decade, Steele might have realized that by deciding to base his new play on Terence's widely popular *Andria* (166 B.C.), he had put himself in a difficult position. Steele had to purge the Roman original of any references resonating with contemporary problems of infanticide and illegitimacy, a particularly challenging undertaking given how integral the anxiety about the unhallowed sexuality is to the plots of both *Andria* and *The Conscious Lovers*. Compounding Steele's already daunting task was his own domestic situation, which I discuss later in this chapter. In 1720, Steele's "natural" daughter, Elizabeth Ousley, was snubbed on the marriage market because of her bastardy, bringing home, so to speak, the issues that his comedy tried to politely circumvent.

In the concluding section, I return to the story of Indiana as a foundling—a story replete with the stale paraphernalia of the traditional foundling narrative: tell-tale tokens, improbable coincidences, and tearful recognitions. I suggest that Steele emphasized those embarrassingly formulaic aspects of his play in order to muffle the disturbing social relevance of *The Conscious Lovers*. I cannot claim that Steele's project of rewriting "bastards" into "foundlings" was altogether successful: in fact, his play seemed to articulate with a new force the anxiety surrounding the transfer of property down the legal line in a society besieged by illegitimacy, even as it made a strenuous effort to disavow this anxiety. I do believe, however, that by uncovering the "bastard" provenance of eighteenth-century foundling fictions, we can qualify the current critical assumption that when eighteenth-century authors framed their plots through the idiom of the classical foundling narrative, they did so because of a certain lack of literary sophistication or imagination. Rather, they did it because, for a variety of pressing public and private reasons, bastardy needed to be rewritten.

Infanticide in Ancient Rome and in Eighteenth-Century England

In 1694, a distinguished literary scholar, Laurence Echard, published a new translation of the plays of Publius Terentius Afer (185–159 B.C.), commonly known as Terence. In the preface to his volume, Echard issued a seemingly puzzling warning for his readers, observing that "Roman plots, often founded upon the exposing of Children and their unexpected Delivery," should not be transplanted onto the English stage.[12] Echard considered Terence "the most Exact, the most Elaborate, and withal the most Natural of all Dramatic Poets," yet he still asserted that the "difference between the Romans and our selves in Customs, Humors, manners and theatres is such, that it is impossible to adapt their Plays to our Stages" (15).

To appreciate the peculiarity of Echard's observation on Terence's unsuitability for the English stage, we have to remember that Terence was a perennial favorite with late-seventeenth- and eighteenth-century readers. Public school students translated him as part of their learning routine.[13] John Dryden proudly claimed him as his role model in the preface to *An Evening's Love*. Terence's plays were constantly in circulation: his *Andria* alone was destined to go through more than one hundred editions between 1700 and 1800. To understand Echard's ambivalence, we may want to take a closer look at the plot of this famous play—the same play that Steele would later select as the basis for his "new" comedy.

Andria tells a story of a young woman named Glycerium who gives birth to the illegitimate child of her lover, Pamphilus. The couple cannot get married because Glycerium's origins are unknown—it is likely that she is not a free citizen—and, anyway, Pamphilus's father has made other matrimonial arrangements for him. Shortly before Glycerium goes into labor, Pamphilus promises her that he will never expose (i.e., abandon in the street) their baby—come what may, even if it is girl!—but will acknowledge it as his and raise it. Nevertheless, in the third act, Glycerium's newborn is put out in the street as part of a complicated plot hatched by Pamphilus's slave Davos in order to prevent Pamphilus's marriage to another woman. As this is a comedy, the infant is abandoned only temporarily, and the play ends with a happy discovery that Glycerium is the long-lost daughter of an Athenian citizen and thus can wed the father of her child.

We can see why the conclusion of the play would not sit well with the late-seventeenth-century critics of theatre (only four years separate Echard's warning and Jeremy Collier's *A Short View of the Immorality and Profaneness of the English Stage*). Terence emphasizes the rediscovered Athenian citizenship of his female protagonist—a point that remained moot for the English audiences because Greek and Roman categories of citizenship did not correlate easily with the British class system. (According to Pericles's law, Athenian citizens could not marry non-Athenians; if they did, the offspring of such marriages were considered illegitimate.) At the same time, Terence allows his fornicating heroine to wed her lover, manifesting a scandalous lack of concern for the notion of female virtue of the kind that came to dominate eighteenth-century belles lettres.[14] Glycerium's story is particularly provoking because she is actually a courtesan-in-the-making—not marriage material even by the standards of Terence's day. Early in the play, we find out that she was adopted by a hetaera (introduced politely as her "sister"), a damning revelation because, as Daniel Ogden points out, it was common for hetaerae to adopt beautiful girls and prepare them for a similar career: "For free hetairai, bearing a girl-child of one's own was a costly alternative (not only in terms of direct expense, but also in terms of one's own looks) to buying a slave-girl.... [Thus Demosthenes refers to a procuress who] is said to have bought ... a number of ... little girls that she judged would grow into beautiful women, in order to rear them as courtesans to keep her in her old age."[15]

The hetaera who takes in Glycerium conveniently dies before the play begins, so we are spared the details of the "sisters'" domestic arrangement and see Glycerium only in the care of Pamphilus (the motif of dependence on one's protector that would make so ambiguous Indiana's position in *The Conscious Lovers*).

Terence's occasionally lighthearted approach to female virtue was one apparent reason to question his plays' immediate suitability for the late-seventeenth-century stage. The main reason, however, as Echard himself pointed out in his preface, was Terence's reliance on the plots of "Exposure and unexpected Delivery of Children." I suggest that Echard saw the Roman plots of exposure as disturbingly relevant to the current English problem of infanticide and could not think of a way to neutralize these plots so as to remove their offensive topical sting.[16]

Echard's careful wording of his brief discourse on "Roman Customs and Manners" implied that the abandonment of newborn children was a thing of a safely contained Roman past, deeply alien to his fellow countrymen, and as such out of place on the English stage. Intentionally or not, Echard, thus, refrained from spelling out the real reasons the contemporary audiences would not appreciate watching staged representations of exposure. Such representations were undesirable not because British audiences could not relate to this antiquated custom, but, unfortunately, because they could relate to it too well. Echard might or might not have been familiar with William Petty's suggestion in the 1680s that England needed a publicly founded institution dedicated to saving the lives of illegitimate children liable to be abandoned or even murdered by their parents, typically, desperate serving-class women trying to avoid the punishment for bringing forth "bastards."[17] But even if we presume that Echard had never heard of Petty's proposals, he still must have been aware of the practice of exposing unwanted illegitimate children, which seemed to increase[18] in proportion with the rapid growth of an urban population and which affected the everyday life of his fellow Londoners.[19] As Toni O'Shaughnessy Bowers points out, by the first decades of the eighteenth century, "abandoned or exposed children—in Augustan slang, children who had been 'dropped'—constituted a social presence that could not be ignored; their bodies, dead or (barely) alive littered London and the countryside."[20] As the choice of contraceptive techniques was as limited in eighteenth-century England as it had been in ancient Rome, to farm an infant out to a "killer-nurse"[21] or to abandon it shortly after birth were often the only options available to an unmarried woman who anticipated being ostracized (and often physically punished) for burdening her parish with a bastard and who had no means for supporting a child on her own. Even though, as Keith Wrightson notes, only a few women among those with the "stringent rational motive to commit infanticide"[22] actually did, the abandonment and murder of newborn children remained a tragically constant feature of the social landscape of the British Enlightenment.[23]

The terms *exposure* and *abandonment* themselves underwent a subtle yet important transformation by the end of the seventeenth century. As Boswell points out, exposure was not necessarily synonymous with infanticide for most of European history. It became so, however, by the late Renaissance, when informal social networks of adoption grew increasingly obsolete and were only partially replaced by parochial provisions for "bastards" and by the spread of foundling hospitals. If we agree with Boswell's argument that the complex "systems of transfer developed in ancient and medieval Europe" ensured that a significant number of "unwanted and burdensome" infants could be "shifted . . . to situations where they were desired or valued,"[24] then we can assume that Roman audiences appreciated the comic potential of the exposure scene in Terence's *Andria* and read this scene as an implicit manifestation of the cohesiveness of their community rather than of its breakdown. By contrast, for late-seventeenth- and early-eighteenth-century British audiences, the sight of the exposed infant would bring on associations with infanticide and the disintegration of community as well as the unpleasant memories of parochial squabbles over the cost of maintaining the abandoned illegitimate children of the poor. (Thomas Bray would aptly express such associations in his 1728 comparison of illegitimate victims of infanticide to "Warts and Wens, and other filthy Excrescencies . . . defacing and weakening . . . the Body Politic" [16]). Paradoxically, it was in part the historical remoteness of the society depicted in *Andria*—and thus the lack of historical context for its exposure references—which made possible the "re-accentuation" (to borrow Mikhail Bakhtin's concept)[25] of those references and infused Terence's comedy with a topicality disturbing for early-eighteenth-century audiences regularly jolted by the "daily sight of infant corpses thrown on the dust heaps of London."[26]

Since we know that the issue of infanticide had not become any less painful by the time Steele turned to Terence's *Andria* in the early 1710s (both illegitimacy and the abandonment of illegitimate children had increased steadily as the century went on[27]), we may ask why Steele chose such an inauspicious literary forbear. If Echard could see that the disturbing parallels between the "Roman custom" of exposure and the English custom of infanticide render plays such as *Andria* unfit for the theatre, why couldn't Steele? My tentative answer to this question[28] is that other considerations had outweighed a possible concern on Steele's part about just how problematic the task of "Englishing" a Roman play dealing with bastardy and abandonment might turn out to be. For Terence did seem—or at any rate was *made* to seem—such a perfect match in other ways! John Loftis characterizes the affinities between the two playwrights as follows: "In Terence, Steele had found out a precedent for his own comic theory, in which the laughter was relegated to a subordinate position. Praising *The Self-Torturer* in the *Spectator*, No. 502, he found it a merit in the play that it did not provoke laughter; rather it was remarkable for 'worthy Sentiments.' Such admiration for the Roman dramatist's humanity doubtless led to his selection of *The Andria* as the source for *The Conscious Lovers*, the Roman play providing ample incident for displaying tender emotions."[29]

The assertion that Terence's "worthy sentiments" and "tender emotions" made him an obvious role model for Steele needs some historical qualification. In claiming *Andria* as a valuable precedent of a comedy that eschewed "transitory laughter"[30] for a more refined sensation of "joy too exquisite for laughter" (Steele 323), Steele followed a tradition established earlier by Restoration playwrights. In 1671, Dryden evoked Terence when he was charged with making "debauch'd persons [his] protagonists . . . and [leaving] them happy in the Conclusion of [his plays,] against the Law of Comedy, which is to reward virtue and punish vice." "I know no such law to have been constantly observ'd in Comedy, either by the Ancient or Modern Poets," Dryden wrote defiantly in the preface to his *An Evening's Love*, adding that "Chaerea is made happy in the *Eunuch*, after having deflour'd a Virgin: and Terence generally does the same through all his Plays, where you perpetually see, not only debauch'd young men enjoy their Mistresses, but even the Courtezans themselves rewarded and honour'd in the Catastrophe" (Dryden 188).

There is an obvious irony in the fact that whereas Dryden used Terence to defend his right to reward "debauchery" at the conclusion of his plays, Steele proceeded to elevate Terence into the patron saint of the new comedy, conceived as a radical correction to the libidinous exuberance of Restoration comedy. Terence clearly was as open to appropriation and subsequent reappropriation as any of the venerable "ancients," and claiming a revered Roman author as his literary forefather enhanced Steele's ambitious self-representation as a reformer of the English stage. These considerations may have helped him to carry on even as—and if—he became cognizant of how difficult it was to chisel his "new" comedy out of a play built around the theme of exposure when his countrymen, in the words of Joseph Addison, did "not know how to speak on such a subject without horror."[31]

And yet, paradoxically, it was Terence's cultural prominence—something that Steele wanted to capitalize on in developing new drama—that must have amplified Steele's troubles. Freeman reminds us that eighteenth-century audience members would form a complicated set of expectations about the play before they "even entered the theater,"[32] and Steele knew that his audiences would be familiar with *Andria* and that at least some of them would compare *The Conscious Lovers* to Terence's comedy (a cultural experience comparable to watching a Hollywood adaptation of a classic novel and filling in details and psychological motivations from the original). What he could not foresee was *how* their knowledge would color their perception of the play, that is, he could not gauge the extent to which they would—intentionally or not—"supplement" his innocent love scenes with the scandalous (and even "unspeakable," to adapt Addison's parlance) innuendoes of the original. It was this uncertainty, I suggest, that led Steele to try to make his play so *irreproachably innocuous* as to be regarded as "ridiculously whimsical" by an eighteenth-century critic (Dennis 533) or "wooden" by a twentieth-century one.[33]

Richard Savage and Elizabeth Ousley

There was yet another complication possibly factored into Steele's endeavor to obliterate the disturbing social relevance of his comedy: the story of Steele's own illegitimate daughter, Elizabeth Ousley, and her failed engagement to Steele's notorious protégé Richard Savage. Steele met Savage sometime in 1718, when the younger man's play, *Love in a Veil*, was being prepared for its Drury Lane production. Savage claimed to be a natural son of Earl Rivers, the product of the earl's adulterous liaison with the Countess of Macclesfield. As Willard Connely nonchalantly notes, there was no doubt that "the fine-mannered but coarse-featured wretch was somebody's bastard . . . , but that he was Lady Macclesfield's no one seemed to be able to affirm but himself."[34] Impressed by the talented young man—and touched by his poignant personal history (the presumed offspring of the peer of the realm was indigent and had to earn his living by his wits)—Steele began patronizing Savage by introducing him to his friends, procuring him writing commissions, and paying him a modest stipend. Steele's devotion to Savage went so far as to offer to him, in 1719, the hand of his daughter, Elizabeth Ousley, in marriage—his "natural" daughter, to be sure, but very well educated and so beloved by her father as to make Betty, his legitimate child, "a little jealous of the fondness Steele showed for his vivacious Elizabeth."[35]

We learn of the treaty of marriage from Samuel Johnson's *Life of Savage* (1743). Johnson tells us that the negotiations came to naught because Steele failed to come up with a promised dowry of £1,000. Savage, however, implies a different reason in *Memoirs of Mrs. Carter*. He claims that he was so averse to the union with the "natural daughter" of Sir Richard that he "could never be induced to see the lady, though [Steele] frequently and warmly pressed [him] to an interview."[36] Interestingly, neither Johnson nor Savage refers to Elizabeth by name; the appellation of the "natural daughter" seems to suffice in both men's accounts of Steele's ill-fated scheme.

That the self-proclaimed "natural" son of Earl Rivers could reject a prospective bride with a curt explanation invoking her bastardy was not at all surprising to those familiar with Savage's propensity for self-aggrandizement and obliviousness. This was the same man, after all, who would write nine years later in his satire *An Author To be Lett* that most Grub Street writers are of "very low Parentage," mock them for "aspiring to the Rank of Gentlemen," and observe smugly that "though bad writers, they might have been good Mechanicks"[37]—all this notwithstanding that, as the anonymous 1727 *The Life of Mr. Richard Savage* reported, he himself had nearly become a "mechanick" when he was "sollicited to be bound Apprentice to a Shoemaker" (7–8), and that his own aspiration, from the days when he pursued his presumed mother to the time when he sponged off Lord Tyrconnel,[38] had always been to be, or to at least live like, a gentleman.

Steele's reaction was also predictable. When "he was officiously informed that Mr. Savage had ridiculed him . . . he was so much exasperated, that he withdrew the Allowance which he had paid him, and never afterwards admitted him to his House."[39] The story gets more interesting, however, when we realize that Steele's disappointment in the matrimonial plan for his daughter coincided with his working on *The Conscious Lovers*. Steele, of course, began thinking of that play long before he met Richard Savage—in fact, Loftis locates Steele's first references to the planned comedy as early as 1710[40]—but the last three years before the 1722 debut of *The Conscious Lovers* saw a number of important revisions, some suggested by Colley Cibber, some informed by Steele's evolving concept of "new comedy." I suggest that given Steele's devotion to his "natural" daughter and his pain and humiliation at Savage's refusal even to "see the lady" let alone marry her, certain crucial details in the plot of *The Conscious Lovers* could be read as reflecting the unfortunate 1719 affair.

One such detail is the play's treatment of the theme of female virtue. On the one hand, Steele conventionally identifies a woman's virtue with her chastity; on the other, he posits virtue in a prospective bride as more valuable than her social class. Or does he? Critics disagree about the significance of the fact that Bevil Junior feels fully committed to Indiana (albeit without informing her about it), *before* she is found to be the long-lost daughter of the rich Mr. Sealand. J. Douglas Canfield argues that while "Sealand and Bevil Junior may both protest that virtue only is their concern in a marriage, . . . each of the nubile characters turns out to be in the right class anyway, so any real challenge to the traffic in women to improve estates proves moot."[41] James Thompson allows Steele something more of social subversiveness:

> Steele insists that the female protagonist's individual worth, her beauty and virtue, must be recognized prior to elevation in class status, prior to the revelation of her birth, and in so doing he clearly ranks individual worth above class status. . . . Potential conflict is resolved by romance conventions: the incognita is eventually recognized as having the requisite genealogical credentials to marry into the male protagonist's class, and so the question of whether individual qualities are determined by class and breeding is, as usual, begged. But unlike a virtuous servant character such as Cherry in George Farquhar's *The Beaux's Stratagem* (1707), a character whose beauty and virtue are recognized but whose value remains debased because of her low parentage, Steele insists that Indiana should be highly valued even if her parentage remains obscure. Class transgression in marriage is eventually avoided, and all of the couples are paired off according to their class status—servant with servant, gentry with gentry—but still Steele is at considerable pains to say that class considerations are secondary.[42]

The story of Elizabeth Ousley's aborted marriage treaty provides a new backdrop for the "considerable pains" that her father took to affirm the primacy of virtue over parentage considerations. The virtue of the play's beauteous foundling seems to be more important than her social standing—or is it a guilt-ridden Steele dreaming about the world in which his daughter's marital pursuits would not be hampered by his youthful indiscretions and by the lack of a ready thousand pounds? The aristocratic Bevil Junior knows true virtue when he sees it and would be willing to take Indiana "as she is," without money or advantageous social position—mark that, Richard Savage, low-bred pretender to gentility harping on the bride-to-be illegitimacy to mask your own cupidity![43] It is not difficult to read *The Conscious Lovers* as Steele's attempt to sublimate his parental heartache through reimagining his rather pressed-for-money "natural" daughter as a legally born offspring of a rich Londoner marrying a man who can afford her delicate sentiments and exquisite education. In 1720, his own Elizabeth wed a glover, one William Aynston, a "prominent villager" of Almeley, Herefordshire, perhaps a bit of a letdown given her "expensive schooling"[44] and her father's earlier ambitions to marry her to a son of an earl, even if illegitimate and not yet acknowledged by his mother.

Bastards, Foundlings, and the Transmission of Property

It has become commonplace in literary criticism to infer a relatively "progressive" bent in eighteenth-century fiction from the curious fact that all those Fidelias, Amelias, Evelinas, "Fatherless" Fannies, and Emmelines receive advantageous marriage proposals on the strength of their virtue alone *just before* their high status and affluence are revealed. I propose that the particular sequencing of events in the eighteenth-century foundling narrative—*first*, the intimation that the heroine is about to marry very much above her station, and *then* the discovery of her own affluence—could be explained, at least in part, by the writers' tendency to downplay the connection between real-life bastards and fictional foundlings. Because the presence of illegitimate children threatened the uninterrupted transfer of property down the legal line, their fictional counterparts had to be portrayed as not even needing the property they would ultimately inherit: greedy mercenary bastards had nothing in common with the idealistic and, as far as marriages go, lucky foundlings.

If part of the appeal of the "first find a rich husband and *then* a rich father" motif of the eighteenth-century foundling narrative was indeed this motif's capacity to both express and assuage the cultural anxiety about the ability of bastards to disrupt the transmission of property to legal heirs, then it is worthwhile to take a closer look at what is going on with property in *The Conscious Lovers*. When Mr. Sealand discovers that Indiana is his daughter, he immediately announces that she will get "a fortune equal to [Sir John Bevil's] hopes" (380), thus cutting in half the inheritance of his other daughter, Lucinda, who until then has been considered the sole heiress to his wealth. The news that Lucinda's estate is halved leads her learned suitor, Cimberton, to break off his courtship: "Why then if half of Mrs. Lucinda's fortune is gone, you can't say that any of my estate is settled upon her. I was in treaty for the whole, but if that is not to be come at, to be sure, there can be no bargain. Sir, I have nothing to do but to take my leave of your good lady, my cousin" (380).

By having Cimberton denounce Lucinda, Steele forces his audience to treat lightly the partial loss of Lucinda's estate. If they take this loss seriously, they are identified with the ridiculous Cimberton; if they ignore it, with the noble Mr. Myrtle, Lucinda's preferred admirer, who hastens to proclaim that "no abatement of fortune shall lessen her value to [him]" (381). A property is well lost if with it goes the "unseasonable puppy" Cimberton (356), the play assures us cheerfully.

Still, if we set aside this manipulation of the audience's emotions, Cimberton's reaction is important because it shows a very real consequence of reintegrating a long-lost child into the family: because Lucinda's estate is halved, her value on the marriage market goes down. What we have to keep in mind is that to have a legitimate child, to lose it, and then to discover it again was the stuff of fiction, and that in real life, a "suddenly discovered" or a "long-lost" child was usually a bastard child, who had simply moved from a hushed-down existence on the outskirts of the family to the room where the will is read and where legitimate offspring gnash their teeth over the sudden diminution of their property. In other words, Steele's eighteenth-century audience could relate perfectly well to a situation in which an extra pretender to family fortunes materializes seemingly out of nowhere and claims his or her share of property and parental affection. Although the play treated Lucinda's financial loss as a personal gain, the underlying socioeconomic dynamics of this "foundling" narrative were recognizably informed by the issue of bastardy.

Here again, as when he felt compelled to neutralize the dangerous topicality of Terence's exposure references, Steele was faced with the challenge of muffling the bastard overtones of his foundling plot. If in the first instance he opted for stressing the sexual innocence of his *conscious* lovers (unlike Pamphilus and Glycerium, Bevil Junior and

Indiana would never have a child out of wedlock!), here he emphasized his plot's reliance on the conventions of the classical foundling narrative, playing up, for example, the role of the material token in the recognition scene.

In the last act of *The Conscious Lovers,* distraught by the conversation with Mr. Sealand (who comes to her house to inquire into the nature of her relationship with Bevil Junior), Indiana throws away a bracelet, which Mr. Sealand immediately recognizes as belonging to his late wife (378). Writing in 1723, John Dennis called the bracelet sequel contrived and completely unnecessary, pointing out that the discovery could have been brought off more convincingly and efficiently if Mr. Sealand's sister, Isabella (who had been lost at sea together with Indiana and has since raised her on her own), acknowledged her brother upon first seeing him at Indiana's house or if Indiana directly answered Mr. Sealand's questions about herself. As Dennis put it, had Steele "known anything of the art of the stage, he would have known that those discoveries are but dully made which are made by tokens; that they ought necessarily or probably to spring from the whole train of the incidents contrary to our expectation" (533–34).

The timing of Dennis's observation could be used to qualify the currently accepted critical view according to which the writer's reliance on such stale conventions of the ancient foundling narrative as tokens should be read as a sign of the relative immaturity of the early-eighteenth-century literary endeavor, a stylistic shortcoming to be gradually overcome and viewed with embarrassment or self-conscious irony by the last quarter of the century. Deidre Shauna Lynch expresses this view eloquently: "In the eighteenth century, the surplus materiality of the means by which [the] scenes of anagnorisis were generated became increasingly embarrassing for writers on literature and theater. By the end of the century critics began to sanction only those recognition scenes that arose from action. They were eager to consign recognitions arising from telltale rings, scars, and other distinguishing features to the debased category of popular entertainment."[45]

Is it really the case that early in the century the use of telltale rings and scars was countenanced as the necessary evidence clinching the anagnorisis? Dennis's assertion that anybody conversant with the "art of the stage" knows that "those discoveries are but dully made which are made by tokens" contradicts Lynch's argument about the evolution in the eighteenth-century critics' reactions to the "surplus materiality" of recognition scenes. Lynch observes that critics began to insist that recognition scenes arise "from action" only "by the end of the century," but Dennis ridiculed Steele's reliance on tokens instead of a "train of incidents" as early as 1723! Indeed, already in 1692, André Dacier had observed in his influential *La Poetique d'Aristotle* that recognition plots with their "marvelous effects" seemed to be "on the wane" among playwrights.[46] These facts should prompt us to reexamine the traditional notion that it took most of the century for authors to grow out of their naive reliance on the formulaic conventions of the classical founding narrative. We should consider instead the possibility that they relied on those conventions both in the early and in the late part of the century *and* both in the newly "respectable" plays and novels and in the fictions produced for "popular entertainment," not because they could not do any better—they could—but because by flaunting those conventions they could hope to calibrate the perceived topicality of their pieces.

Dennis is absolutely correct in his view of Steele's bracelet maneuver as superfluous: Indiana and her father would have indeed arrived at the discovery of their consanguinity in the course of their conversation, and if not, Aunt Isabella would have set the matter straight. In fact, Dennis's critique is so germane that we have to ask why the expert playwright, the author of *The Funeral*, *The Tender Husband*, and *The Lying Lover*, would have recourse to such *superfluous* gimmicks. This was, after all, the same Steele who made fun of foundlings and their tokens—their "marks"—in his *The Tender Husband* (1705), in which Biddy Tipkin, whose head runs on romances, informs her aunt that she is "not satisfied in the point of [her] nativity. Many an infant has been placed in a cottage with obscure parents, till by chance some ancient servant of the family has known it by its marks" (218). Steele did not need Dennis to enlighten him as to the exact aesthetic value of a "mark" as a dramatic device; why then did he leave himself so openly vulnerable to the charge of theatrical amateurism?[47]

I suggest that by deploying the contrived bracelet gimmick, Steele intended to signal the "literariness" of his play at the expense of its social relevance. The tale about a "suddenly found" daughter of an affluent merchant assimilated itself all too easily to the pernicious and well-known real-life scenario, and one possible way to deflect the audience from that identification was to emphasize the stylized bend of the plot. Indiana as an antiquated foundling somewhat out of place on the early-eighteenth-century stage (a stage, according to Dennis, too sophisticated for nodding at stale conventions) was still better than Indiana as a covert bastard too much at home with eighteenth-century anxiety about the effects of illegitimacy on the transmission of property.

There was no age of innocence, then, in eighteenth-century literary history in which the conventions of the ancient foundling narrative were taken at their face value or at least tolerated because of the presumed paucity of dramatic devices available to the writer. I suspect that we could push the time when such naive reception was indeed possible much further back than is currently accepted. Already in *An Ethiopian Romance* (c. 250–380 A.D.), Heliodorus coyly comments on the artificiality of the convention of anagnorisis when Charicleia is dramatically reunited with one of her adoptive fathers, Calasiris, at the house of the merchant Naucicles. Amidst the happy cries—"Oh, father!" "Oh, daughter!"—Nausicles remains "dumbfounded" as he sees Calarisis "embracing Charicleia as hard as he could and weeping," for he can "make nothing of the recognition scene, *so like a stage play,* until Calarisis, warmly embracing and kissing him," explains the situation (118–19; emphasis added). Charicleia's meeting with Calasiris represents just one of many similarly histrionic reunion scenes sprinkled generously throughout *An Ethiopian Romance,* whose characters are acutely aware of the stylized, literary nature of those occasions. When Calasiris is finally reunited with his two biological sons, who are on the brink of killing each other, his appearance is described as a "novel episode" of the "*tragedy being enacted*" (164). Calasiris is said to enter "like a *deus ex machina*" (165); and the onlookers who witness the anagnorisis (for there are always appreciative spectators at hand) say "nothing and [do] nothing but [stand] like statues . . . enthralled by the *spectacle,* when the *inner curtain* [opens] on a new *character*—Charicleia," who is on the way to one of her own miraculous reunions (165–66; emphasis added throughout).

Along these spectacular performances of familial sentiment runs the novel's more low-key but nevertheless persistent preoccupation with succession and legacies. Calasiris's sons fight bitterly over the right to inherit their father's priestly post. Also, upon first hearing Charicleia's claims to his paternity, her biological father, King Hydaspes, does not believe her and fears that he would be tricked into making this "suppositious and illegitimate[48] child [his] successor" (254), thereby delivering the throne of Ethiopia to his enemies and rivals. Thus the problem of inheritance, as Robert Markley observes, still "lies at the conceptual center" of *An Ethiopian Romance.*[49] The use, or, rather, the pointed overuse, of literary conventions, such as anagnorisis, testifies to the novel's tongue-in-cheek negotiation of anxieties surrounding the passing of economic resources and political power.

Bastard Daughters and Foundling Heroines

The reliance on such conventions does not become less self-conscious as we move further back into ancient history. As Jean-Joseph Goux points out, another foundling narrative of antiquity, the story of Oedipus (c. 430 B.C.) is in fact a literary "anomaly," a parody of the "regular heroic myth."[50] Following the earlier study of Bernard Knox, who insisted on the "polemical significance" of Sophocles's tragedy in Periclean Athens and demonstrated that "the play can be read as a declaration of rejection of the new concepts of the fifth-century philosophers and sophists,"[51] Goux argues that Sophocles deploys literary formulas to draw attention to them, and that this literary self-consciousness is critical for the play's reflection on the emerging new class of philosophers-autodidacts.

Historicizing the ancient foundling narrative is beyond the objectives of the present study. The quick glance at *An Ethiopian Romance* and *Oedipus Rex* was intended merely as a reminder of how easy it may be for us to ascribe literary naiveté to certain historical periods and how mistaken such ascriptions could be. Returning to the English Enlightenment and its dealings with wives, concubines, the liberated and "obstructed" glands, and the "little ones o'both sides" (Sterne 451), we should consider the possibility that throughout the eighteenth century—not just at its end—writers employed conventions of the foundling romance both to evoke and disavow a wide host of troubling issues related to illegitimacy. We see both of these impulses at work in *The Conscious Lovers,* in which Steele gave voice to the "unspeakable" issue of infanticide and to the thousands of everyday familial crises over the transmission of property, while simultaneously burying these jarring voices under the stylized surface of his "innocent" foundling comedy (322).

The next chapter considers a novel written at the same time as *The Conscious Lovers,* whose author also relied on the conventions of the foundling narrative to mediate his story of bastardy and infanticide. In his case, however, the effect was very different, for, unlike Steele, who took pains to camouflage his play's social topicality, Daniel Defoe wanted his readers to hear and to understand and to act upon his references to child murder. *Moll Flanders* thus emerges as a novel that cannot quite make up its mind about the status of its title heroine, who is now represented as a bastard, a bastard-bearer, and a spokesperson for the infanticide prevention campaign, and now as a foundling with a convenient amnesia about her origins and adventures—a dangerous ambiguity, as it turns out, in a literary culture increasingly using gender as a guarantee of the character's legitimacy.

-2-

MOLL FLANDERS AND THE ENGLISH "SHELTER FOR BASTARDS"

*D*aniel Defoe's *Moll Flanders* appeared in 1722, the same year as Richard Steele's *The Conscious Lovers*, but here the similarities would seem to end. Neither the eighteenth-century reading and theater-going public nor twentieth-century literary critics have ever thought of seeking parallels between Defoe's "debauched from her youth"[1] heroine and Steele's paragon of "merit and virtue" (Steele 376). Yet Defoe's frequent allusions to the classical foundling narrative (such as the recognition scene between the long-lost child and the parent, when Moll meets her mother in Virginia) compel us to consider aligning Moll with other eighteenth-century foundlings, such as Indiana, Fidelia, Evelina, and Emmeline.

As a thought experiment, such an alignment can be surprisingly illuminating. Moll's picturesque list of transgressions—she fornicates, commits incest, lies, steals, cross-dresses, and steals again—appears to set her apart from these irreproachable maidens. Yet *Moll Flanders* represents an early and important articulation of the question that perplexed many later eighteenth-century authors of the admittedly more "polite" foundling fictions: was it possible to portray a female foundling as ultimately not tainted by the problems associated with bastardy at a time when the renewed cultural interest in foundling narratives pointedly reflected the painful necessity to deal with socioeconomic and moral repercussions of illegitimacy on an everyday basis? In *Moll Flanders*, Defoe did not manage, nor perhaps try very hard, to sustain such representational separation. He used the rhetoric of the early-eighteenth-century infanticide prevention campaign to introduce his repentant heroine; he made Colchester—the site of a sensational

Moll Flanders *and the English "Shelter for Bastards"*

seventeenth-century infanticide case—her adopted hometown; and he depicted a network of wet nurses who took unwanted bastard infants off their mothers' hands, thus documenting the existence of informal social institutions that had evolved to deal with illegitimacy.[2] In other words, if, with our vantage of hindsight, we consider both *Moll Flanders* and *The Conscious Lovers* as artifacts of a culture expressing its anxiety about illegitimacy and infanticide through the idiom of the foundling narrative, we can say that whereas Steele nearly succeeded in camouflaging this anxiety, Defoe allowed it to take over his foundling plot.

Moll is thus an uneasy hybrid. From the point of view of the eighteenth-century differentiation between legally born fictional foundlings and bastards, she is both a bastard and a foundling. As an (arguably) illegitimate daughter of a convict, she is a poster child for the campaign for the opening of an English foundling hospital, actively promoted by Defoe in his journalistic writings. At the same time, as an innocent victim of circumstances beyond her control (an image that she assiduously cultivates), unexpectedly discovered by her mother in a faraway land, she is a throwback to the heroine of the classical foundling romance. Although we cannot be certain that Defoe consciously intended the "foundling" plot of *Moll Flanders* as a corrective for its "bastard" plot, the complex dialogical relationship between the two is indicative of the precariousness of the eighteenth-century strategy of reimagining the treacherous issue of illegitimacy through the presumably safe medium of a classical foundling story.

In what follows, I begin with the "bastard" plot of *Moll Flanders*. I outline the history of the early-eighteenth-century infanticide prevention campaign and discuss the rhetoric of "national interest" and "public good" used by its champions, such as Joseph Addison, Thomas Coram, Thomas Bray, and Defoe. I then show that, written at the early stages of the anti-infanticide crusade, *Moll Flanders* expressed its political message, critiquing the impotence of traditional authorities in the face of the growing practice of child murder, but it could not and would not sustain the impersonal tone of Addison's essays, Coram's petitions, and Defoe's own pamphlets, such as *The Generous Projector*. As a novel, *Moll Flanders* necessarily had to foster the readers' emotional involvement with its title heroine, which meant giving the practice of abandonment of bastard children by their mothers a human face and a psychological motivation. Such a human touch complicated the public discussions of child murder that tended to conform to the "new standards of polite discourse,"[3] which focused on the ways in which infanticide threatened "public good" and "national interest." I further

CHAPTER 2

examine the foundling plot of the novel and conclude by suggesting that, in contrast with Steele's *The Conscious Lovers,* the framing of *Moll Flanders* as a conventional foundling narrative did little to neutralize its disturbingly personal treatment of the double themes of infanticide and illegitimacy.

The People's Campaign against Infanticide[4]

Even a cursory look at the history of illegitimacy and infanticide in early modern England shows that the infanticide-preventive measures practiced by state and church were often at cross-purposes with the measures supposed to curb illegitimacy.[5] On the one hand, the Acts of 1575 (18 Eliz.c.3) and 1609 (7 Jac.1c4) stated that mothers of bastard children might be corporally punished or placed in a House of Correction,[6] and the notorious 1650 "Fornication" Act made incest and adultery capital offenses. On the other hand, a 1624 Jacobean statute (the *only* English law dealing with infanticide until the Lord Ellenborough's Act of 1803) dispensed with the presumption of innocence and declared that if an unwed woman concealed the birth and death of her child, she would be automatically accused of child murder.[7] In practical terms, this particular combination of laws meant that the fear of corporal punishment and public ostracism would often prompt the unwed woman (particularly of the serving class) to conceal her pregnancy and try to get rid of the child as soon as it was born even though the 1624 statute targeted precisely this sort of behavior.[8]

The archdeaconry courts of Anglican England complemented the efforts of justices of the peace by enforcing public penance for illegitimacy.[9] Such penance took different forms in different regions of the country, ranging from the denunciation of the offending woman from the pulpit, to her placement in a so-called "stool of repentance" in front of the congregation, to the excommunication of the unwed parent and the denial of baptism to the child.[10] Again, as in the case with punishments meted out by justices of the peace, the fear of being shamed in front of her co-parishioners and of having her reputation ruined could lead a woman to conceal her pregnancy and to murder her child.[11] As Keith Wrightson points out, a "thorough investigation of infanticide . . . raises the disturbing possibility that . . . Christian social morality . . . may have exacerbated the resort to infanticide to avoid the stigma of illegitimacy."[12] The ecclesiastical attempts to prevent infanticide included regularly preached sermons condemning child murder[13] and the encouragement of neighborly snooping and reporting to ministers about suspected pregnancies.[14]

Also, some parishes—though perhaps not the same ones that practiced excommunication and denial of baptism as punishment for illegitimacy—attempted to forestall child murder by modifying the practice of register keeping so as to include both the birth date and the baptism date of every child instead of the baptism date alone. The Prayer Book of 1662 extended the permissible interval between the date of birth and the date of baptism to fourteen days, which was already a substantial extension of the seven-day interval stipulated previously. However, as scholars working on reconstitution demographics have discovered, the real intervals between birth and baptism varied, for example, from about eighteen days in the late seventeenth century to 111 days in the late eighteenth century in the Derbyshire and Nottinghamshire parishes, and from twenty-seven days in the late seventeenth century to 444 days in the late eighteenth century in the Cambridgeshire parishes.[15] The custom of recording baptism dates as birth dates meant that the children who died unbaptized were not recorded at all, which offered ample opportunity for infanticidal parents to do away with their unwanted offspring.[16] The overt purpose of recording the birth dates and the baptism dates separately was to shame tardy parents into baptizing their children sooner. Less explicitly, this practice also served to mitigate the problem of child murder by ensuring that fewer newborns would end up as anonymous victims of infanticide.[17]

It is difficult to estimate the effectiveness of the combined efforts of church and state to prevent, and if such prevention failed, to punish infanticide. What is important for the purposes of this study is the early-eighteenth-century view of the *perceived* success of state- and church-sponsored anti-infanticidal measures, and we have sufficient evidence that by the early 1720s, infanticide had come to be viewed as a "Pest to the Public" that religious and state authorities could neither prevent nor punish. Thomas Coram's complaint about the "daily sight of infant corpses thrown on the dust heaps of London"[18] captures well the outraged helplessness felt in the face of this crime by his early-eighteenth-century contemporaries. As William Burke Ryan notes, London parks, ditches, and garbage heaps were the typical places where onlookers could come across dead infants (43). Those strolling close to waterways could expect to see the bodies of drowned children, as the Thames was the favorite depository for unwanted infants.

FIGURE 1. *Study for the Foundlings* by William Hogarth (1697–1764); pen, ink, and wash; 4³/₈ by 8³/₈ in. (11.1 by 21.3 cm). Reproduced with permission of the Yale Center for British Art, Paul Mellon Collection.

Moll Flanders *and the English "Shelter for Bastards"*

William Hogarth's 1739 engraving, *Study for the Foundlings* (figure 1) unapologetically lists some of the methods for disposing of such children: stabbing, drowning, or abandoning them in common pathways in hopes that someone would pick them up. (The engraving was part of the fundraising campaign for the London Foundling Hospital, but notwithstanding its intended shock value, the untoward activities it depicted had unmistakable real-life references.)

Compared to what people saw in the streets and heard rumors about, the number of infanticide cases tried in the courts of law must have seemed ludicrously low. According to the Old Bailey Sessions Papers, the actual number of cases brought before the jurors was less than one a year. In the period 1707–1787, there were fifty-seven such cases registered in Middlesex and London. The records of the Northern Circuit assize courts between 1720 and 1799 contain the description of 207 cases, which comes to fewer than three cases per year.[19] Similarly, recently uncovered records of the Court of Great Sessions of Chester show the following reduction in the number of prosecuted infanticide cases:

> The period 1700–49 witnessed less than half the prosecutions experienced within the previous fifty years, and prosecutions roughly halved again between 1750 and 1799. The 1680s experienced the highest level of prosecutions (eighteen), but during the eighteenth century, no decade experienced more than eight prosecutions and the average for that century was about five per decade. Overall, then, the Cheshire evidence would suggest a situation in which infanticide was . . . a crime fairly regularly prosecuted in the later seventeenth century but which, in statistical terms, declined steadily over the eighteenth century.[20]

The meager number of infanticide cases reaching the courts prompted Addison to observe in a 1713 article in *The Guardian* that although "there is scarce an assizes where some unhappy wretch is not executed for the murder of a child . . . , many more of these monsters of inhumanity [go] wholly undiscovered, or cleared for want of legal evidence."[21] Defoe concurred in 1731: "But alas! What are the exploded Murders to those which escape the Eye of the Magistrate, and dye in Silence?"[22] The feeling that the legal response to infanticide did not address the problem adequately was compounded by the realization that the traditional measures directed at preventing illegitimacy in fact spurred infanticide. As John Brownlow, an alumnus and the first historiographer of the London Foundling Hospital, would note in 1858, the "Fornication" Acts and Poor Laws ensured that the mother of a bastard was "punished with the infamy of years . . . for the error of the day. . . . A woman with a sense of honour expected being left to the reproach of the world and her own conscience, and [perceiving] no other means of saving her character, [would vent] her fury on the consequences of her seduction—the child of her seducer!"[23]

It was in this atmosphere of growing public dismay over the spreading practice of exposing unwanted infants and the perceived impotence of church and state authorities to do anything about it that Addison decided to call the people of England to action:

> I shall mention a piece of charity which has not been yet exerted among us, and which deserves our attention the more, because it is practised by most of the nations about us. I mean a provision for foundlings, or for those children who, through want of such a provision, are exposed to the barbarity of cruel and unnatural parents. One does not know how to speak on such a subject without horror: but what multitudes of infants have been made away with by those who brought them into the world, and were afterwards either ashamed or unable to provide for them! . . . [This crime] certainly deserves the utmost application and wisdom of a people to prevent it.[24]

It is significant that Addison appeals to the "utmost application and wisdom of a *people*" and not that of justices of the peace or of concerned clergymen. Addison's language implied that the traditional authorities, such as the church and state, had forfeited their "monopoly of interpretation" (to adopt Jürgen Habermas's concept)[25] in the case of newborn child murder: the daily eyesore of "infant corpses thrown on the dust heaps of London" appeared to testify to their inability or unwillingness to resolve the problem.

Crucially, Addison did more than just tap into the brewing feeling of communal dissatisfaction and point to the usual suspects—inept clergymen and corrupted jurors; he also shaped this feeling, gave it an appropriate voice, and established its legitimacy. What right had the "people" to interfere with the life and death of someone else's children? What right had they to police other people's reproductive behavior? The church had that right because of its concern with the victims' and perpetrators' salvation. The state had that right because it was supposed to protect the lives of its citizens and punish criminals. Above all, the agents of the church and state who dealt with infanticide (from the pulpit or in the court of law) were permitted to delve into these private and painful issues precisely because they functioned as disinterested representatives of larger institutions that had presumably sprung up as natural expressions of an underlying and unquestionable moral order. Priests and judges were configured as devoid of their own (reproductive) agendas and of petty human curiosity. Not so with the "people"—private, unaffiliated persons. Who appointed *them* to censor other people's vices and devise new charities?

Addison answered this question as he made an effective rhetorical move from infanticide as something private and unspeakable—and hence belonging to the jurisdiction of an impersonal institution represented in each particular case by a functionary lacking any private agenda—to a problem in which every Englishman appeared to have a stake. Apart from lamenting "the greatness of the crime," he invited his readers to "consider it as [robbing] the common-wealth of its full number of citizens," for as such, it certainly warranted "the utmost application and wisdom of a people to prevent it." Addison noted that "Paris, Milan, Madrid, Lisbon, Rome, and many other large towns" had already built great hospitals and thus had ensured that "many [were] by this means preserved, and [did] signal services to their country." Infanticide thus became a touchstone of national self-definition: were British citizens to stand and watch helplessly as their country's precious human resources were being depleted while other countries (mostly Catholic ones, too[26]) worked to resolve their infanticide problem?

The appeal of Addison's approach was manifest in the frequency with which the rhetoric of *public good* and *national interest* cropped up in subsequent print discussions of child murder. In his *Fable of the Bees*, Bernard Mandeville wrote that a *"civiliz'd Nation"* could not tolerate a woman whose "mind [was] capable of divesting itself so entirely of Humanity" (65; emphasis added). Jonathan Swift's *Modest Proposal* also tapped into the perception that newborn babies constituted a valuable public asset. His satire implicitly acknowledged the seriousness of the infanticide problem. Mindful of the "public good of [his] country" (a formula quickly becoming a must in any discussion of infanticide), the "proposer" asserts that his scheme "will prevent . . . that horrid practice of women murdering their bastard children alas too frequent among [his countrymen]" (2182).[27] Thomas Bray, arguing for the necessity of "Erecting in the City of London . . . a Hospital for the Reception of Poor Cast Off Children," claimed that such a measure would enable the saved children to become "useful Members of the

Commonwealth" (16). In his *Generous Projector or a Friendly Proposal to Prevent Murder and Other Enormous Abuses by Erecting an Hospital for Foundlings and Bastard-Children,* Daniel Defoe bemoaned the negative effect that infanticide was imagined to have on British demographics: "Thus is the World [robbed] of an Inhabitant, who might have been of use; the King of a Subject; and future generations of an Issue not to be accounted for, had this Infant lived to have been a Parent" (10).[28] Finally, Thomas Coram, who had been lobbying for opening a foundling hospital in London since the early 1720s, in his first personal petition to the king in 1737 (the petitions of the previous decade had been orchestrated by Coram but signed by Noblemen and Gentlemen, or "Ladies of Quality and Distinction") described the victims of infanticide as deprived of their chance of becoming "Useful Members of ye Common Wealth."[29]

The prevalence of the rhetoric of "public good" and "national benefit" is indicative of the very special position the self-appointed champions of the infanticide prevention campaign occupied in relation to the women that they represented and the powers that they hoped to influence. A part of the moral cachet of movers and shakers of the public sphere, such as Addison, Defoe, and Coram, came from their perceived ability to serve as a conduit between the disenfranchised, voiceless part of the population and those in possession of enough money and power to change the state of things, in this case, the king, Parliament, and the rich donors supporting the idea of the British "House of Orphans." This conduit function was especially prominent in the case of the infanticide prevention campaign. Information and propaganda concerning the handling of this crime always flowed in one direction: from journalists and writers (such as Addison and Defoe) and unaffiliated private citizens (such as Coram) to their middle- and upper-class audience. Those immediately implicated in child murder and abandonment (working-class women) had no access to the information produced and discussed in the public sphere, and they could not participate in shaping public opinion on the issue. Seemingly present in the public discussion (being, after all, its subject) they were, in fact, glaringly absent from it, allowing other people to represent their case in any way they wanted.

The pamphlets, petitions, and newspaper articles dealing with the problem of child murder thus contained almost no reference to concrete situations involving particular women; it would have been very difficult, indeed nearly impossible, to talk about "public good" and "national interest" after presenting the case of, say, Hannah Warwick, who had kept her pregnancy and the birth—and death—of her child secret because she was mortally afraid of her parents' wrath and her bullying brother's sermons,[30] or that of one Mary Doe, "a good-natured, inoffensive, and modest girl," made pregnant by her own father, and accused of "strangling and choking" her bastard infant shortly after delivering it.[31] We do not know if the champions of the infanticide prevention campaign ever consulted the depositions at the Old Bailey and read the sad histories of the mothers of the potentially "useful members of the Commonwealth," but whether they did or not, their public writing on the subject contained no reference to such personal histories. The absence of any mention of specific situations seemed to further legitimate their right to deal with the problem of child killing, as they appeared commendably devoid of idle curiosity and concerned with the well-being of their country rather than with gossipmongering. The latter was the presumed prerogative of numerous broadsides, pamphlets, and ballads, such as "The Bloody Minded Midwife," "The Cruel Mother," "Blood for Blood," and "Inquest after Blood," describing in gory detail incidents of child abandonment and murder.[32]

Another topic typically skirted in the polite discussion of infanticide was the sexual behavior of men who fathered illegitimate children. Although the image of the "seducer" does figure in such discussions, it remains vague: the man appears out of nowhere, ruins a hapless female, and vanishes forever.[33] The lack of interest in fathers typical for the discourse concerning infanticide in the first half of the eighteenth century is suggestively corroborated by a pattern emerging from the contemporary parish registers. Among each hundred cases of recorded illegitimate births in the northwest part of the country in the period from 1538 to 1650, both the mother and the father are named in 61 cases, the father alone is named in 27, and only the name of the mother is listed in 12. By contrast, in the period from 1651 to 1754, both parents are listed in 40 cases, the father alone in 12, and the mother alone in 48. In the east region of the country, in the period from 1538 to 1650, both parents are listed in 18 cases, only the father in 9, and only the mother in 73. In the period from 1651 to 1754, both parents are listed in 20 cases, fathers alone in 5 cases, and mothers alone in 76 cases. Apart from the curious difference in the regional attitudes toward parental responsibility, these numbers demonstrate that from the second part of the seventeenth century, "bastardy was felt increasingly to be the sole responsibility of the mother of the child."[34]

Although it is risky to extrapolate too much from this data,[35] it does seem to correlate with the tacit consensus shared by the champions of the infanticide prevention campaign that child murder would remain a problem as long as there were no suitable facility where working-class mothers, abandoned by their sexual partners and newly mindful of their country's needs, could deposit their unwanted children instead of killing or abandoning them clandestinely. Such an approach concentrated squarely on the behavior of unwed women and ignored larger social problems, such as the particular combination of public attitudes toward illegitimacy and legal measures that seemed in many cases to promote infanticide rather than forestall it. By ignoring such issues and presenting instead a blueprint for a practical local measure such as the English "House of Orphans," Addison, Bray, Defoe, and others managed to develop an ideologically appealing and aesthetically acceptable way of speaking about the Unspeakable.

Moll as a Bastard and Bastard-Bearer

Moll Flanders enters the early-eighteenth-century discourse on infanticide immediately upon introducing its title heroine. The novel opens with Moll's glowing description of the French L'Hôpital des Enfants-Trouvés[36] ("the House of Orphans," as Defoe puts it), the charitable institution designed to take in the children of convicted criminals:

> I have been told, that in one of our neighbor nations, whether it be in France or where else I know not, they have an order from the king, that when any criminal is condemned, either to die, or to the galleys, or to be transported, if they leave any children, as such are generally unprovided for, by the forfeiture of their parents, so they are immediately taken into the care of the government, and put into an hospital called the House of Orphans, where they are bred up, clothed, fed, taught, and when fit to go out, are placed to trades, or to services, so as to be well able to provide for themselves by an honest, industrious behavior. (7)

Moll then complains that no such institution existed in her native England when she was left to shift for herself at the tender age of six months: "Had this been the custom in our country, I had not been left a poor, desolate girl without friends, without clothes, without help or helper, as was my fate" (7).

Moll Flanders *and the English "Shelter for Bastards"*

Defoe's contemporaries must have immediately recognized the rhetorical alignments of Moll's opening speech. Her complaints about the sluggishness of the English government in establishing a "House of Orphans" in the fashion of "one of our neighbor nations" as well as her reference to the "honest, industrious behavior" of the hypothetical inmates of such a "House" repeat almost verbatim the arguments advanced in the press in the early stage of the infanticide prevention campaign by such figures as William Petty, Addison, and Bray. Note that Defoe attempts to soften the frankly propagandist tone of the "House of Orphans" passage by having Moll remark that she is not quite sure whether it is France or some other neighboring nation that takes care of its abandoned children in such an enlightened way. Moll's coquettish ignorance must have struck eighteenth-century readers as disingenuous because the Paris Foundling Hospital, established in 1670, was treated throughout the English infanticide prevention campaign as, first, the most conspicuous model for, and, after 1739, as the most conspicuous rival of, the London Foundling Hospital. In the 1720s, Bray was known to praise the French "Princesses and Duchesses, and other Ladies of the Prime Nobility of Paris . . . [who] entered into a Confraternity to manage [L'Hôpital des Enfants-Trouvés]" (28). The 1749 engraving by Samuel Wale, entitled *A Perspective View of the Foundling Hospital with Emblematic Figures I*, featured a group of aristocratic visitors promenading by the Hospital and a "sneering Frenchman" envying the splendor of this charity. The little poem underneath the image brought the point home: "Though Frenchmen sneer, their boasted first Design, / Brittish Benevolence shall far outshine."[37]

"Left a poor desolate girl without friends," Moll wanders "among a crew of those people they call gypsies" (8),[38] and then settles at Colchester, Essex, in the care of a parish nurse. Defoe's choice of Colchester as Moll's adopted hometown is remarkable, for Colchester was notorious in late-seventeenth- and early-eighteenth-century England as the site of a multiple infanticide case: in the late 1630s, one of its inhabitants "buried one child, poisoned another, [and] smothered a third"—all of them illegitimate. During a series of depositions following her crimes, she confessed to trying first to abort her children with the help of her lover, who "by phisick [had] often assayed to destroy the same child within her," but did not succeed.[39] As Pat Rogers points out, "Defoe had extensive links with [Colchester], sixty miles north-east of London, and bought the lease of several hundred acres of land there in August 1722. . . . His plans for the site included a tile factory. It is clear

CHAPTER 2

from his *Tour thro' Great Britain,* vol. 1 (1724) that he made many trips to this region around this time."[40] It is likely that Defoe was familiar with the infamous highlight of Colchester history involving the triple infanticide and that he selected Colchester as a scene for Moll's earliest adventures for this particular reason. Note that Moll's initial encounter with the concept of illegitimacy takes place in Colchester when she naively chooses as a role model a neighboring "gentlewoman" who mends lace and washes "ladies' laced heads," and is then told by her nurse that she, Moll, "may soon be such a gentlewoman as that, for [this woman] is a person of ill fame and has had two bastards" (12). The history of Colchester's murderous mother of bastards provides a context for Moll's first discovery of illegitimacy and foreshadows her future dealings with a network of wet nurses who take care of bastard children.

The intimations of the existence of such a network align Defoe's novel with the newspaper and coffeehouse discussions, which called for the "people" to attempt to resolve the problem of infanticide since the traditional methods used by state and church seemed to have had proven inadequate. When Moll finds herself pregnant with a child whose father is gone, she knows that the only impact that the intervention of official authorities could have on her life at this juncture is to make it much more difficult. Defoe (via Mother Midnight) euphemistically refers to that intervention as "the parish impertinence usual in such cases" (129), meaning "the right of the parish to remove an unmarried woman who was pregnant to her place of settlement, if not the place of her birth then the parish from which she had most recently come."[41] Moll confesses that her fear of the parish is stronger than even her concern of "how to dispose of the child when it comes" (129)—a damning testimony to the adverse role played by the official authorities in the dilemma faced by unwed mothers. And because the forced removal to the place of settlement (and what would it be for the itinerant Moll: Colchester? Virginia? Bath?) is the only "service" which the parish could offer to Moll at this point, she comes to rely instead on Mother Midnight and her helpers. In the ironic reprise of Addison's rallying call for the "people" to step in where the church and state had proved impotent, Defoe's novel prominently features the informal network of "people" as the only resource available to an unmarried pregnant woman wishing to escape public disgrace.

The "people's" network consists of the women who put pregnant women in touch with Mother Midnight and the wet nurses who work for her. In Moll's case, it is her landlady who functions as a go-between

Moll Flanders and the English "Shelter for Bastards"

for Moll and Mother Midnight: "It seems the mistress of the house was not so great a stranger to such cases as mine was as I thought at first she had been, as will appear presently; and she sent for a midwife of the right sort—that is to say, the right sort for me.... My landlady... said to her, "Mrs. B——, I believe this lady's trouble is of kind that is pretty much in your way, and therefore if you can do anything for her, pray do, for she is a very civil gentlewoman" (128).

Moll is quickly impressed by her new acquaintance's bookkeeping (Mother Midnight carefully tailors her bills of fare to different levels of income), and she gradually learns about a larger system behind that bookkeeping.[42] Moll, of course, first proclaims that to give an "account of the nature of the wicked practices of this woman... would be but too much encouragement to the vice, to let the world see what easy measures were here taken to rid the women's burthen of a child clandestinely gotten," only to proceed with such an account with the typically Defoesque relish[43] for a smoothly functioning organization:

> This grave matron had several sorts of practice, and this was one, that if a child was born, though not in her house (for she had the occasion to be called to many private labours), she *had people always ready*, who for a piece of money would take the child off their hands, and off the hands of the parish too; and those children, as she said, were honestly taken care of. What should become of them all, considering so many, as by her account she was concerned with, I cannot conceive.
>
> I had many times discourses upon that subject with her; but she was full of this argument, that she saved the life of many an innocent lamb, as she called them, which would perhaps have been murdered; and of many a woman, who, made desperate by the misfortune, would otherwise be tempted to destroy their children. I granted her that this was true, and a very commendable thing, provided the poor children fell into good hands afterwards, and were not abused and neglected by the nurses. She answered, that she always took care of that, and *had no nurses in her business but what were very good people, and such as might be depended upon.* (133; emphasis added)

It appears from Mother Midnight's description that her underground "business" prevents infanticide more efficiently than the system of preventive and punitive measures evolved by church and state, and that in any case, it makes much more sense for an unwed pregnant woman to turn to Mother Midnight (provided she could afford it) than to try to do away with a bastard infant on her own.

What must have rendered the novel's account of Mother Midnight's network simultaneously more compelling and more unsettling for Defoe's eighteenth-century readers was that wet nursing constituted one of the key elements of the period's "informal economy"[44] and as such contributed to one of the earliest known proto-professional organizations of women. As Gillian Clark has demonstrated in her edited *Correspondence of the Foundling Hospital Inspectors in Berkshire, 1757–68*, the London Foundling Hospital was able to implement its program of taking in illegitimate infants precisely because it could rely on "women's networks [functioning] in the occupation of wet nursing."[45] Clark argues that the correspondence of inspectors shows "very clearly . . . that there was active co-operation between nurses." Although women's networks

> are seen [in the correspondence] through the relationship of the nurses with the representatives of the single organization [the Hospital], . . . there is a strong sense that co-operation would have thrived without this focus and that nurses employed by private families would have worked together in just the same way. . . . Nurses of the foundlings . . . acted individually and collectively by protecting each other against the employer, asking for their rights as employees to pay and rewards. . . . Their common interest in rates of pay and in bonus payments were subjects of discussion across the country network of relations and neighbours and on journeys together to and from London. It was, for example, the nurses who in 1764 told their inspectors of the differential pay rates between those [working for one particular inspector] and those in the neighbouring areas; their neighbourhood and kinship networks are thus very apparent.[46]

There is something quietly ironic in Defoe's portrayal of Mother Midnight's network of wet nurses as a successful "grassroots" alternative to the failing anti-infanticidal efforts of the traditional authorities. It seems that the network designed to take care of unwanted children is already in place; all that is needed now is to legitimize it with a Royal Charter and some Parliamentary grants and to replace the old headmistress, Mother Midnight, with a respectable public figure, preferably a titled male (such as his Lordship the Duke of Bedford, the first official head of the Foundling Hospital after it became an incorporated charity in 1739).

Moll Flanders *and the English "Shelter for Bastards"*

It is unlikely that Defoe consciously intended this kind of rhetorical effect: The procuress and stolen-goods-taker Mother Midnight and the "Persons of Compassion and Generosity," whom he envisions in his *Generous Projector* as "hiring a House" where the "innocent Children" of the "wicked Parents" could be raised, *have to* belong to the opposite ends of his moral universe (10). Nevertheless, his novel does seem to underscore a similarity between Mother Midnight's organization and the House of Orphans as envisioned by Bray, Coram, and Defoe himself.

Such similarity primarily concerned the negative effect that the presumed lack of accountability for their sexual trespass would have on the morals of women. From the early days of the crusade to establish a "House of Orphans" in England, its opponents argued that by taking the infant off the mother's hands, no questions asked, the "shelter for bastards" would encourage "irresponsibility and licentiousness."[47] Coram complained in a private letter, soon after the opening of the London Foundling Hospital, that when an acquaintance of his requested his wife to hand over some money to the Hospital, she replied that "she would by no means encourage so wicked a thing."[48] Troublingly, *Moll Flanders* seemed to substantiate those apprehensions as the availability of a network enabling a woman to get rid of her children frees Moll for further adventures (i.e., marriage to an unsuspecting banker from London and a subsequent career as a cross-dressing thief). The "gentlewoman" from Moll's hometown gives birth to two bastards, but since there is no Mother Midnight to make her children disappear, her sexual history becomes public knowledge and as such a social handicap; in contrast, aided by the "Old Beldam," Moll can dispose of her child swiftly and clandestinely and continue her "depredations upon mankind" (3) with perfect impunity.[49] Moll's progress through the circles of gentility thus seemed to substantiate the apprehensions voiced throughout the campaign for the establishment of the English House of Orphans that in a misguided attempt to increase the number of "useful citizens," Coram and his supporters would shatter the bedrock of social stability: the age-honored practice of regulating women's social mobility though the control of their reproductive behavior.[50]

The ideological valence of the hypothetical English House of Orphans thus seems to undergo a metamorphosis as Moll changes from a "poor, desolate girl" to a sexually active woman. For the infant Moll, the presence of a House of Orphans would have meant not only that she would have been sheltered from any immediate danger but also that her future social ambitions would have been severely circumscribed. None of the champions of the infanticide prevention campaign had envisioned a foundling hospital as providing anything but the most basic education for its charges, and when the London Foundling Hospital opened in 1739, special care was taken to prepare the children for a life of menial labor and instigate in them the proper social humility. Had Moll grown up in such an institution, she would not be able to speak French, play the spinet, and generally behave like "quality." For the adult Moll, however, the presence of a House of Orphans would have meant the exact opposite: an increased social mobility, made possible by the availability of the repository for her illegitimate children. One can speculate about ways to resolve this ambiguity (e.g., had Moll been brought up in the House of Orphans, she would have been humble and "virtuous" and wouldn't have needed to get rid of her own children), or chalk it to up to the essentially "heteroglot" nature of novelistic discourse. The writer may try to advocate his favorite social project in his novel, but he cannot hope to rein in the multiplicity of conflicting readings and ideological inferences resulting from such "incorporation of genres."[51]

Moreover, a novel can highlight, in a rather controversial fashion, the hitherto obscured aspects of that social project. *Moll Flanders* complemented the "public good–national benefit" rhetoric of the infanticide prevention campaign with a vivid picture of a specific woman poised on the brink of infanticide. Although Moll never actually commits child murder or abandons her child in the street, her story was one of the rare instances of early-eighteenth-century literature presenting the point of view of the abandoning mother herself.[52] This point of view was quite different from the one implied by the newly accepted polite way of talking about the crime. Where Mandeville, for instance, would settle for a glibly impersonal description of the infanticidal mother as a woman divested "entirely of Humanity," Defoe painted an all-too-human heroine trying to think rationally and yet deeply depressed by her dilemma.

First, Moll argues very reasonably that keeping the child would annihilate her marriage prospects, a sacrifice which she is not up to: "I knew there was no marrying without concealing that I had had a child, for he [the banker, her intended husband] would soon have discovered by the age of it that it was born, nay, and gotten too, since my parley with him, and that would have destroyed all the affair" (137).[53] Second, she enlists her readers' empathy by describing her pregnant self as being in "extreme perplexity," full of "apprehensions," growing "very melancholy," falling "very ill, [with her] melancholy really increasing [her] distemper" (127–28).[54] Moll's matter-of-fact reasoning about the dire personal consequences of keeping the child as well as her emotional appeal to the reader explore approaches to infanticide very different from the one adopted by such people as Addison, Bray, and Coram, who focused on the negative effects that the early deaths of potentially "useful citizens" could have on the national well-being. Moll, as Toni O'Shaughnessy Bowers points out, was "locked into cultural assumptions and material relations that [made] infanticide, symbolic and actual, a necessary condition of maternal survival."[55] There was no room, however, amidst the discussion of "national good" and "public benefit," for the articulation of these "cultural assumptions and material relations," particularly from the point of view of the infanticidal mother herself, just as there was no room for referring to personal plights of the teenage child murderesses Hannah Warwick and Mary Doe.

Moll Flanders might not have much in common with those unfortunate girls; indeed, as John Richetti observes, Moll is a "female impersonator," masculine in her "skill and cunning for survival, . . . [and] untouched by the special quality of female experience."[56] At the same time, if we compare her down-to-earth talk about how unwanted motherhood could impact her life to the lingo of "public good" and "national benefit" used by the champions of the infanticide prevention crusade, we realize that "male creation"[57] though she may be, her perspective on child murder expressed striking empathy with mothers faced with excruciating personal choices and fostered an emotional identification with such women hardly available through other public discourses on the subject. One wonders, moreover (thinking of eighteenth-century "polite" audiences' rejection of *Moll Flanders*) if the cultivation of such empathy in print was particularly welcome in a culture that has just found a relatively acceptable, impersonal way to speak about these unspeakable, personal matters.

Moll as a Foundling

If the second paragraph of the novel proper introduces Moll as a poster child for the infanticide prevention campaign—an illegitimate baby abandoned by her mother—the third paragraph blurs that image by casting doubt on Moll's bastardy. Here is Moll carefully glossing over the issue of her illegitimacy:

> My mother was convicted of felony for a petty theft, *scarce worth naming*, viz. Borrowing three pieces of fine holland of a certain draper in

Cheapside. The circumstances *are too long to repeat*, and I have heard them related so many ways, that *I can scarce tell* which is the right account. However it was, they all agree that my mother pleaded her belly; and being found quick with a child, she was respited for about seven months. . . . This is too near the first hours of my life *for me to relate anything of myself* but by hearsay . . . *nor can I give the least account* how I was kept alive, other than that, as I have been told, some relation of my mother took me away, but at whose expense, or by whose direction, *I know nothing at all of it*. (8; emphasis added)

Moll never states explicitly that her mother was not married at the time of her birth (neither does the question of her paternity come up in Moll's subsequent conversations with her mother in Virginia), and she cuts herself off every time she comes perilously close to blurting out that she is illegitimate.[58] Moll assures the reader that the circumstances surrounding her birth are "scarce worth naming . . . , too long to repeat"; that she cannot "relate anything" of herself "but by hearsay," that she cannot "give the least account" of what was going on; and that plainly she knows "nothing at all of it."[59] This, incidentally, is coming from a person who had a detailed account of her birth from her own mother, and who has a prodigious memory that allows her to remember the price of the hundreds of trinkets that passed through her hands during her highly productive career as a thief.

That Moll's evasive account of her early days is indeed aimed at obscuring her bastardy is corroborated by the mirror opening of Defoe's novel *Colonel Jack*, written in the same year. Like Moll, Jack is an indigent bastard intent on moving up in the world, dreaming "of nothing but being a Gentleman Officer, as well as a Gentleman Soldier" (105), who begins as a London criminal and ends as an affluent plantation owner in Virginia. Like Moll, Jack goes through several troubled marriages (as the novel's subtitle explains, the Colonel "married four Wives, and five of them prov'd Whores") and tries on various social disguises (such as passing "for a natural Spaniard" in front of Spanish merchants). Consider, however, the opening paragraphs of Jack's story. As he informs his audience, "my Nurse told me my Mother was a Gentlewoman, [and] my Father was a Man of Quality, and she (my Nurse) had a good piece of Money given her to take me off his Hands, and deliver him and my Mother from the Importunities that usually attend the Misfortune, of having a Child to keep that should not be seen or heard of" (3). Here Defoe's language admits of

Moll Flanders *and the English "Shelter for Bastards"*

no ambiguity. There are no strategic pauses, equivocations, or interruptions that would allow us to question Jack's illegitimacy later. And no such questioning would ever be needed: we are squarely in the domain of Mother Midnight and her efficient wet nurses, and no anagnorisis awaits Jack somewhere in the middle of his mad dash through continents, languages, and identities.

Jack's gender is the decisive factor in his unapologetic illegitimacy. That Defoe had no qualms about allowing Moll to lie, steal, and fornicate but would not allow her to remain as unquestionably illegitimate as her male counterpart aligns *Moll Flanders* with other eighteenth-century works of fiction that conceptualized bastardy as a fate reserved primarily for male characters. However, unlike Frances Burney, Charlotte Smith, Maria Edgeworth, and other writers for whom the correlation between the legitimacy and gender assumes the status of a moral absolute, Defoe never fully commits to this correlation: Moll, after all, is neither absolutely legitimate nor absolutely illegitimate. Still, Defoe's reluctance to leave Moll a bastard indicates his awareness of the pressures of a literary market that would not countenance illegitimacy in romantic heroines heading toward a *happy* resolution of their troubles. I emphasize "happy" because when eighteenth-century novels did feature avowedly illegitimate female characters, such as the Mushroom sisters in Agnes Maria Bennett's *The Beggar Girl,* Eliza in Jane Austen's *Sense and Sensibility,* and the nameless daughter of Lady V. from Tobias Smollett's *Peregrine Pickle,* such personages were denied happy marriages, emotional tranquility, and, sometimes, even life itself.

But given what Defoe attempts to accomplish in *Moll Flanders,* perhaps it is inevitable that he would have difficulties with the tradition that aligns the gender of the heroine with her legitimacy and that legitimacy with her "deserved" happy fate. Defoe depicts an infanticidal mother, herself perhaps a product of an illegitimate union,[60] who fights for survival in a world hostile to poor women, to single mothers, to older women, and to bastards lacking useful family connections, and he endeavors to tell her essentially modern, difficult, and dark story through the idiom of the foundling romance. This idiom, of course, had always been susceptible to re-appropriation and parody (witness Heliodorus's treatment of each anagnorisis scene as a miniature theatrical performance), but in *Moll Flanders,* it begins to feel downright surreal. When Moll meets her long-lost mother in Virginia, the recognition is clinched by a token very different in its meaning from the nobility-confirming rings or scars of the classical romance: the mother's Newgate scar is a sign of a woman branded for her criminal strivings in the service of economic survival. Similarly, when Moll realizes that she has committed incest with her own brother—a revelation that would completely destroy the protagonist in the classical foundling narrative—she simply shakes off that unpleasant experience and goes on with her eventful life. Moll must go on, or, rather, rush on her story must, for any stasis is as fatal to it as is passivity to an unprovided-for middle-aged woman in the 1720s.

When it comes to heritable property—the cornerstone of the eighteenth-century literary endeavor to camouflage bastards as foundlings—Moll's position as quasi-bastard/quasi-foundling translates into a relationship with economic assets that resists any neat classification. On the one hand, like every fictional foundling of the Enlightenment, who secures an aristocratic spouse prior to inheriting parental property and thus differentiates herself from the beggarly real-life bastard by not really needing her inheritance, Moll marries a "Noble Lord" before coming back to Virginia and learning that her mother left her "a plantation on York River . . . with the stock of servants and cattle upon it" (266). On the other hand, Moll's Noble Lord turns out to be moonlighting as an indigent highwayman, and if she does not need her inherited property so desperately at the end, it is because she has accumulated enough independent wealth by stealing.

In Virginia, Moll's "bad" wealth—gotten at someone else's expense—gets mixed with the "good"—legally inherited—property until we can no longer decide on the emotional coloration of the resulting hybrid. Mocking, perhaps unintentionally, Locke's *Second Treatise of Government,* Defoe has Moll cultivating her plantation with tools bought both with stolen money and the money inherited from her mother, and rewarding her dutiful son Humphrey—the one who has kept her land in good shape—with the gold watch that she "stole from a gentlewoman's side, at a meeting-house in London" (268).[61] Moll means well with both her farming enterprise and her gift to Humphrey, and yet one wonders how, if at all, she fits into the system described by J. G. A. Pocock, in which the "moral personality . . . and the opportunity of virtue" are directly contingent upon inheriting landed property.[62] Is Moll more virtuous now that she invested parts of her loot into the inherited land that she will eventually pass on to her son? Or has she in fact violated the law once more and shall transgress even further in the future by making Humphrey her heir, for, as William Blackstone's

Moll Flanders *and the English "Shelter for Bastards"*

Commentaries reminds us, bastards could neither inherit nor will property (she does both)?

Deeply ingrained into the plot, these troubling questions remain unanswerable, even if the novel does attempt to use conventions of the foundling romance to mediate the issue of Moll's virtue. Moll intersperses the account of her "depredations upon mankind" with musings about that "evil counselor within her," which prompted her and hurried her on, that "busy devil that drew [her] in [and] had too fast hold of [her] to let [her] go back (153)."[63] She insists that she "knew not what fate guided her," and that her "fate was strangely determined" (134). Such evocations of fate aim at softening Defoe's opportunistic heroine into "a victim of circumstance,"[64] a familiar literary figure, because the majority of legitimate foundling heroines from Heliodorus's Charicleia to Smith's Emmeline were not allowed to learn about their origins and firmly establish their legitimacy while sitting placidly at home with their adoptive parents. Instead, they went out into the world, risking their lives and more importantly, their reputations.

The female foundlings' particular brand of unwilling heroism had long been useful for the writers faced with the challenge of producing titillating, commercially viable stories while keeping the young unmarried heroines of those stories miraculously untainted by their expeditions.[65] (After all, as Miss Glanville of Charlotte Lennox's 1752 novel *The Female Quixote* would perspicaciously observe, marriageable "young ladies" do *not* have "troublesome adventures" [87–88].) Having been thrust into the wide wild world as helpless infants and brought up by strangers, such heroines could not help going through their gripping—and often erotically charged—"adventures" to reinscribe themselves into the familial and social order; thus framed as reluctant heroines, they retained their claims to respectable, upwardly mobile marriages.

Note, then, how similar Moll's rhetoric is to that of another early-eighteenth-century foundling, Indiana, from Steele's *The Conscious Lovers*. Indiana's turbulent past should, in principle, disqualify her from a successful performance in the marriage market: after all, she has been "plundered" in her cradle, "tossed on the seas," and made "an infant captive"; she lost her mother, heard "but of her father," was adopted, lost her adopter, and was "plunged again in worse calamities" as the brother of her late benefactor sexually assaulted her. But since Indiana cannot be held responsible for her past—"twas Heaven's high will" that as a "helpless infant" she was exposed to "such variety of sorrows"—she is allowed to marry the impeccable Bevil Junior

(377–78). Though the appeals to fate sound much less convincing in Moll's case than they do in Indiana's, they are symptomatic of Defoe's attempt to recruit the literary tradition of "forgiving" the itinerant virgins for the "troublesome adventures" that they have to go through prior to finding their legal families and acquiring upscale spouses.

Yet, there is a typically Defoesque twist to Moll's talk about fate. In the early parts of her story, the nameless, faceless, unfathomable fate has something approaching a name, face, and public accountability: it is identified with the inept British State. Moll claims that had her government been mindful of the well-being of its citizens and made provision for an English House of Orphans, she would not have been "left a poor, desolate girl without friends, without clothes, without help or helper, as was [her] *fate* . . . by which, [she] was not only exposed to very great distresses, even *before [she] was capable either of understanding [her] case or how to amend*, but brought into a course of life, scandalous in itself, and which in its ordinary course tended to the swift destruction both of soul and body" (7; emphasis added).[66] In other words, whereas a typical eighteenth-century fictional foundling, such as Indiana, tearfully blamed fate for inflicting upon her a past that was a bit too interesting, Defoe's ambitious heroine aimed at both excusing her past and sticking it to the British government for not taking care of the bastard children of the poor.

Could she indeed do both? And, generally speaking, could a novel lobby for the opening of an English "shelter for bastards" by portraying an abandoned bastard child, who grows up into a mother prone to leaving her own bastard children behind her, and still claim the protection of the representational tradition that allowed the female protagonists some adventures (provided those adventures bore the stylized marks of the ancient romance)? The literary fate of *Moll Flanders,* a book that remained excluded from the "highest literary company"[67] of its era, suggests the negative answer to this question. *Moll Flanders* went too far in its engagement with the issues of bastardy, and no appeal to the foundling romance could redeem it in the eyes of "polite" reading public.

At the same time—especially when compared with *The Conscious Lovers*—the uneasily cohabiting bastard and foundling plots of *Moll Flanders* raise the possibility that there was something about the novel as a literary genre, as opposed to drama, that made it in principle less amenable to camouflaging the bastard origins of its foundling plot. Novels and plays seemed to mediate differently the dialogic tension

Moll Flanders *and the English "Shelter for Bastards"*

implicit in a story of a legitimate, lucky foundling making her way in a society both invested in and deeply ambivalent about its discrimination against bastards. The next chapter considers this possibility by tracing references to illegitimacy in Edward Moore's 1747 play, *The Foundling,* and Samuel Richardson's 1747–48 novel, *Clarissa.*

-3-

KICKING OUT THE CUBS
The Wrong Heirs in Richardson's Clarissa

The plot of Samuel Richardson's *Clarissa* is propelled into action by a last testament "not strictly conformable to law, or the forms thereof."[1] As a woman and the youngest child in the family, Clarissa Harlowe is not supposed to inherit her grandfather's estate over the heads of her father, her uncles, her brother, and her older sister. The novel could thus be viewed as a complex narrative justification of this rude disappointment of family expectations. As the story progresses, we are encouraged to think that if the purpose and indeed the excuse of affluence is to lighten the burden of other, less fortunate, people, then the benevolent and charitable Clarissa *deserves* to be the heir, and if the customs of the realm and "the forms" of the law favor instead her covetous, vicious, and selfish relatives, then something is wrong with the law and the socioeconomic system it supports.

Yet Clarissa is not the only wrong heir of the story. As Robert Lovelace gushes to Jack Belford about his progress (or the lack of such) with his "goddess," Belford responds by reporting a bitter disappointment that has befallen their fellow rake Thomas Belton. Having lived with his beloved mistress, "Thomasine," for many years in precisely the kind of "honorable" arrangement that Lovelace hopes to foist on Clarissa, Belton has discovered that Thomasine might have been unfaithful to him all along, that their teenage sons might have been sired by another man, and that what needs to be done now is to evict the boys from the house that they, in their bastardly impudence, have dared to consider their home. Belton, alas, is too sick to do it himself, so Belford, reliable friend that he is, undertakes to kick the mother and her two "sturdy cubs" (1187) out of Belton's house and to keep them off the property until Belton's own sister can move in and take possession of the estate. The endeavor requires some struggle. Thomasine, "who was once so tender, so submissive, so studious to oblige, that [Belton's friends] all pronounced him happy, and his course of life . . . eligible, . . . is now . . . termagant [and] insolent . . . , and her boys threaten anybody who shall presume to insult their mother" (1089). Still, Belford succeeds in "driving out" Thomasine and her children. These "fruits of blessed keeping" (1089) will not inherit the dying man's estate, even if he is their father (and who can tell now?).

Although critics have commented extensively on the "centrality of property"[2] in *Clarissa*, the episode involving the dispossession of Belton's illegitimate children never figures in this discussion. Its main topic remains Clarissa and the ways in which her grandfather's decision manifests a "modern, bourgeois attitude"[3] that challenges the period's trend to consolidate property and power "in the hands of a single magnate,"[4] such as James Harlowe. Yet the novel contains a series of suggestive parallels between Clarissa's fate and that of Belton's illegitimate sons, particularly when it comes to their respective relationship with heritable property. It appears that Richardson's conceptualization of Clarissa as a person both deserving and capable of managing the disputed estate implicitly relies on a view of bastards as deprived a priori (by the virtue of their illegitimate origins) from appealing to the same "progressive version of possessive individualism."[5]

Moreover, the overlap between the story of Thomasine's "cubs" and that of Clarissa intervenes into the novel's complicated set of literary allusions to the classical foundling narrative. Richardson uses such allusions to mediate the main protagonists' struggle for rhetorical dominance, for both Lovelace and Clarissa like comparing Clarissa to famous fictional foundlings in order to strengthen their competing interpretations of their troubled romance. The novel cannot sustain, however, the separation between its foundling and bastard discourses, as evidenced by Lovelace's anxious reassurance, at one point, that Clarissa herself is certainly legitimate.

I begin by discussing the foundling subplots of *Clarissa*, one of which is introduced by the intricate theatrical reference that brings together Terence's *Andria*, Richard Steele's *The Conscious Lovers*, and Edward Moore's 1747 play, *The Foundling*. I argue that Lovelace employs this reference in an attempt to represent his and Clarissa's story as following a stereotypical comic plot—one similar to the plot of *The Foundling*—in which the rake "tries the virtue" of the young woman in his protection, is repulsed by her in his vile stratagems of seduction, and is ultimately forgiven both by the woman herself and by her newly found father on the condition of immediate "reformation." I also show that Clarissa herself uses a reference to drama featuring a foundling—in her case, John Dryden and Nathaniel Lee's 1678 tragedy, *Oedipus*—as part of her tormented endeavor to explain and perhaps excuse the series of fatal missteps that have led her away from her father's house and into a brothel in London.

I further focus on the novel's treatment of bastards—the two sons of Belton and Thomasine—and discuss the implications of the similarities between the respective stories of the "cubs" and Clarissa if we are to conceive of Richardson's novel as an "ideologically progressive" narrative. I conclude by proposing that these, most likely unintended, similarities epitomize the difficulties faced by eighteenth-century novelists who deployed the foundling trope to broaden the evocative potential of their narratives and yet wished to keep the foundling elements separate from the novels' discussion of the problems caused by illegitimacy. It appears that eighteenth-century playwrights, including Steele, Moore, and George Colman the Elder (to whose 1767 play, *The English Merchant,* featuring yet another virtuous heroine lost as a child and found as a young woman, I turn at the end of this chapter) were, on the whole, more successful in submerging the "bastard" connotations of their foundling plots than were novelists, such as Daniel Defoe and Richardson.

Clarissa and the Eighteenth-Century Foundling Comedy

Roughly one-third of the way into the novel, vexed by his lack of progress with the captive Clarissa, Lovelace announces to Belford that he "will write a comedy": "I have a title ready; and that's half the work. *The Quarrelsome Lovers.* 'Twill do. There is something new and striking in it. Yet, more or less all lovers quarrel. Old Terence has taken notice of that; and observes upon it, that lovers falling out occasions lovers falling in; and a better understanding of course. 'Tis natural that it should be so. But with us, we fall out so often, without falling in once" (571). Lovelace refers here to the scene in Terence's *Andria,* in which Pamphilus's father, Simo, wants to convince his neighbor Chremes that Pamphilus has broken off his affair with a young hetaera (i.e., Glycerium, the "girl from Andros") and is therefore ready to marry the good girl his father had in mind for him all along: Chremes's daughter Philumena. Chremes is in no hurry to bestow his only child on a possibly profligate young man. Lovelace's "lovers falling out occasions lovers falling in; and a better understanding of course" is a paraphrase of Chremes's cautious response to Simo's announcement that his son has quarreled with his mistress: "lovers' quarrels are a renewal of love."[6] What is interesting about Lovelace's classical allusion is the title of the hypothetical play he wants to write—*The Quarrelsome Lovers*—and the modest Lovelacean aside that "there is something new and striking about" such an idea. Lovelace, as it turns out, is alluding here to the controversial early reception of Moore's *The Foundling*. The play premiered at Drury Lane in February 1748, but rumors of its presumed plagiarism had been circulating among theater-going Londoners since the preceding fall. Moore had been accused of copying Steele's *The Conscious Lovers*, which itself was a sanitized version of Terence's original comedy featuring a foundling and her temporarily exposed illegitimate infant. Lovelace's intention to bring forth a "new and striking" comedy that would improve on Steele and Terence thus ironically echoes the theatrical world's accusations that Moore had slavishly imitated Steele's adaptation of Terence's *Andria*.

To gauge the justness of such accusations, let us consider the plot of Moore's play. The action of *The Foundling* takes place in the house of Sir Roger Belmont (a character similar to Steele's Sir John Bevil), whose son, young Belmont (corresponding to Bevil Junior) is a fashionable rake. Prior to the beginning of the play, Belmont introduces into his father's household Fidelia (the Indiana figure), a young woman of beauty and sense whose origins remain a mystery. Belmont claims that Fidelia is the sister of his late college friend, Jack, who bequeathed her to Belmont's guardianship. Belmont's own sister, Rosetta (somewhat reminiscent of Steele's Lucinda[7]), believes this improbable story, but Sir Belmont is nonplussed that Fidelia was brought to his house in the middle of the night and that her family name and circumstances are shrouded in secrecy. The audience is informed that Fidelia had been lost by her father, who had to flee England for political reasons, and was brought up by a nurse who found her a "helpless infant at her door." When Fidelia was twelve years old, the avaricious nurse sold her to one Villiard "for the worst of purposes." After soliciting in vain Fidelia's sexual favors for several years, Villiard finally had "resource to violence." Fidelia's cries brought in Belmont Junior, who was "accidentally passing" (191) their house at midnight, just in time to save her from being raped. (Steele's Indiana was saved by Bevil Junior shortly after being dragged "by violence to prison" (337) by her latter-day guardian, who had failed to seduce her with promises and menaces and decided to prosecute her for allegedly refusing to pay him back for her maintenance since childhood.)

The difficulty of Belmont Junior's situation is that after carrying Fidelia away from her guardian-ravisher and installing her at his father's house, he realizes that in these circumstances he cannot safely seduce her—something that he has intended since he first saw her. Belmont has to find a way to remove Fidelia to a separate lodging. He attempts this removal by arranging for a letter injurious to her reputation to be delivered anonymously to his sister, so that, worried about associating so closely with a woman of presumably questionable virtue, Rosetta will withdraw her friendship from Fidelia and insist on her leaving their house. The plan backfires. Sir Charles Raymond, father of Rosetta's military admirer, Colonel Raymond, discovers that the young Belmont is at the bottom of this vile stratagem, confronts the rake, and accuses him of abusing his status as Fidelia's protector. The older man is willing to take Fidelia into his own house to guard her against the younger man's advances (the familiar motif of father and daughter meeting in a sexually ambiguous situation). Belmont Junior is jealous of Sir Charles and angry with himself for mistreating Fidelia. In a fit of repentance, he renounces his aversion to marriage and proposes to the indignant and hurt Fidelia, just as her former "owner," Villiard, turns up to claim his lawful "property." (Note that as in most eighteenth-century foundling narratives, the offer of marriage precedes the revelation of the heroine's identity and affluence.) A duel between Villiard and Belmont Junior as well as Sir Roger Belmont's cruel mortification at having a penniless daughter-in-law are averted by Sir Charles's announcement that he has just been informed by the dying and penitent nurse that Fidelia is really his long-lost daughter. The play ends with a double wedding (Fidelia marries Belmont Junior, and Rosetta, Colonel Raymond) and Belmont's self-proclaimed conversion into a man of "Honour."

Moore's play is similar to *The Conscious Lovers* in so far as both comedies feature an attractive and virtuous young woman of unknown origins under the protection of an amorous young nobleman, a woman who finally discovers her long-lost father in a friend of the family and turns out to be well-born as well as rich. For many eighteenth-century playgoers, those parallels were enough to charge Moore with plainly copying Steele. After watching *The Foundling,* Horace Walpole wrote that he liked "the old *Conscious Lovers* better, and that not much. The story is the same, only that Bevil of the new piece is in more hurry [more impatient], and consequently more natural."[8] It took Henry

Fielding's spirited defense of Moore's piece in his *The Jacobite Journal* to put the issue of plagiarism somewhat at rest. Fielding pronounced "the comedy of the *Foundling* to be a good Play" and "adjudged" it to "be represented and received as such," noting that as "to the malicious Insinuations of Plagiarism, they do not deserve an Answer: They are indeed made in the true Spirit of modern Criticism" (209).

In fact, as several scholars have noted, *The Conscious Lovers* might not have been as important an influence on *The Foundling* as was Richardson's *Pamela*. Moore himself advertised his play's indebtedness to Richardson's first novel by having Belmont tell his confidant Colonel Raymond that to resolve to marry the portionless, obscure Fidelia he should "read *Pamela* twice over first." What if, muses the reluctant Belmont, Fidelia is "but the Out-case of a Beggar, and oblig'd to Chance for a little Education,"—to which his upright friend, the colonel, replies: "Why then her Mind is dignified by her Obscurity; and you will have the Merit of raising her to a Rank which she was meant to adorn—And where's the mighty Matter in all this!—You want no Addition to your Fortune, and have only to sacrifice a little necessary Pride to necessary Happiness" (144–45). Luckily, those exalted egalitarian sentiments are never put to the test because, unlike Pamela, Fidelia is revealed to be a lady of birth and fortune and the colonel's own sister. The weak attempt at a social critique contained in the colonel's speech is neutralized, even before he opens his mouth, by the telltale title of the play.

What was Richardson's relationship with Moore at the time he inserted his covert reference to *The Foundling* into his *Clarissa*? Though not a confidant to the degree of Aaron Hill, Moore grew increasingly friendly with Richardson in the late 1740s. We get our first glimpse of the two men together in 1748 when Richardson helped Moore revise *The Foundling* for its Drury Lane debut. Though the greater part of the play was written between July 1746 and May 1747, Moore continued working on it well into the next year. In the summer of 1747, he made a number of corrections suggested by David Garrick, and in January 1748, he met with Richardson, Joseph Spence, Colley Cibber, and a "very pretty young lady, that writes verse"[9] in the Green Room for a reading of the comedy. This meeting precipitated additional corrections before Moore could submit the manuscript of *The Foundling* to the Lord Chamberlain later that month. It is tempting to think that Richardson had proved a sympathetic and helpful reader because Moore invited him later for a similar read-through of his next play, *The Gamester* (1753), although it is also possible to view the latter invitation in the context of Richardson and Moore's personal friendship or the prestige that the presence of the author of *Pamela* and *Clarissa* would lend to such a conference.

In September 1748, Richardson sent Moore the fifth volume of *Clarissa*. The tenor of the letters exchanged on the occasion between the two writers is informal and friendly. Moore rallies Richardson (the letter written on October 1 is a long praise couched in the form of an elaborate rebuke) and confesses his affection for him. He warns the author of *Clarissa* that if the enthusiastic ladies who have read the novel were so lucky as to spend an "hour with Mr. Richardson . . . [his] Turn of Ravishment might be next."[10] In his next letter, Moore voices his doubts about the way Richardson represented Clarissa's and Lovelace's deaths, prompting the famous five-page reply in which Richardson supplies an elaborate explanation of why Lovelace could not have been called on to comment upon his fatal duel with Morden.[11] Moore was so impressed with *Clarissa* that he wanted to make a tragedy out of it. According to Anna Laetitia Barbauld, "Richardson mention[ed] in one of his letters that Mr. Moore, author of *The Foundling*, had an intention of bringing the story of Clarissa upon the stage, and that Garrick told him he should with great pleasure be the Lovelace of it" (1:cvii). (This plan never materialized.[12]) At the end of 1748, Richardson wrote to Hill, who needed to be reassured about David Garrick's intention to produce Hill's tragedy *Merope*, about a meeting he had with "Mr. Moore . . . one of Mr. Garrick's principal confidants." Richardson "took Occasion . . . on Mr. Moore calling upon [him] to ask . . . what he knew as to the acting or not acting Merope this Season . . . [and Moore] had, as in Confidence" assured Richardson that Garrick "was very desirous" of bringing the play on.[13] The last currently available reference to the Moore–Richardson relationship comes from Richardson's letter to Lady Bradshaigh in 1753. Richardson writes that he "heard the greatest part of the *Gamester* read by Mr. Garrick, before it was brought upon the stage. On the whole, [he] much liked it [and] thought it a very affecting performance. There are faults in it; but [it is] a moral and seasonable piece" (*Selected Letters*, 224). Although Alan Dugald McKillop suspects that by 1754, Richardson's "friendship with Edward Moore had cooled," his evidence for such a breach is largely circumstantial.[14]

We can thus only speculate on the exact emotional coloration of Richardson's allusion to the rumors of plagiarism that sullied the debut of his friend's play. On the one hand, having participated in its Green Room read-through, Richardson must have had some sort of personal investment in the success of *The Foundling*. He must have also been flattered by *The Foundling*'s tribute to *Pamela*. It is very likely then that Lovelace's promise to write a "new and striking" comedy was a friendly in-joke rather than a casual jab at Drury Lane's practice of recycling successful old plays. On the other hand, we do not know how Richardson felt about Moore's close friendship with his rival Fielding and about Fielding's active involvement in Moore's professional and personal life. Besides contributing to *The Foundling*'s ultimate success, Fielding published praises of Moore's poem *The Trial of Selim the Persian, for Divers High Crimes and Misdemeanors,* and later he applied to Lord George Lyttelton (the sympathetic subject of the poem) for assistance in procuring Moore the position of Deputy Licensor to the Stage, the income from which would allow the then indigent playwright to marry the woman he loved.[15] (Anthony Amberg has even suggested that when Moore did marry Jenny Hamiliton, they named their only child Harry after Fielding.[16]) Although it is by no means certain that by having Lovelace expostulate about the "new and striking comedy," Richardson was expressing any subconscious annoyance about Fielding and Moore's chumminess, we cannot completely ignore that possibility.[17]

But whether a friendly or not-so-friendly in-joke, Lovelace's evocation of *The Foundling* serves an important function in *Clarissa* as it participates in what William Warner calls Lovelace and Clarissa's "struggle for interpretation." Lovelace strives to cast his pursuit of Clarissa in comic terms whereas Clarissa frames the story of their relationship in a "tragic mode,"[18] or, as several scholars have suggested, in a hagiographic mode, in which, as a Christian martyr, she moves inexorably toward her tragic and instructive end.[19] Lovelace's and Clarissa's competing genres and styles translate into competing ideologies aligned inversely along the categories of class and gender. The aristocratic Lovelace wishes to write a comedy—a "low" genre compared to tragedy—as a subtle sexual putdown of his upper-middle-class "goddess," whose family, as he never tires repeating, "is beneath [his] own" (426). Clarissa is committed to the tragic "high" style of hagiography that would ultimately make irrelevant both her sexual vulnerability and her disadvantageous—in contrast to Lovelace's upper-class kin—social standing. That Lovelace's idea of a play called *The Quarrelsome Lovers* is part of his attempt to "make their story his comedy" (77) has been suggested by Warner and elaborated by several scholars since;[20] what I want to add to their insights is that Lovelace has in mind a specific comedy, a comedy with a "foundling" plot, and, moreover, one more similar to the play written by Moore than to the original *The Conscious Lovers*.

As even Walpole acknowledged in his criticism of Moore's play as a mere spin-off of Steele's original, "Bevil of the new piece is in more hurry, and consequently more natural" (quoted in Caskey, 39); in other words, Moore's indisputable contribution to the plot of the old *Conscious Lovers* was to transform the proper, even "wooden," Bevil Junior into the "more natural" rake, Belmont. The story of Belmont's relationship with Fidelia is thus precisely the comedy that Lovelace imagines reenacting: a dashing young nobleman saves a girl of unknown origins from an obnoxious suitor; the young lady is unmistakably in love with her savior (Moore's Fidelia is open about her feelings, and Belmont is certain about her sexual attraction to him); the rake wants to persuade her to cohabitation, applies a devious stratagem, fails—and having thus been reassured about her virtue—marries her with a sincere wish to make the best of husbands. Moore's comedy ends with Fidela's father, who until now had condemned Belmont's behavior, conceding Belmont his daughter's hand in marriage: "Take her, Mister Belmont, and protect the Virtue, you have try'd" (195). The elements of this scenario that must particularly appeal to Lovelace's fancy include, first, the sexual vulnerability of the heroine, apparently abandoned, or "exposed," by her "natural friends" (Lovelace is fond of using the word *exposure* in speaking about Clarissa's family—"Have they not willfully exposed her to dangers? . . . And had they not thus cruelly exposed her, is she not a single woman?" [717]); second, her unmistakable love for the hero, which is not shattered even by his despicable plotting (precisely the reaction that Lovelace hopes for); and, third, the final respectful submission by the father of the bride to the rake he formerly held in contempt (an unthinkable outcome in the case of Harlowe Senior, but Lovelace likes contemplating fantastic resolutions that elevate him and humble his enemies).

There is one detail in *Clarissa* that could, despite some reservations, be read as Lovelace's direct projection of Moore's Belmont onto himself. Lovelace, as we know, occasionally gets so deeply into the role that he is playing at the moment that he maintains it even when there is no obvious reason to do so, and so it seems that he "plays" Belmont in a conversation with his cousin Charlotte that takes place at Lord M.'s. When Charlotte scolds Lovelace for his "stratagems," he diverts her by hinting at the possibility of a little incestuous dalliance between them:

> They [Lovelace's cousins] are smart girls; they have life and wit; and yesterday, upon Charlotte's raving against me upon a related enterprise, I told her that I had had it in debate several times, whether she were or were not too near of kin to me: and that it was once a moot point with me whether I could not love her dearly for a month or so: and perhaps it was well for her that another pretty puss started up and diverted me, just as I was entering upon the course. . . . I told Charlotte that . . . I was sure I should not have been put to the expense of above two or three stratagems (for nobody admired a good invention more than she), could I but have disentangled her conscience from the embarrasses of consanguinity.
>
> She pretended to be highly displeased. . . . (1024)

Lovelace consistently attempts to show that other people share his worldview even if they are not honest enough to admit it. Here he strives to make it sound as if Charlotte actually participated in his fun and, being a "smart girl" who has to repress her "life" and "wit," even appreciated the opportunity to act out some of her forbidden fantasies with her incorrigible cousin. This theme grows even stronger in the third edition of the novel (1751), in which Lovelace claims that in response to his jokes about incest, his cousins "were forced to put on grave airs, and to seem angry, because the Antiques [i.e., their elders] made the matter of such high importance. Yet so lightly sat anger and fellow-feeling at their hearts, that they were forced to purse in their mouths, to suppress the smiles [that Lovelace] now-and-then laid out for."[21]

This conversation between Lovelace and his cousins echoes one in *The Foundling* in which Belmont tells his sister Rosetta that, accomplished coquette that she is, she would have been particularly vulnerable to his rakish charms had he not been her brother. Rosetta replies in kind, and they part mutually pleased with their incestuous exchange:

> BELMONT: Nay, Child, if a Coquet be so useful in the System of Morals, a Rake must be the most horrid Thing in Nature—He was born for her Destruction—She loses her Being at the very Sight of him—and drops plum into his Arms, like a charm'd Bird into the Mouth of a Rattle-snake.
>
> ROSETTA: Bless us all!—What a Mercy it is, that we are Brother and Sister!

> BELMONT: Be thankful for't Night and Morning upon your knees,
> Hussy—for I shoul'd certainly have been the Ruin of you.... (157)

We have no direct evidence on the exact textual effects that the Green Room read-through of *The Foundling* had on the manuscript of *Clarissa*.[22] However, it is known that even at the time of that read-through, Richardson was already revising *Clarissa*, intending to blacken Lovelace's character,[23] so it is quite possible that he decided to adopt some of Belmont Junior's libertine sentiments for his own rake. Furthermore, whereas we cannot ascertain that the motif of incestuous joking between a rake and his attractive female relative was Moore's own invention and thus the only source for the scene in *Clarissa*,[24] we do have some circumstantial evidence that such exchanges were not common in the literature of the time. Lady Mary Wortley Montagu, who was exceptionally well-read and would have recognized Lovelace's flirting with his cousin as a mere literary convention—had it been such—was shocked by it: "Such Libertys as pass between Mr. Lovelace and his cousins are not to be excus'd by the relation," she wrote to her daughter, Lady Bute, adding that she "should have been much astonish'd if Lord Denbeigh should have offer'd to kiss [her], and [she should hope that] Lord Trentham never attempted such an Impertinence to [Lady Bute]" (422).

If we agree that the "Libertys" that pass between Lovelace and Charlotte are borrowed from *The Foundling*, then the scene containing such borrowings can also be considered in the context of Lovelace's comic reimagining of Clarissa's fate. Positioning himself as a new Belmont, the rake who flirts with his cousin/sister and tries to seduce the beauteous foundling in his protection, while the role of that virtuous but ultimately forgiving foundling is reserved for Clarissa, is Lovelace's way to assure himself and his audience that he will succeed—has to succeed, for such are the laws of the genre within which he is working—in convincing Clarissa that she should marry him notwithstanding his earlier plots and contrivances.

Scattered throughout the novel, Lovelace's expostulations on Clarissa's "foundling" status thus can be read in relation to his strategy of casting Clarissa as the Fidelia of his comedy. Early in the novel, he describes Clarissa by evoking the image of a child "laid to" a strange family which then raises it as its own: "But here's her mistake . . .—she takes the man she calls her father . . . ; she takes the men she calls her uncles; the fellow she calls her brother; and the poor contemptible she calls her sister; *to be* her father, *to be* her uncles, her brother, her sister . . ." (145). Later, appropriating the foundling narrative's rhetoric of exposure, he claims that Clarissa's friends have "willfully *exposed* her to dangers . . . —yet must know that such a woman would be considered as lawful prize by as many as could have the opportunity to attempt her . . ." (717; emphasis added). In other words, Lovelace uses eighteenth-century revivals of the classical foundling narrative, such as Moore's and Steele's plays, to insist that his treatment of Clarissa fits the mode of romantic comedy and should be judged and rewarded accordingly (i.e., by marriage, if Lovelace chooses to marry).

Richardson does something very similar here to what he did in *Pamela,* in which, according to William Warner, he has Mr. B. initially conceptualizing Pamela as a heroine of a traditional romance of amorous intrigue and Pamela resisting such framing for her story and "teaching" Mr. B. to "read" her correctly, that is, in the context of the new domestic novel: "Because of its own manifold similarity to the novels of amorous intrigue, the text of *Pamela* must ward off the sort of novelistic reading it might inadvertently court. In order to prevent his readers from doing to Pamela what Mr. B. does to its heroine—namely, read within the codes of the novels of amorous intrigue—Richardson . . . represents the genesis of his own proper reader, the reformed Mr. B."[25]

Too little too late, Lovelace also becomes a reformed reader. Clarissa triumphs in their ideological battle by finally stifling Lovelace's comedic interpretation of their story and imposing upon him her hagiographic reading: after Clarissa's death, the distraught Lovelace demands a lock of her hair and her heart, which he "will keep in spirits," while her "bowels . . . shall be sent down" to her family (1384)—a sentimental charge transmogrifying into the hunt for the relics of a deceased saint.[26]

Lovelace is not alone in trying to appropriate a foundling narrative for his ideological purposes: Clarissa and those who support her in her discursive struggle with Lovelace do it as well. Early in the novel, Clarissa muses, "How happy I might have been with any other brother in the world but Mr. James Harlowe; and with any other sister but *his* sister" (65–66)—the first stirrings of the dream of being really the child of a different, and better, family that comes full circle later when Clarissa exclaims that "by some unaccountable mistake, [she] must have been laid to a family that, having newly found out or at least suspected the imposture, cast [her] from their hearts with the indignation that such a discovery would warrant" (986). Anna Howe joins enthusiastically in Clarissa's first fantasies of not really belonging to her family: "And do they [James and Arabella] not both bear [your father's] stamp and image more than you do?" (67); and when, later, Clarissa reports having written to James that she "should endeavor to assert [her] character, in order to be thought less an *alien,* and *nearer of kin* to [James and Arabella], than either of [them] have of late seemed to suppose [her]" (227), Anna responds passionately: "[You are] an alien. You are not one of them" (237).

The most striking instance of Clarissa's evocation of the foundling romance takes place when she explicitly aligns herself with the classical foundling of antiquity, Oedipus. As she observes to Anna:

> It were an impiety to adopt the following lines, because it would be throwing upon the degrees of Providence a fault too much my own. But often do I revolve them for the sake of the general similitude which they bear to my unhappy yet undersigned error.
>
> To you, great gods! I make my last appeal
> Or clear my virtues, or my crimes reveal.
> If wand'ring in the maze of life I run,
> And backward tread the steps I sought to shun,
> Impute my errors to your own decree;
> My FEET are guilty; but my HEART is free. (568)

Adopted from John Dryden and Nathaniel Lee's *Oedipus* (1678), these lines immediately precede Lovelace's reference to Terence, Steele, and Moore and are thus strategically positioned in the text of the novel as a suitably tragic counterpart to Lovelace's comic reading of the situation. Clarissa's identification with Oedipus reveals the ideological stakes behind her talk about being an "alien," a "laid-to" child, an "impostor" in her own family. If Lovelace turns to the foundling narrative to strengthen the comic mode of the story, Clarissa uses it to negotiate the responsibility for her adventures. As argued in the previous chapter, the foundling status of the heroine in eighteenth-century fiction enabled her to be a reluctant heroine, not responsible for her best-selling peregrinations, thus retaining her claim to respect and to a socially ambitious marriage. Both Indiana and Moll Flanders emphasize that because their fate was predetermined at birth by having been abandoned or lost by their parents, they cannot help their subsequent titillating adventures: "twas Heaven's high will" that as "helpless [infants]" they were exposed to "such variety of sorrows" (377–78). As several critics have demonstrated, Clarissa is obsessed with whether or not—and exactly how—she is responsible for what befell her. The appeal to the foundling romance implicitly supports her melancholy observation that she seems "to be impelled, as it were, by a perverse fate which [she is] not able to resist" (332) and that "a poor *lost* creature . . . [she] cannot charge herself with one criminal or faulty inclination" (565; emphasis added). Clarissa's identification with Oedipus is paradigmatic in this respect, as she first introduces it by saying that it "were an impiety to adopt the . . . lines [spoken by that tragic foundling], because it would be throwing upon the degrees of Providence a fault too much [her] own," but then "adopts" those lines anyway, claiming the "general similitude which they bear to [her] unhappy yet undersigned error." The outcome of Clarissa's positioning herself as a foundling is that like Oedipus, she can now legitimately ask "great gods" to "impute [her] errors to [their] own decree" and not to her misguided judgment.

The question of property, the key concern of the eighteenth-century foundling narrative, underwrites in complex ways Clarissa's meditations on fate and Providence. One of the first instances of such underwriting comes when Clarissa realizes that her family will not stop pressuring her to marry Solmes. Clarissa tells Anna that while there remains any hope, however remote, that her relatives can be persuaded to give up that ill-conceived match, she "should think the leaving [her] father's house, without his consent, one of the most inexcusable actions [she] could be guilty of, were the protection to be ever so unexceptionable; and *this notwithstanding the independent fortune willed to [her] by [her] grandfather*" (242–43; emphasis added). Note the intentional ambiguity of Clarissa's meaning, conveyed by the terms *fortune* and *willed*. It seems that the grandfather had not only left Clarissa his estate—the sentence would have looked very different had Clarissa used those simple words—but he had also predetermined (willed) her fate (fortune).[27] Thus even while claiming that she would never leave her father's house, Clarissa begins to explore the rhetoric of fate that she will be able to rely on in the future should she indeed run away from her family. Clarissa's grandfather is tentatively cast here as one of Oedipus's "great gods," to whose "decree" (i.e., his bequest of estate) her "errors" can be "imputed" (568).

The implicit alignment of property with fate—via the word *fortune*—adds a new dimension to the novel's fascination with the "wrong" heirs. As Clarissa's grandfather admits in his will, his bequest of the estate to his youngest granddaughter is "not strictly conformable to law, or the forms thereof." By leaving it to her in spite of the "prior right" (as Uncle

Antony puts it) of Clarissa's other relatives, he preordains—"wills" in Clarissa's "foundling-speak"—the future ordeals that will establish her right to the estate on terms other than those "strictly conformable to law." That Clarissa fulfills this unspoken clause of the will is suggested by her own final testament: whereas for most of the novel, she recoils at the thought of claiming her estate, at the end, she feels fully entitled, first, to give "all the real estates in to which [she has] any claim or title ... to [her] father ... rather than [her] brother and sister, to whom [she] had once thoughts of devising them" and, second, "to dispose ... absolutely" (1413–14) the income from her grandfather's estate (e.g., to leave six hundred pounds to Mrs. Norton).[28] The right to bequest is the most eloquent testimony of the right to own. The terms of ownership have been adjusted: although both the opening and the closing wills are viewed as incongruous, the incongruity of the former is framed in legal terms (the youngest daughter gets the property that should have gone to one of the male heirs), but the incongruity of the latter, in affective, emotional terms (a dying teenage girl "devises" an estate to a surviving parent).

Clarissa, Belton's Bastards, and the Problem of Inheritance

The eighteenth-century obsession with bastardy provides a crucial context for Clarissa's transformation from a legal oddity to a rightful testatrix. Dangerously, the same rhetoric that describes Clarissa as a foundling could be read as doubting her legitimacy. Nobody in the novel would go so far as to imply that Clarissa is illegitimate. Yet we have to realize that the language used by people around her to describe her situation sounds much more innocuous to us today than it did to eighteenth-century readers attuned by their daily dealings with bastardy to the potential double meaning of phrases doubting or affirming too shrilly a person's paternity. When the incensed Clarissa promises her brother that she will "assert [her] character in order to be thought less an alien, and nearer of kin to [him]" (227), or when she wants to show him that she has "something in [her] of [her] father's family, as well as of [her] mother's" (105), or when she writes in her will that she was "nobody's" (compare to the legal definition of bastard—*filius nullius*—the son of nobody), her language indicates that the treatment she receives from her family would be more understandable had they had doubts about her legitimacy. (We should remember here that in

Kicking Out the Cubs

Peregrine Pickle, published three years later, Tobias Smollett did not have to say once that Peregrine was not really Gamaliel Pickle's son: the revulsion with which his mother treats Peregrine as he grows older and begins, presumably, to look more and more like his unnamed real father proves his bastardy better than any direct explanation would have done.) That eighteenth-century readers were aware of the ambiguous overtones of Clarissa's rhetoric is shown by Lovelace's explicit assertion of Clarissa's legitimacy in the midst of his epistolary complaints about her "mistaken" thinking that her father *is* her father. When Lovelace writes to Belford that Clarissa "takes the man she calls her father (*her mother had been faultless, had she not been her father's wife*) ... to be her father ..." (145; emphasis added), he knows that the aside about Clarissa's mother's "faultlessness" is absolutely necessary to ensure that his claim that Clarissa's father is not really her father would not be taken literally.

One effect of such rhetorical experimentation with the issue of Clarissa's legitimacy is that readers—specifically, eighteenth-century readers—may well have begun to feel even more exasperated by the unreasonable Harlowes: Clarissa is treated almost as if she were a bastard, while, according to the logic of the novel, as expressed by Belford, only children who really are illegitimate deserve to be abused in such a heinous fashion. Here is Belford describing approvingly the handling of the two "sturdy ... cubs" born to the unholy union of Belton and Thomasine, who must be kicked out of their father's house because the longer they stay, the better their chances of inheriting Belton's estate will be:

> [Thomasine's] boys (once [Belton] thought them his) are sturdy enough to shoulder him in his own house as they pass by him. Siding with the mother, they in a manner expel him; and in his absence riot away on the remnant of his broken fortunes. ...
>
> I have undertaken his cause. He has given me leave, yet not without reluctance, to put him into possession of his own house; and to place in it for him his unhappy sister, whom he hitherto slighted, *because* unhappy. ...
>
> Though but lately apprised of [Thomasine's] infidelity, it now comes out to have been of so long continuance, that he has no room to believe the boys to be his: yet how fond did he use to be of them!
>
> Her boys threaten anybody who should presume to insult their *mother*. Their *father* (as they call poor Belton) they speak of as an

unnatural one. And their probably *true father* is for ever there, *hostilely* there, passing for her cousin, as usual: now her *protecting cousin*. (1088)

Belford then compares Belton's situation with that of the ancient Sarmatians, who, returning home after many years of absence, had to get rid of their unfaithful wives; their slaves, who had been their wives' lovers all those years; and the now adult children born to those adulterous unions, who are resolved to defend their mothers and fathers:

> Noble Sarmatians, scorning to attack their slaves with equal weapons, only provided themselves with the same sort of whips with which they used formerly to chastise them. And attacking them with them, the miscreants fled before them.... (1089)
>
> Tourville ... will let you know the difficulty we had to drive out this *meek* mistress and *frugal* manager [Thomasine], with her cubs, and to give the poor fellow's sister possession for him of his own house; [Belton] skulking meanwhile at an inn at Croydon, too dispirited to appear in his own cause.
>
> But I must observe that we were probably but just in time to save the shattered remains of his fortune from this rapacious woman and her accomplices: for, as he cannot live long, and she thinks so, we found she had certainly taken measures to set up a marriage, and keep possession of all for herself and her sons.
>
> ... I was forced to chastise the quondam hostler [Thomasine's alleged cousin] in her sight, before I could drive him out of the house. He had the insolence to lay hands on me: and I made him take but one step from the top to the bottom of a pair of stairs. I thought his neck and all his bones had been broken. And then, he being carried out neck-and-heels, Thomasine thought fit to walk out after him. (1187)

Although it is highly unlikely that Richardson intended his readers to draw any conscious comparisons between the "cubs'" eviction and Clarissa's forced elopement from her father's house, in his choice of words in describing both the real illegitimacy of Belton's sons and the metaphorical illegitimacy of Clarissa, the two situations speak to each other with ironic urgency. First, in both cases, the persecution of the "wrong" heirs is fueled by the growing suspicion that if left unattended, those heirs will get more than they are entitled to. Belford is certain that he has come "just in time" to keep Thomasine and her sons from arrogating "the remains of [Belton's] shattered fortune"; similarly, James and Arabella Harlowe are convinced that their "little siren" of a sister "is in a fair way to *out-uncle* as well as *out-grandfather*" (80) them (that is, to inherit, her uncles' estates in addition to her grandfather's). Second, both fathers rely on other people to drive their children out. Belton "skulks" at an inn at Croydon, "too dispirited to appear in his own cause," while Belford and Mowbray effect the eviction for him; Clarissa's father decides to "wholly commit [the handling of Clarissa] to [his] Son James . . . and to Bella, and to [his] brother . . ." (327). Third, Belford's unproven assumption that Belton's sons are really the children of Thomasine's "cousin"-lover echoes both Anna's claim that James and Arabella bear "stamp and image [of Harlowe Senior] more than [Clarissa does]" (67) as well as a series of similar avowals of Clarissa's "difference." Thomasine's "cubs" are too "broad-shouldered" to be their father's sons (Belton is but a slight man), and Clarissa is too "good" to be her hard-hearted father's daughter.

Considerations of social class subtly enter Belford's conceptualization of the boys as not worthy of Belton's estate. It is important that, in Belford's view, Belton's sons are not even human. They are "cubs," and their presumed father is, conveniently, a hostler, a former handler of horses, who himself transmogrifies into a beast of burden fit to be driven away with a whip. Belford never says that he used the whip on Thomasine's lover, but he does report "chastising" the "quondam hostler" and making "him take but one step from the top to the bottom of a pair of stairs" (1187). Here, the repetition of the word *chastise*, used earlier by Belford to tell the story of the Sarmatians, superimposes the image of the righteous Sarmatian chastising his slave with a whip onto the description of the scuffle on the stairs of Belton's house. In other words, unlike Clarissa, who is granted an opportunity (ironic as it may sound, given the sufferings this opportunity entails) to prove herself morally worthy of her inheritance, Belton's children are debarred from inheriting their father's estate and even from having the potential for earning a moral right to that estate. They are destined to remain legal and moral outcasts, demonized now as "cubs," now as the offspring of a "slave," for no observable reason other than for being devoted to their mother and resenting those who mistreat her.

The contrast between the treatments afforded to the differently wrong heirs should qualify the critical view of *Clarissa* as essentially progressive in its view of real property. Several scholars, including Christopher Hill, Theodore Albert, John Zomchick, and April London, have argued that via the grandfather's will, Richardson's novel embodies a "modern, bourgeois attitude"[29] toward the essentially feudal custom of entail. In his study of family and the law in eighteenth-century fiction, Zomchick has pointed out that:

> As an unassimilated historical effect, the will instigates the narrative by creating a problem to be solved. Ideologically progressive, it redistributes wealth to the deserving . . . and is in accord with William Blackstone's belief that the freedom to alienate one's lands at will was conducive to economic growth. A commercial nation fared best, Blackstone writes, with "a number of moderate fortunes engaged in the extension of trade." . . . Viewed in this manner, the bequest supports a progressive version of possessive individualism by working against the concentration of wealth and power in the hands of an already empowered elite. The grandfather justifies the bequest, furthermore, by his affection for a deserving granddaughter. The motive for this historical event, then, embodies the two most important values of bourgeois society: familial affection and meritorious labor.[30]

How are the considerations of familial affection and meritorious labor factored into the story of Thomasine's "cubs"? Belton "used to be . . . fond" of his sons, and Thomasine used to be known as a "frugal manager" of Belton's estate, but neither the memory of past affection nor the acknowledgment of past labor seems to have any bearing on the present decision to kick the bastards out and forget about them. The bourgeois redistribution of wealth does not apply to illegitimate children; the question of what they would do with their hypothetical share of the estate—would they "engage in the extension of trade" or would they "riot [it] away"? (most likely the latter, given their villainous bastard natures)—appears irrelevant and so is never contemplated. Significantly, it is Belford who effects both the devaluation of Thomasine as a manager of Belton's estate and the retroactive secondary bastardization of her "cubs": it is according to Belford that, however unholy Belton and Thomasine's union might have been, Thomasine's sturdy cubs do not belong even to that union. Throughout *Clarissa*, Belford appears to be obsessed with the theme of illegitimacy, condemning the bastard-breeding practice of "keeping" as frequently and vociferously as Lovelace extols it[31] (and perhaps one is bound to be perceived as shrilly obsessed when faced with the difficult task of providing a counterpoise to the charming and witty Lovelace, who is given far more space in the novel to express his views), and as readers, we are invited to accept Belford's demonizing of bastards as the only moral alternative to Lovelace's cheerful depravity. Richardson's novel may thus be progressive in its treatment of its heroine—signaling her difference from everybody in her family and positioning her as a living challenge to the ossified system of patriarchal values—but it seems to be much more conservative in its view of illegitimate children.

By the mid 1750s, Richardson must have become less comfortable with bastards remaining beyond the pale of the fiction's humanist interrogation of the socioeconomic status quo. He did offer a slightly more humane solution to the bastard problem in his *The History of Sir Charles Grandison* (1753–54), in which Sir Charles still drives the illegitimate children of Sir Thomas Grandison and Mrs. Oldham off the estate but at the same time provides for them financially, making it possible for them to engage "in the extension of trade." Richardson's adjustment of attitude toward bastards in his fiction might have been predicated upon his compassion for the illegitimate children of the poor: in 1754 he was elected as one of the governors and guardians of the London Foundling Hospital. He might also have envisioned Sir Charles's position as a balanced compromise between the demonizing of illegitimate children in *Clarissa* and what he considered to be the scandalous pandering to fornicators in Fielding's *Tom Jones*.

"Rewriting" Bastards on Stage and in the Novel

Richardson's use of the theatrical representations of the foundling motif in his novel raises the important issue of genre-related differences in the period's fictional treatment of illegitimacy. While *Clarissa*'s engagement with the plays of Dryden, Steele, and Moore substantiates David Marshall's and Jean-Christophe Agnew's observation that "the novel achieves a distinctive form in the eighteenth-century by virtue of its internalization of 'the figure of theater,'"[32] it also opens the possibility that the Enlightenment's preoccupation with bastardy presented playwrights and novelists with distinctly different representational challenges. It seems that such preoccupation intervened in novelistic discourse much more forcefully than it did in the drama, making it more difficult for the novelist to separate the foundling elements of his plot from the characters' concerns about illegitimacy.

It is true, of course, that we can still recover in *The Conscious Lovers* Steele's anxiety about the fate of his own "natural" daughter and about the disturbing topicality of Terence's exposure references. It is also true that Moore's fleeting reference to Fidelia as a possible "Out-case of a Beggar" and his mention of the corrupted nurse who sold "the helpless infant" she had found "at her door" as soon as the foundling approached sexual maturity must have given pause to an eighteenth-century audience attuned to the distinction between the well-recommended nurse employed by a respectable household to take care of a legitimate child and the shady personage—a Mother Midnight figure—paid to take an unwanted bastard off the parent's hands. Fidelia's avaricious caregiver seems, troublingly, to belong to the latter category. At the same time, Moore carefully modifies the history of his heroine's father so as not to substantiate our suspicions about the circumstances of her birth. Indiana was conceived immediately upon Mr. Sealand's abandoning the wicked ways of a "Man of Pleasure about the Town"—a detail implying that she has narrowly avoided the fate of being a "natural" child. Fidelia's father, on the other hand, had never been a rake. Driven into banishment by his mistaken political zeal rather than by a profligate's need to recover a wasted estate, Sir Charles is the picture of moral uprightness; if anything, the political naïveté that had caused him to be loyal to a lost cause strengthens this favorable impression. By the end of the play, we have no choice but to take at its face value the story about the misguided nurse who mistakenly treated the legitimate daughter of a gentleman as a common bastard abandoned by her parents.

George Colman the Elder's *The English Merchant* (1767) replicates Moore's strategy of explaining why "a young lady of great beauty and virtue"[33] could possibly find herself in the unseemly position of a "wretched vagabond" (16) suspected of being a "strolling princess . . . , [even if] more frugal of [her] favors than the rest of [her] sisterhood, merely to enhance the price of them" (20). Because Sir William Douglas, the father of Colman's heroine, Amelia, had formerly supported the cause of "disloyalty and resurrection" (11), he is now "proscribed, condemned, attainted (alas, but too justly!)" (10), and forced to conceal his identity and whereabouts. "Abandoned by the relation who succeeded to [her guardian's] estate" (10), Amelia lives alone in London, supporting herself with "the work of her own hands" (22), exposed to "dishonorable proposals" from "presuming" lords (14). Like Moore, Colman substitutes a father's political misdemeanors for sexual ones, a strategy that appeared to gain popularity among eighteenth-century playwrights groping for a respectable explanation for a strange denouement in which a man suddenly "discovers" his daughter in a boardinghouse after not seeing her for twenty years. Infusing the traditional foundling plot with political meaning helped Moore and Colman to further obscure the potentially indelicate "bastard" contexts of their plays.[34]

But the main reason that Steele, Moore, and Colman were able to deploy the conventions of the foundling narrative and (in the case of Moore and Colman) strategically situated political allusions to neutralize the connotations of illegitimacy forcing their way into their dramas was the relatively limited, when compared to novels, scope of their plots. The typical foundling play focused on two or three nuclear families and made a point of never featuring any secondary illegitimate characters, whose presence might precipitate an unwelcome comparison between the respective ontological statuses of the bastard and the foundling characters. By contrast, the period's novelists dealt with multiple and extended families and rarely failed to include or at least mention an illegitimate child born to one of the numerous secondary personages. The trademark of the novelistic discourse—its "thick" description of imagined reality—called for and facilitated the admittance of multiple episodic characters, including the inevitable bastards.

We have already seen that even those eighteenth-century writers who explicitly signaled their characters' affinity with the foundlings of antiquity—as Defoe did in *Moll Flanders*—failed to keep the foundling elements of their plot impervious to the corrosive impact of contemporary anxiety about the socioeconomic and ethical repercussions of bastardy. Under these conditions, no novelist could foresee and control all the suggestive inferences and titillating misreadings made possible by the complex cross-wiring between the foundling and bastard sequences of the novel. The very attempt to control such inferences could instead increase their number exponentially. Whereas in *The Foundling*, the discussion of Fidelia's possible illegitimacy, and indeed *any* further discussion of illegitimacy, was forcefully foreclosed by Sir Charles's account of his former political difficulties, in *Clarissa*, Lovelace's nervous aside on Mrs. Harlowe's "faultlessness" duly asserted the legitimacy of the title heroine but at the same time implicitly reminded readers of numerous other mothers in the story who were certainly "faulty." The images of those mothers, such as Thomasine and Lovelace's former mistresses, were left to haunt the cultural imagination of the "century of illegitimacy."

-4-

TOM JONES

Resisting the Mythologization of Bastardy

Looking for bastards in *Tom Jones* is a highly gratifying endeavor. One finds them at every turn of the plot and, at the end of one productive search, puts the novel away with a pleasant anticipation of discovering more of those stinking "misbegotten Wretches"[1] upon the next rereading—an impression perhaps intended by the author. The current list, supported by the analysis of such scholars as Robert Alter and Hugh Amory, includes Tom; his half-brother Blifil;[2] Goody Seagrim's eldest daughter; Molly Seagrim's child; Nancy Miller;[3] and Nancy's first child. (Then there is also the fascinating family of the Fitzpatricks, the Gaelic prefix "Fitz" meaning "bastard son.") Several of those characters—Blifil, Molly Seagrim's older sister, Nancy, and Nancy's future child—may not qualify as illegitimate under early modern law because their mothers are made "honest women" (i.e., they marry their lovers) some time after their "lapses"; however, because the narrator, for whatever reason, chooses to inform readers about those lapses, we should have no scruples about adding these four to our inventory of bastards.[4]

What is remarkable about Henry Fielding's illegitimate characters—apart from the fact that there are so many of them—is how unremarkable they are. The novel consistently rejects the venerable literary tradition of portraying bastards as either preternaturally evil, treacherous, and murderous or extraordinarily gifted, vivacious, and charismatic; as revoltingly ugly, or breathtakingly handsome; as atheistic to the point of sacrilege, or devout to the point of prophetic holiness and martyrdom; as leading players in doomed political melodramas, or bemused outsiders commenting with easy penetration on the foolish passion of other characters. I am lifting these categories, which I have loosely arranged into binaries, from Alison Findlay's *Illegitimate Power: Bastards in Renaissance Drama,* in which she demonstrates that what remained constant amidst the rich variety of early modern representations of bastards was the insistence on their extraordinariness. Good or evil, bastards were different from everybody around them by being superlative in whatever qualities were to define their personalities, and Fielding's illegitimate characters do not fit this pattern.

This chapter argues that the pointedly ordinary bastards overpopulate the novel for a specific reason. Fielding explores the gap between illegitimacy as a widespread social phenomenon and illegitimacy as a cultural fantasy, challenging the literary tradition of mythologizing what had long become an inescapable and commonplace fact of life for early modern men and women. In the case of his secondary characters, he does it by denying them any special, "bastardy-related" features or fates; in the case of his main protagonist, he compounds this denial by making his readers expect the plot to turn one way or another depending on Tom's legitimacy and then disappointing these expectations. Fielding's experimentation with his readers' assumptions about what the bastard or the foundling status of the character could entail makes Tom Jones a particularly problematic candidate for being perceived (as he often is today) as the paradigmatic bastard of eighteenth-century belles lettres and, moreover, the embodiment of eighteenth-century "criticism of aristocratic ideology."[5]

Eighteenth-Century Bastardy: Narratives of Excess

Fielding's main protagonist, as Terry Castle has argued, represents "the archetype of uncomplicated good nature . . . the lucid, even banal moral type."[6] On the other hand, the same critic has characterized Tom's success with women as "magical;"[7] and the novel does seem to prod us gently toward marveling at Tom's kindness, extraordinary good looks, and sexual charisma. To understand what is at stake in the novel's cultivation of these seemingly contradictory readings of its title hero, we have to focus on Tom's illegitimacy and reconstruct the literary and social background against which he is configured as transcending and destabilizing the categories of "bastard" and "foundling."

To measure Tom's personal "magic," we can compare him to the three characters representing a wide spectrum of eighteenth-century fictional attitudes toward illegitimacy: the first is Richard Savage's literary persona, the "Bastard," who proclaims his bastardy from the rooftops as a selling point for his personality; the second is Tobias Smollett's Humphry Clinker, who treats his status as a "natural" child as a fact of life, not to boast or shed tears or even think too much about; and the third is Smollett's Peregrine Pickle, who remains blissfully unaware of his mother's lapse and his own status as an impostor on his father's property. All three cases demonstrate that the Renaissance tradition of depicting the bastard as a prodigy in whatever capacity he chooses to impress the world had not become extinct by the eighteenth century, although it had acquired a distinct tenor of self-conscious literariness. Savage, Clinker, and Pickle are antithetical to Tom in the sheer intensity of their talents and obsessions yet are recognizable as displaying extreme versions of Tom's own contradictory impulses.

Savage, whose aborted marriage treaty with Elizabeth Ousley was discussed in the first chapter, calculatedly capitalized on the image of the bastard as a prodigy when he wrote in his famous autobiographical poem, *The Bastard* (1728),

> Blest be the Bastard's birth! through wondr'ous ways,
> He shines eccentric like a Comet's blaze.
> No sickly fruit of faint compliance he;
> He! stampt in nature's mint of extasy! (89)

Every metaphor in this stanza is a conscious reference to the traditional literary discourse on bastardy. Comparing the protagonist to "a Comet's blaze" taps the custom of associating bastards with political disturbances. Just as the appearance of a comet portended a social cataclysm, so did—in works of fiction—the emergence of a bastard as an official or unofficial leader of a political formation. The lines "No sickly fruit of faint compliance he; / He! stampt in nature's mint of extasy!" echo Shakespeare's *King Lear*, in which Edmund claims that a bastard could "in the lusty stealth of nature, take / More composition, and fierce quality, / Than doth within a dull, stale, tired bed / Go to th' creating a whole tribe of fops, / Got 'tween asleep and wake,"[8] and *Cymbeline*, in which Posthumus Leonatus muses that perhaps his father was somewhere else when Posthumus was "stamped" [conceived], and that perhaps he is really a "counterfeit," a progeny of some sly "coiner with his tools."[9] After this bravura opening, Savage goes on to describe his "cruel" natural mother (the Countess of Macclesfield refused to admit the clamorous impostor into her family in lieu of her long-dead infant son[10]), the murder that he committed while inebriated, and the kind surrogate mother (the Queen of England) whom he claimed to have acquired as a result of publicity from his murder trial. Savage's goal throughout the poem is to convert the shock value of his illegitimacy, augmented by the familiar metaphors of libidinal excess, into monetary and social value. He is selling not just his poetry, but himself—the occasionally murderous and yet too-sensitive-for-his-own-good and sensationally talented social misfit.

Savage's self-marketing strategy brilliantly prefigures what Marie MacLean describes in her study of social rebels of nineteenth- and twentieth-century French literature as a conscious attempt on the part of such writers as Flora Tristan, Gerard De Nevral, Charles Baudelaire, and Jean-Paul Sartre to translate their illegitimacy—real or invented—into literary and financial currency: the writer's claim to the "name of the mother," the only claim that the bastard child could make with certainty, becomes "not only a public scandal but a paying business."[11] When Tristan calls herself "Pariah"; Nevral, "Peregrinus"; Baudelaire, "Monster"; and Sartre, "Bastard," those sobriquets tap—as did Savage's "Bastard" in 1728—the powerful self-mythologizing potential of illegitimacy generated by the hundreds of years of rhetoric of sexual and political excess. Tom Jones, of course, does not fit this paradigm of valorized overflow. At the same time, his three guilt-ridden love affairs—*his* main claim to excess—do relate, if only parodically, to the emerging paradigm of bastardy as a trope conscripted to the service of personal myth making.

Smollett's Humphry Clinker is another eighteenth-century bastard, but his unassuming bastardy is antipodal to Richard Savage's illegitimate glamor. To borrow an image from Richardson's *Clarissa*, Clinker would be perfectly happy to "slide through life unobserved," but he is blessed—or cursed—with a gift of preaching that exalts and complicates his humble existence. Jacques Derrida observes that "every male bastard can rejoice in an immaculate conception,"[12] and Clinker is a perfect embodiment of yet another stereotype of excess associated with bastardy that Derrida has in mind here: he is a religious visionary who cannot help preaching what he believes in, which wins him both a devoted following and the threat of martyrdom. During his stay (on false charges) in Clerkenwell prison, Clinker evangelizes with a passionate self-abandon, converts his fellow prisoners to Methodism, earns the reputation of a "saint," and then nearly condemns himself to death during the hearing of his case, by insisting on conflating the terms of spiritual and criminal guilt. Nor is Clinker altogether safe from religious persecution at home, as his inability to contain his spiritual impulses earns him a severe reprimand from his master/father. Clinker claims to be moved to preach Methodism by "an inward admonition of the spirit" and the "new light of God's grace"—professions that lead Matt Bramble, deeply distrustful of religious zealotry, to proclaim that he "will have no light in [his] family but what pays the king's taxes" (a reference to the window tax) and that Humphry's "new light of grace" is a "deceitful vapour, glimmering through a crack in [his] upper story" (135). Clinker's "persecution" by his father is simultaneously parodic and touching in its unmistakable reference to scriptural stories of seers who were dismissed by their shortsighted domestics as crazy and embarrassing. Again, Tom Jones by no means measures up to the intense spirituality of saintly illegitimates, on whom Clinker is modeled, tongue-in-cheek. At the same time, eighteenth-century readers must have read Tom's relative unworldliness as the novel's implicit nod toward the cultural tradition associating bastardy with holiness.

Smollet's Peregrine Pickle differs from both Savage's "Bastard" and Smollett's Clinker in that he never finds out that he is illegitimate. We deduce his bastardy from the eagerness with which his maternal grandfather wants to marry his apparently pregnant daughter off to the unsuspecting Gamaliel Pickle; from the occasional "slips" of the narrator, as when, for example, he refers to Peregrine as "the child of passion" (594); and from Peregrine's mother's condemnation of her firstborn as a "monster" and "impostor" (as Aileen Douglas has argued, Sally Pickle hates her son "in the voice of property, according to which he is, indeed, a monstrous impostor"[13]). Since nobody but the mother can proclaim with certainty Peregrine's bastardy—and she is not at all eager to destroy her reputation—Peregrine remains in his own eyes and the eyes of the world the legal heir to his father's landed property, which he duly inherits when Gamaliel dies intestate. R. G. Collins was the first scholar to argue that Pickle is a bastard;[14] and recently Douglas has suggested that Peregrine's "odd" (i.e., the satirical transmogrifying into the cruel[15]) treatment of human bodies is grounded in his illegitimacy: "forced to go through life without the 'least mark of maternal regard,' Peregrine uses satire to demonstrate that the bodies of others are, like his own, not what they seem."[16]

Douglas's analysis focuses on psychological effects of illegitimacy: Peregrine's mother abhors him, and, in response to her rejection, he becomes indifferent to or even titillated by other people's pain. I want to consider a related trait of Peregrine's personality grounded directly in the early modern literary stereotyping of bastards. Douglas observes that Peregrine's "distinctly unpleasant . . . practical . . . satire involves disguise, cross-dressing, imposture, and mimicry."[17] According to Findlay, one characteristic trait of the early modern fictional bastard was his acting ability.[18] The bastard's personality could be inherently protean, and Peregrine's ability to mimic other people is indeed uncanny. On one occasion, when he and his friend Godfrey Gauntlet want to punish a farmer's wife for resisting Gauntlet's amorous advances, Peregrine finds "means to make himself acquainted with the farmer's voice and manner of speaking," so that when he and Gauntlet come to the farmer's house—the host being absent—Peregrine is able to demand entrance "in the rustic tone of the farmer . . . [and] the wife never doubting that her husband was returned," lets them in (169). On another occasion, Peregrine reads in his tutor's private journal and, finding the entries insipid as well as mildly unflattering to himself, decides to get even with the writer by "interlining" several phrases "betwixt two paragraphs, in manner that exactly resembled the tutor's hand-writing" (354). Furthermore, upon meeting Emily Gauntlet's merchant uncle and wishing to ingratiate himself into his good graces, Peregrine proceeds "by help of his natural sagacity" to adapt himself "wonderfully" to the humor of the older man:

> In the progress of the discourse, he consulted the merchant's disposition; and the national debt coming upon the carpet, held forth upon the funds like a professed broker. When the alderman complained of the restrictions and discouragement of trade, his guest inveigled against exorbitant duties, with the nature of which he seemed as well acquainted as any commissioner of the customs; so that the uncle was astonished at the extent of his knowledge. . . . Pickle laid hold of this opportunity to tell him [falsely] that he was descended from a race of merchants. (399–400)

Pickle's eerie talent for mimicking to perfection other people's voices, handwritings, and "races" functions simultaneously as the evidence and the consequence of his illegitimacy. Smollett's readers, familiar with the literary tradition of "protean" bastards, could see Peregrine's superhuman adaptability as yet another proof of Gamaliel Pickle's abused paternity and as a slightly fantastic but still recognizable confirmation of a bastard's general "difference."[19] As with Peregrine's other qualities—his charm, sexual appeal, beauty, and agility—his adaptability is excessive, unsettling in its image of multiple personalities bubbling in Peregrine's body and seeking other human frames to latch onto and claim as their own.

CHAPTER 4

From Savage's attempts to cash in on his notorious bastardy and Clinker's larger-than-the-humble-me spiritual inspiration, to Pickle's exuberant parasitizing on the "host" bodies of his acquaintances, excess is what all eighteenth-century fictional bastards have in common, and excess is what Tom lacks. His vices are tamable, his virtues are proportionate, and he has no special talents to boast of. It appears that Tom's bastardy is really the most fascinating thing about him because it throws into an interesting relief features that would otherwise add up to the generic eighteenth-century designations of a "pretty fellow," a "fine young man," a "young rogue" who needs to sow his wild oats before settling into benevolent country squiredom in the manner of his uncle. Following the footsteps of his admired Augustans, Jonathan Swift and Alexander Pope, Fielding sets up a trap for an unwary reader: if we insist that Tom is different from everybody around him, then we have to say that it is his kindness, generosity, and generally sound moral instinct that make him exceptional, and if we do say so, then it is a fine world we live in and a high standard by which we judge ourselves and other people.

Turning to Michael McKeon's assertion that, "although of gentle lineage, [Tom] is truly a bastard," we should thus ask ourselves what criteria we use to gauge "true" bastardy of fictional characters. Compared with other prominent bastards of eighteenth-century belles lettres, Tom is an odd man out, pointedly unexceptional in both his faults and merits, and thus perhaps unfit for being considered a paradigmatic expression of that particular literary type. We may also want to qualify Claude Rawson's observation that Fielding could have made Tom "a legitimate foundling like Joseph Andrews, . . . [but he] must have known that it was in some ways bold and unorthodox to make his hero a bastard and keep him so."[20] It appears that Fielding's bold and unorthodox move was not simply to leave his hero a bastard—that was done frequently enough in the case of male protagonists—but rather to conceptualize Tom's bastard status in terms very different from those commonly used in eighteenth-century belles lettres both before and after the publication of *Tom Jones*.

Bastards and Foundlings in the Fictional Chronicles of Political Upheavals

In the famous exchange of letters between Richardson and Aaron Hill's daughters, Astraea and Minerva, the Hill sisters complain to the author of *Clarissa* about the "familiar coarseness" of the title of Fielding's novel."[21] This complaint is puzzling. It would have made sense had Astraea and Minerva simply disliked the book like those readers who condemned wholesale Fielding's "motely [*sic*] History of Bastardism, Fornication and Adultery."[22] The sisters, however, though also initially prejudiced against the novel, eventually found themselves won over by the "Humanity of its Intention" and its "extremely moving Close."[23] The title still bothered them, nevertheless, and in trying to understand what it was that they found so "coarse" about it, we begin to sense the feeling of a conceptual vertigo induced in eighteenth-century readers by Fielding's experimentation with the conventional ways of representing bastardy in belles lettres.

The word *foundling* in the title of the story could not by itself be considered either "familiarly coarse" or even mildly provocative; nobody murmured, for example, when Moore used it to indicate the representational tradition to which his comedy belonged and to assure his audience of the happy conclusion to Fidelia's ordeals. "Tom Jones" would also agree with the usual custom of naming the novel after its main protagonist. True, such a name would signal the hero's modest origins—perhaps even his illegitimacy—as "Moll Flanders," "Colonel Jack," and "Humphrey Clinker" do, but that in and of itself would not necessarily be problematic. "Tom Jones" and "Foundling" together are more troubling because a *legitimate* protagonist of the foundling narrative ought to have a more noble-sounding name, such as Fidelia, Indiana, or Evelina (note that Clarence Hervey, the hero of Maria Edgeworth's 1801 novel, *Belinda*, can't abide the "vulgar" name of his fair foundling, Rachel, and promptly renames her Virginia). Even this infelicitous combination, however, could be forgiven were the protagonist of the story indeed to turn out to be a foundling—a legitimately born offspring of a noble but ill-starred union—renamed by his poor adoptive parents, who didn't know any better, the simple souls. To decide that the title "The History of Tom Jones, a Foundling" is "familiarly coarse," one has to read the novel to the end, to be smacked on the head, as Tom is by the wine bottle, by the hero's illegitimacy only to reflect back and realize that Tom does not look like any other literary bastard and that the mongrel title is only too typical for the story's multilayered categorical miscegenation. "Coarse," in other words, functions in Astraea and Minerva's letter as a code for frustration provoked by Fielding's subversion of the literary categories of "bastard" and "foundling," a frustration that at the time of their writing lacked both a vocabulary and an agreed-upon conceptual framework for expressing itself.

Eighteenth-century readers might have well been at a loss as to what to make of the character called "Foundling," whose adventures contain recognizable references to the conventions of the classical foundling narrative,[24] but who remains illegitimate, though without a clear-cut ideological meaning attached to his illegitimacy. For not only does Fielding make Tom fall short in the department of private excesses (which would have aligned him with stereotypical bastards), but he also mocks his readers' implicit assumptions about the relationship between the hero's legitimacy and his politics.[25] By using the 1745 Jacobite rebellion as a historical background for his tale, Fielding evokes the literary convention of first associating a character of unknown origins with a social transformation/upheaval and then making sense of that upheaval on the personal level by correlating its success or failure with this character's legitimacy. This convention was already present in the ancient foundling narrative and later, in Renaissance plays, and still viable in the 1740s. Heliodorus's Charicleia, for example, is a lawfully born foundling, and the social change that she precipitates—her countrymen's abandonment of the "savage" religious rite of their ancestors, the human sacrifice—is clearly viewed by the author as positive. In contrast, the anonymous Renaissance plays, *The Life and Death of Jack Straw* and *Claudius Tiberius Nero*, featured protagonists who were retroactively bastardized by the respective authors: the dangerous charisma of the "vile" bastards was thus enlisted to "explain" what were officially considered inauspicious turns in their respective communities' political past. Shakespeare's *King John* exploits the same correlation; when Philip the Bastard joins the king, the king's cause is doomed. In 1744, Eliza Haywood published *The Fortunate Foundlings*, whose bastard hero, Horatio, enlists in the army of the Swedish King Charles XII and proceeds to do "extraordinary service" (226) to his liege: "More than once had the conqueror been indebted to this young warrior, for turning the point of the destructive sword from giving him the same death he was dealing to others" (258). Still, Horatio's joining the "gallant Sovereign's" troops is peculiarly timed because the hitherto undefeatable Charles is on his way to being beaten by the "Muscovites" (259). In other words, the fictional bastard can be a strong fellow, with an appealingly overdeveloped sense of the ridiculous and a "trick of Coeur-de-lion's face,"[26] but a king should think twice about taking such a one into his service if he wants to survive and win the war.

Tom's short-lived career as a soldier (one of the most frequently discussed episodes of the novel[27]) thus parodies both the familiar "bastard goes to war" and the "foundling goes to war" scenario, according to which the bastard's—or the foundling's—entrance into the fray precipitates a momentous change in the course of history. Had Fielding been writing a more traditional "bastard" story in the vein of his Renaissance predecessors or one similar to Haywood's *The Fortunate Foundlings,* his illegitimate hero would have joined the Pretender's army and inadvertently contributed to its tragic defeat.[28] Had he planned to legitimate his foundling hero at the end, Tom would have enlisted the royal troops and led them into a glorious assault on the army of Bonnie Prince Charlie.[29] As it is, however, Tom Jones, who is neither the conventional bastard nor foundling, joins His Majesty King George's army on the eve of its victorious April 16 battle at Culloden only to be immediately hit on the head with a wine bottle and thus prevented from any further military exploits.[30]

Note that there is a crucial difference between saying (as I do) that Fielding refuses to link the political crisis of 1745 and Tom's illegitimacy into a mutual meaning-conferring system and saying (as Joe Alison Parker does) that "from the outset [Tom's] foundling state, which renders him a virtual blank slate, provokes others to attempt to confer meaning on him, and his subsequent lack of fixed meaning provides further provocation."[31] On the one hand, I agree with Parker's point that the uncertain birth status of a protagonist invites people to speculate about his social valence and to project onto him, often with grotesque results, their own fantasies (from Savage to Sartre, writers have used the status of a bastard as a leaky depository of cultural dreams and nightmares in order to promote themselves and their work.) On the other hand, the range of such speculations and projections has always been relatively limited and, within certain cultural contexts, connected to the character's legitimacy. Neither the fictional foundling nor the fictional bastard is ever a "blank slate" in the sense that, at any given turn of the plot, such a personage bears a burden of readers' expectations that have more to do with his literary-historical pedigree—that is, the literary tradition of which he is a supposed part—than with his personal lineage. Had not Astraea and Minerva associated a certain set of plot possibilities with the legitimate protagonist and another set with the bastard protagonist (even if they would not have been able to articulate those associations in such terms), they would not have found the story so disorienting and would not have to pin their frustration about their disappointed expectations onto the (really, rather innocuous) title of the novel.

CHAPTER 4

Secondary Characters: More Bastardy without Meaning

Fielding's decision not to invest Tom's illegitimacy with an explicit political meaning is consistent with his treatment of other bastards in his novel. After letting his readers know, however indirectly in some cases, that many of his characters were conceived out of wedlock, he then pointedly refuses to explain their behavior and respective fates through their bastardy. One covert bastard, Blifil, could easily have been cast as a stereotypical villain, dripping with venom simply on the grounds of his illegitimacy, yet his villainy is always pragmatic and hardly generated by that formulaic irrational "bastardly" need to be evil. In the long run, Blifil is not more malevolent than any legitimately born scoundrel in the novel. Moreover, if medieval and Renaissance stories of evil bastards typically ended with their death or their irrevocable excision from the community, Blifil at the end of the story is busily working his way back into comfortable upper-middle-class existence by laying up money to purchase a seat in Parliament and courting a rich widow.

In the case of his female characters, Fielding occasionally appears to adhere to the literary tradition of correlating the chastity of daughters with that of their mothers, but then he refuses to punish or even censure either mothers or daughters for their sexual trespasses, making the reader wonder if the initial correlation was there for no other reason than to create an opening for a pun or a juicy repartee. The pregnant Nancy Miller is wittily described as having "had a mind to be as wise as her mother" (667), and the pregnant Molly Seagrim has the satisfaction of pointing out to her mother, who claims that Molly is the first of the family "that ever was whore," that she herself gave birth to Molly's older sister "within a week" after her wedding (158). Nancy, moreover, is characterized by the admiring narrator as the "best-tempered girl in the world" (867), second only to Sophia in her appearance and manners. Her affair with Mr. Nightingale is crowned by a brilliant and, as readers dare to hope, mutually satisfying marriage. Nor is Nancy's mother, the "worthiest creature in the world" (790), punished for conceiving her daughter out of wedlock—her marriage to her late husband, a clergyman, is reported to have been very happy. Molly Seagrim is likewise rewarded for her youthful slip with marriage to Partridge, "one of the best-natured fellows in the world and . . . master of . . . much pleasantry and humor" (71), and, moreover, in possession of "£50 a year" that Jones settles on him (870). It is true that Molly's mother, Goody, is not very content with her husband, but in the context of the novel's moral economy, she gets her comeuppance not for sleeping with George before matrimony but for being quarrelsome and avaricious. Similarly, we are led to believe that Bridget Allworthy might have been happy had she married the father of her first illegitimate child, Mr. Summer; it is her snobbish rejection of that worthy but poor young man (who later dies of smallpox) that leaves her open to the amorous assails of the hideous Blifil brothers. In other words, the novel's rewards and punishments are allotted in proportion to the women's amicability and not to their legitimacy or chastity. Stripped of its mythical aura, illegitimacy is treated as simply yet another aspect of everyday sexuality mediated by the far-from-perfect social conventions.

As a circumstances-driven, rather than a character-driven, event, being a bastard or bearing a bastard child does not determine the person's virtue. Even in the case of his most irreproachable virgin, Sophia, Fielding slips a number of double entendres which imply that her moral worth would not be judged solely by her sexual behavior. When Mrs. Fitzpatrick arrives with her morning visit to Lady Bellaston, Sophia is described as lying in bed in a different apartment in the house, wide awake, while "Honour [is] snoring by her side" (608). By portraying Sophia as separated in her sentience from her fast-asleep "honour," Fielding hints slyly that Sophia's virtue is contingent on factors other than her ability to keep her "honour" perennially awake; it is defined by her kindness, courage, and personal integrity, qualities thrown into a particularly stark relief by the insidious plotting going on between Mrs. Fitzpatrick and Lady Bellaston. Given slightly different circumstances, it is possible that Sophia would have lived with Tom before marriage and gotten away with it, just like Mrs. Miller and her daughter get away with living with their respective lovers before marrying them.

We may thus want to reconsider and perhaps take at its face value Richardson's notorious observation that Fielding has made his hero "a natural child because his own first wife was such" (*Selected Letters*, 198). The author of *Clarissa* must have intended it as an insinuation that Fielding simply did not have enough imagination for writing fiction and thus slavishly copied real life in all its, however unattractive, aspects, but something else comes through in that dismissive remark. Fielding might have indeed made his main protagonist and many other characters in the novel illegitimate and, moreover, has treated their illegitimacy as simply a fact of life rather than a scandal in need of reimagining and mythologizing, because for his own first wife, for him, as well as for hundreds of thousands of other people living at the time in England, it was a fact of life. By denying a special status to fictional bastards, Fielding reaffirmed the everyday humanity of real-life "natural children" and their mothers and fathers.

"Tommy" Jones and the Foundling Hospital's "Tommies"

There were certain boundaries, however, that even Fielding, committed as he was to demythologizing bastardy, would not cross. Although he routinely draws on the imagery associated with the London Foundling Hospital, his novel makes clear that his protagonist, an educated son of a clergyman and a wealthy gentlewoman, has nothing in common with bastard children of the serving-class poor sheltered by the Hospital. The humanity of the novel's bastards is predominantly the middle-class humanity, facilitated by good breeding and amply allowing for social mobility, two properties hardly associated in the public mind with the inmates of the Foundling Hospital.

Tom Jones contains several references to the eighteenth-century infanticide prevention campaign, from Mrs. Deborah Wilkins's infanticidal suggestion that the child found in Squire Allworthy's bed should be left at the church door and the narrator's observation that Mrs. Miller was as careful in telling Allworthy about the history of Nancy's marriage "as if she had been before a judge, and the girl was now on her trial for the murder of a bastard" (794), to the mention of Allworthy's support of "an hospital" (33)[32] and the comment on Lady Bellaston, who would rather pay for the upkeep of a sexy "young Fellow" than contribute to such "Hackney Charities of the Age . . . [as] Hospitals" (633). Indeed, the very name of the novel's protagonist—Thomas—may have reminded some eighteenth-century readers of the most prominent and controversial charity of their times (though we have no way of knowing if Astraea and Minerva Hill were aware of this particular connotation, and whether it should be factored into their disapproval of the title). One of the rules of the London Foundling Hospital was that every infant had to be given a new name immediately upon being admitted. The names, especially during the first decade, were those of the charity's benefactors, and its most distinguished benefactor—under whose portrait the children grew and, according to the Hospital's lore, to which they even prayed, thinking that it was the depiction of God Almighty—was its founding father, Captain Thomas Coram. Even after Coram's estrangement from the Hospital in the spring of 1742, he continued to attend its baptismal ceremonies. For example, between October 1747 and March 1751, he "stood godfather to twenty children."[33] As a staunch supporter of the Foundling Hospital keenly interested in its affairs,[34] Fielding knew how popular the name Thomas was within its walls, and it is not implausible that he was thinking about it when he made Allworthy the godfather of the little foundling and bestowed upon the child Allworthy's "own name of Thomas" (69).

And yet the novel's suggestive allusions to the infanticide prevention campaign notwithstanding, the affinity between Tom Jones and "Coram's children" runs only name-deep. The numerous "Tommies" of the Hospital were early instructed to know their modest social station, to be content with it, to learn only the rudiments of reading and writing, and to be prepared to work hard to achieve a modicum of economic independence in the future. As such they ultimately had nothing in common with their Horace-reciting fictional namesake who ends up inheriting one great estate and marrying the heiress of another.

To fully grasp the ideological stakes of Fielding's strategy of evoking his countrymen's philanthropic impulse as a suggestive backdrop for a story of an abandoned child while at the same time ensuring that this child's fate will have nothing in common with that of the poor objects of public charity, one may consider the amplification of that strategy by a late-eighteenth-century writer. In her 1797 novel, *The Beggar Girl and Her Benefactors*, Agnes Maria Bennett concludes her description of the beggar girl, Rosa Buhanun, whose accomplishments grow as she moves from one benefactor to another, with a paean to Rosa's beauty and her multiple guardians' benevolence: "Such was the exterior of the miserable outcast Charity had rescued from the dunghill on which it was cast; and such, no doubt, would be the transformation of many other deplorable objects, were there hearts to make the trial" (1:224). Predictably, however, by the end of the novel, Rosa turns out to be the long-lost daughter of a kind and sophisticated countess and the only real heiress to the titles and riches of two prominent aristocratic families, an upscale version of the revelation that Tom's father was a gentleman and that, upon marrying Sophia, Tom will be in possession of two great estates.

Bennett's admirable belief in the ameliorative effect that works of charity can have on the "deplorable objects" rescued from the "dunghill"[35] thus goes the way of the noble advice that Colonel Raymond from Moore's *The Foundling* gives to his rakish friend Belmont, when he suggests that Belmont should marry the accomplished and virtuous Fidelia even if she is "the Out-case of a Beggar." However attractive, neither sentiment can be truly put to the test within the context of the eighteenth-century tradition of translating the difficult issues bound up with serving-class and middle-class illegitimacy into tales of aristocratic or fabulously rich foundlings.

Fielding thus works both within this tradition, given the outcome of Tom's story, and against it, given how different Tom is from other fictional bastards and foundlings of the period. Seeing Tom's character as both grounded in and resisting the prevalent cultural discourses on bastardy makes it increasingly difficult for us to believe that as a "true bastard" who "makes good, Tom is much closer to the model of the progressive protagonist than anything Fielding had previously attempted" (McKeon 418). Whether we define a "true bastard" as an inmate of the Foundling Hospital; an illegitimate fictional adventurer (e.g., Savage's "Bastard," Haywood's Horatio, and Smollett's Peregrine Pickle); or a presumed natural child revealed to be a legally born foundling (e.g., Burney's Evelina, Smith's Emmeline, and Bennett's Rosa), Tom does not fit into any of these categories. He emerges instead as a fantastic hybrid partaking of competing cultural attempts to reimagine bastardy without committing to any of them, which is why we should be cautious about deciding univocally on his ideological significance and pronouncing him either a progressive or a conservative icon. Paradoxically, as we attempt to reconstruct the cultural history of early modern illegitimacy, the supposedly paradigmatic bastard of eighteenth-century belles letters continues to remain its most elusive personage.

-5-

FEMALE PHILANTHROPY, THE LONDON FOUNDLING HOSPITAL, AND RICHARDSON'S *THE HISTORY OF SIR CHARLES GRANDISON*

On April 24, 1750, William Hogarth put his painting *The March to Finchley* (see figure 2) up for auction, the proceeds from which were to go to the London Foundling Hospital. What happened next, according to the *Gentleman's Magazine*, was that a "certain lady" discovered herself "the possessor of the fortunate number" and decided to present the painting to the Hospital. She was dissuaded, however, from doing so directly, "some person [having suggested] what door it would open to scandal, were any of her sex to make such a present."[1] One possible rationale behind the prudent suggestion might have been the subject matter of the painting. The central characters in the painting are a handsome grenadier about to depart for battle, his jealous wife, and his young mistress. One of Hogarth's friends, Justice Welsh, described the younger woman as "debauched, with child, and reduced to the miserable employ of selling ballads, who, with a look full of love, tenderness, and distress, casts up her eyes upon her undoer, and with tears descending down her cheeks, seems to say, 'sure you cannot—will not leave me!'"[2] The painting intended as a gift to the public charitable institution thus depicted a poor woman pregnant with an illegitimate child—a potential inmate of the same institution. Awkward as this circumstance appeared to be, it was not this awkwardness that informed the reaction to the generous lady's initiative. In fact, we know that the lady (her name remaining unknown) handed *The March to Finchley* over to the artist, and Hogarth gave it to the Hospital in his own name; it was gladly accepted and proudly exhibited in the General Court Room. Thus it was specifically the gender of the donor, independently

CHAPTER 5

FIGURE 2. CF 1852 *March of the Guards to Finchley*. 1750 by William Hogarth (1697–1764). Coram Foundation. Foundling Museum. London. UK/Bridgeman Art Library.

from the dubious erotic charge of the painting, that provoked the fear of scandal in the auction participants.

Notably, any mention of the lady philanthropist was erased from the two other contemporary accounts of the auction, one provided by the *London Evening Post* on May 1, 1750, the other by the *Minutes* of the Court of Governors on May 9. The *London Evening Post* reported:

> Yesterday Mr. Hogarth's Subscription was closed, 1843 Chances being subscribed for. The remaining Numbers from 1843 to 2000 were given by Mr. Hogarth to the Hospital for the Maintenance and Education of exposed and deserted young Children. At Two o'Clock the Box was open'd, and in the Presence of a great Number of Persons of Distinction, and the fortunate Chance was drawn, No. 1941, which belongs to the said Hospital; and the same Night Mr. Hogarth deliver'd the Picture to the Governors. His Grace the Duke of Ancaster offer'd them 200l. for it before it was taken away, but it was refus'd.[3]

According to the Court of Governors, "The Treasurer acquainted the

Female Philanthropy and the London Foundling Hospital

General Court, that Mr. Hogarth had presented the Hospital with the remainder of the tickets Mr. Hogarth had left, for the chance of the picture he had painted, of the *March to Finchley*, in the time of the late Rebellion; and that the fortunate number for the said picture being among the tickets, the Hospital had received the same picture."[4] Apparently, neither the *Post* nor the Court of Governors chose to mention that it was a "certain lady" who, upon drawing a "fortunate Chance," decided to give up her prize for the benefit of the Hospital. In fact, the story was edited so carefully that there was no room left for the depiction of the generous outside donor; in the *Post*'s report, the winning number is said to turn up among the tickets belonging to "the same Hospital," but the lady vanishes without a trace.

To appreciate the peculiarity of this story, we have to remember how assiduously the champions of the English infanticide prevention campaign had courted the support of gentlewomen at its early stages. Inspired by the prominent role played by women in the establishment and functioning of French, Italian, and Dutch foundling hospitals, the tireless Thomas Coram made the participation of Ladies of Quality a cornerstone of his anti-infanticide crusade.[5] It was by his instigation that in 1735, twenty-one upper-class women signed a petition to the king about the need for a foundling hospital in London. This made it possible for Coram to start his next petition by pointing out "That many Ladys of Quality and Distinction [are] deeply touched with Concern for the frequent Murders committed on poor Miserable Infant Children at their Birth by their Cruel Parents to hide their Shame and for the Inhumane Custom of exposing New born children to Perish in the Streets."[6] Later Coram would claim that, in effect, the whole campaign for the opening of the Hospital had been the initiative of the ladies, who were subsequently supported in their noble undertaking by gentlemen.[7] In November 1739, at a public ceremony inaugurating the official establishment of the new charity, Coram opened his speech with the following paean to the ladies: "It is with inexpressible pleasure, I now present your Grace, as the head of this noble and honourable Corporation, with his Majesty's Royal Charter, for establishing an Hospital for exposed children, free of all expense, through the assistance of some *compassionate great ladies, and other good persons*."[8] The early history of the Foundling Hospital was thus marked by the commitment to include women and even go as far—at least rhetorically—as to present them as the primary moving force behind the establishment of this public charity. In light of this history, the account of the 1750 auction, with its fear of scandal surrounding the initiative of the anonymous lady, looks like a puzzling aberration.

To unravel some parts of this puzzle, we have to reconstruct the cultural history of the London Foundling Hospital at mid-century, for it seems that the story of Hogarth's painting was not an isolated accident; on the contrary, it was only too representative of the general exclusion of gentlewomen from a public role in the affairs of the Hospital starting in the 1740s. In what follows, I discuss several possible explanations for such exclusion, considering them in particular within the context of the recent feminist revisions of Jürgen Habermas's paradigm of the bourgeois public sphere. I also show how the gender politics of the eighteenth-century infanticide prevention campaign influenced—and were influenced by—the works of contemporary fiction. Here I first consider briefly the reference to the Foundling Hospital in Tobias Smollett's *Peregrine Pickle* (1751) and then discuss in detail the allusions to infanticide and illegitimacy in Samuel Richardson's *The History of Sir Charles Grandison* (1753–54). I argue that we could read Richardson's portrayal of illegitimacy as indicative of his ambivalent take on the issue of female philanthropy. On the one hand, his novel appears to articulate emotional reasons behind the reluctance of Ladies of Quality to lend their names to the Hospital starting from the 1740s; on the other, *Grandison* stops short of giving to this reluctance an unqualified moral imprimatur. Instead, Richardson evokes a cultural fantasy in which the bastard children and their mothers—whose claims to financial and emotional support regularly disrupt the stability of the upper-middle-class household—could be neutralized and removed from the immediate field of vision of the threatened legal family. This ideal arrangement (that is, from the point of view of the Grandison women) both demands the wife's vigilant attendance on the family—uninterrupted by her independent excursions to the public domain (including the domain of public philanthropy)—and commends men who build and support public charities in which transgressing women and their base-born children could be confined and reformed.

Legitimating the "Shelter for Bastards"

By the early 1740s, when the rush of excitement from receiving the public imprimatur in the form of the Royal Charter and taking in the first groups of illegitimate infants had somewhat subsided, the governors and guardians of the London Foundling Hospital found themselves dealing on an everyday basis with the problem of defending both the moral outlook of the new charity and its continuous claim to public financial support, which, until 1756, came exclusively in the form of private donations. By mid-century, the Hospital emerged as a genuinely controversial cultural institution. On the one hand, it embodied the best humanitarian impulses and provided an outlet for the complex civic ambitions of eighteenth-century Englishmen; on the other, it reflected the deep-seated class and gender anxieties of the British Enlightenment.

The Hospital's prominent place in the English cultural imagination was captured by Fielding's 1752 "compliment to the present Age for two glorious Benefactions . . . that to the use of Foundling Infants and that for the Accommodation of poor Women in their Lying-In."[9] As the first national joint-stock charity, the London Foundling Hospital served as a model for other philanthropic institutions, such as the Lying-in Hospital, Magdalen House, the Marine Society, and Lock Hospital, all of which sprang to life in the 1740-1760s. The Hospital's foundational promise to provide the empire with "useful citizens"—the much needed soldiers and workers—responded to fears about the rumored depopulation of the country[10] and appealed to the British sense of patriotism. Its overwhelming dependence on private donations offered to city merchants a gratifying opportunity to reconcile their "new-found wealth with the dictates of Christian and classical morality" by creating a "public sphere united by bonds of sympathy and benevolence—a body to which everybody possessed of a modicum of education and property might ostensibly belong."[11] Its carefully selected location and architectural outlook,[12] the prominent social position of many of its governors, and its much publicized contribution to national arts—the Foundling Hospital's annual art exhibition was a precursor of the Royal Academy of Painting and Sculpture—turned a visit to the Hospital into "the most fashionable morning lounge in the reign of George II."[13]

The art exhibition was a brilliant stroke. Not only did it attract potential donors to the Hospital and generate positive publicity, but it also subtly contributed to the impression that the Hospital was open to—indeed, welcomed—public scrutiny. As David Solkin points out, "if people were to be persuaded to part with their money, strategies had to be devised to bring them on to the premises, so that they could see concrete evidence of [an important] task well done."[14] In fact, Michel Foucault's succinct characterization of the underlying principles of the eighteenth-century insane asylum—"Surveillance and Judgment"[15]—

rings equally true for the Foundling Hospital. Its governors and guardians made panoptical transparency the grounding principle of the institution's relationships with the outside world. Foundlings grew up, in Samuel Johnson's words, "much accustomed to new spectators."[16] Visitors could see the children at work or play—a public diversion that turned out to be so popular among Londoners but so disruptive for the children that in 1751 the governors had to issue a special order that children were not to be observed after their bedtime.[17] As to the "Judgment" part, any visitor could take it upon himself to criticize the Hospital's routine and to offer suggestions for improvements; such civic-minded interventions would be heeded with respect, no matter how high-handed and irritating they might seem to the governors.[18]

More ambivalent—and rarely discussed by cultural historians—was the Hospital's strategy of legitimating itself through the manipulation of the cultural categories of "bastard" and "foundling." On the one hand, the very name of the institution, the *Foundling* Hospital, as well as the selection of paintings welcoming visitors in the General Court Room, implied that the objects of the Hospital's charity—the bastards— were to benefit from the mythopoetic aura that informed classical and early modern representations of foundlings. On the other hand, the Hospital had to tread a fine line between banking on some aspects of this myth (i.e., the ultimate social and sexual conformity of the fictional foundling) and rejecting others (i.e., the foundling's dizzying social mobility). Governors and guardians of the Hospital deployed the cultural differentiation between bastards and foundlings so as to simultaneously present the institution designed to take care of illegitimate children as the means of an enlightened containment of otherwise unruly sexual and social forces and to assure the paying public that their young charges knew well their humble place in the social hierarchy.

Next to the portraits of British statesmen, poets, and composers, the sumptuously decorated General Court Room of the Hospital featured a series of paintings on biblical themes depicting children receiving relief and benediction from strangers: the exposed Ishmael perishing in the desert with an angel hovering above him; the dying son of the widow of Zarephath revived by Elijah; the infant Christ showered by the magi's "gifts, gold, and frankincense, and myrrh,"[19] and Moses brought before the benevolent daughter of the Pharaoh. One distinguishing characteristic of all the children portrayed in these paintings is their relative "maturity," especially striking in the case of Moses, who looks like an unusually sturdy three-month-old in Francis Hayman's

Female Philanthropy and the London Foundling Hospital

FIGURE 3. CF 71802 *The Finding of the Infant Moses in the Bullrushes*. 1746 (oil on canvas) by Francis Hayman (1708–1776). Coram Foundation. Foundling Museum. London. UK/Bridgeman Art Library.

painting (see figure 3). Such touching-up of biblical stories was not accidental: the age of the abandoned child had historically been one of the key criteria used by English parish clerks to decide whether the child was illegitimate. Bastard children were typically abandoned immediately after birth or "as soon as the lying-in period was complete."[20] When the abandoned child was more than two months old, it was likely that factors other than illegitimacy—such as poverty and widowhood—prompted its parent(s) to part with it. This consideration was reflected in the admission policy of the Foundling Hospital: as the Hospital was to provide safe haven exclusively for illegitimate children, only infants under the age of two months were allowed to be taken in. The "daily crowd of [visitors] in their splendid equipages"[21]—the potential donors of the Hospital—were thus presented with the pictures of the *visibly* legitimate children crucially dependent on the kindness of strangers.

CHAPTER 5

What could be accomplished by projecting the *presumed* legitimacy of biblical foundlings onto the children of the Hospital? (I use "presumed" because several of the paintings' characters weren't unquestionably legitimate; for example, Christ had been regularly gracing the popular lists of the "good" bastards published throughout the early modern era.) The parallel association of the Hospital's bastard charges with literary foundlings, and of the moneyed visitors of the Hospital with biblical benefactors, represented an innovative rhetorical strategy adopted to fortify the Hospital's own claims to ideological legitimacy and to other people's money. The champions of the Hospital tapped the cultural view of the fortunate foundling, someone who transcends his or her temporary ordeals of abandonment, poverty, and rumored shameful birth to be at last safely contained within publicly sanctioned sexual and social boundaries. The cultural availability of the old literary tradition discriminating between vile bastards and benign foundlings implied that the Hospital deserved credit for taking in bastards—the would-be agents of social destruction, atheism, and sexual deviance—and turning them into foundlings—hard workers, devout Protestants, eligible marriage partners, and good citizens of the commonwealth.

The legitimacy of many fictional foundlings also allowed the champions of the Hospital to implicitly strengthen their claim that by taking in illegitimate children, they were returning the children's mothers to the path of virtue. It was hoped, as Brownlow puts it, that after being "preserved" from the "desperate crime" of infanticide, the "wretched parent [would], by her penitence and future rectitude, [maintain] the cause of virtue, and once more [enjoy] the pleasure of reputation after having tasted the ill consequences of losing it."[22] By entering the Hospital and becoming a foundling instead of a bastard, a child was thus meant to serve as a guarantee of his mother's future adherence to the sexual norms of her community, thus directly counterbalancing the old charge that by taking illegitimate children off their mothers' hands, the Hospital removed the strongest check to female promiscuity.

Its evocative name and predilection for a certain style of pictorial representation notwithstanding, the Hospital needed to distance itself from one particular aspect of cultural myth: the fantastic social mobility of the foundling. The young charges of the charity were not to entertain any high-flown ideas about their birth or destiny, and neither were the visitors to the Hospital to receive an impression that the children were "coddled" and being brought up above their station. That the

Hospital was readily suspected of such indulgence is clear from the advice to the governors proffered by the author of the anonymous 1761 pamphlet, *Some Objections to the Foundling Hospital Considered by a Person in the Country to Whom They Were Sent*. The pamphlet recommends the governors bring the foundlings up "in such a manner as will fit them to bear any hardships"—feed them on "simple fare," dress them in "cheap" and "light" garments (19). In response, perhaps, to such external pressure, the governors made a point of contrasting the lavishly decorated General Court Room with the Spartan look of the children's quarters. As Rachel Ramsey points out, the former "was the epitome of mid-century luxury and elegance. The difference between it and the rooms occupied by children are striking, but, of course, that was exactly the point. No contributor . . . could fail to compare the two vastly different decorative schemes without being convinced of the carefully maintained distinction between those who gave generously and those who received humbly."[23] The governors also complemented the simple diet, moderate exercise, and useful pastimes (winding silk, netting purses, knitting, and spinning) of their children with such recreational activities as learning a variety of hymns that referred pointedly to their illegitimacy, some written especially for the Hospital, some adapted from biblical Psalms. A typical hymn (quoted in full above, in the introductory chapter) featured a child who "confessed" that "each part of [her] sinful frame [had been] form'd in Guilt" and pleaded to God to "wash off" the "foul offence" bestowed upon her by her fornicating parents.[24]

In her comprehensive 1981 account of the history of the London Foundling Hospital, Ruth McClure points out that such hymns were representative of the overarching project of socializing the inmates of the Hospital to their modest station in life and notes that other eighteenth-century charities relied on similar methods to help children to "early imbibe the Principles of Humility and Gratitude to their Benefactors, and to learn to undergo with Contentment the most Servile and laborious Offices."[25] Apart from this general strategy of teaching children to know their place, the hymns that reminded them about their sin and guilt perhaps provided a necessary counterpart to the rhetorical message sent by the paintings exhibited in the General Court Room that identified the charges of the Hospital with legendary foundlings.

And yet despite the high social profile of many of the Hospital's governors and donors, its willingness to submit to rather troublesome public scrutiny, and its rhetorical strategy of manipulating the cultural categories of "bastard" and "foundling," the Hospital never managed to shed its association with sexual and social transgressiveness. The grumbling that the "shelter for bastards [encouraged] irresponsibility and licentiousness"[26] continued unabated, taking different forms as the century went on.[27] It was widely rumored that its champions wanted to swindle the public into paying for the upkeep of their own illegitimate children; the 1750 pamphlet *The Scandalizade, A Panegyri-Satiri-Comic-Dramatic Poem* claimed that Coram conceived of the Foundling Hospital because he "had many a Lass grappl'd under the Lee." In 1760, when several other charitable institutions copying the Hospital's joint-stock model were opened in London, the Foundling Hospital was often presented by its ill-wishers as part and parcel of a larger confederacy aimed at debauching the nation's morals. As a popular pamphlet entitled *Joyful News to Batchelors and Maids: Being a Song, in Praise of the Fondling Hospital, and the London Hospital in Aldersgate-Street* [one of London's Lying-in Hospitals] proclaimed, now "young Maids may safely take a Leap in the dark with their Sweethearts; and if they should chance to be with child may go to Aldersgate-street and lie-in, and when their month is up, they may go to the Foundling Hospital and get rid of their Bantling, and pass for pure Virgins."

"Ladies of Quality" and the London Foundling Hospital

The history of the Ladies of Quality's involvement with the London Foundling Hospital is symptomatic both of the Hospital's and the Ladies' ambiguous position in the eighteenth-century public sphere. On the one hand, Coram made a point of presenting the campaign for the opening of the Foundling Hospital as initiated and strongly supported by upper-class women. Furthermore, after the establishment of the Hospital, prominent upper- and middle-class women actively participated in its affairs by serving as inspectresses of the country nurses hired by the Hospital to take care of the young children. Among those who took it upon themselves to monitor, without any remuneration (or, more important for the present argument, any public ado) the work of country nurses were Martha Vansittart ("one of the beauties of the court of George II [whose] father, Sir John Stonhouse, had been a Privy Councillor and Comptroller of the Household to Queen Anne"[28]); Anna Maria Poyntz (the maid of honor to Queen Caroline, whose husband was a "Privy Councillor and at the accession had been 'high in favour and confidence of the new King George II,' and who had been appointed Governor to the Duke of Cumberland, the king's then nine year old son"[29]); and Juliana Dodd (whose brother was "a great friend of Mrs. Thrale and Miss Burney" and whose husband was a close friend of Horace Walpole—one of the Hospital's early governors.[30]) Juliana Dodd's persuasive arguments in September 1759 led the governors to abandon the contemplated initiative of paying the nurses an extra three pence a week to enable them to buy the children's clothing themselves instead of receiving it from the Hospital.[31] The surviving correspondence between the Hospital's inspectors and its governors attests to the crucial role played by women, such as Vansittart and Dodd, in the functioning of the charity.

On the other hand, once there was no Coram to drag them into the spotlight,[32] women ceased to lend their names to the public support of the Hospital altogether. As McClure points out, "over the years many women contributed generously to the Foundling Hospital, visited it, served as godmothers to its children and as inspectresses of its country nurses, and offered suggestions to improve the conduct of its affairs, but none of them ever sought to participate officially in its administration."[33] McClure's explanation for their reluctance to participate in the Hospital's administration is that "English women, unaccustomed to the burden of governing a public charity, might have refused nomination to official position had they been asked." She also suggests that it is likely that those in charge of the public image of the Hospital were reluctant to include women in its governing body, thinking "their new project sufficiently controversial without risking any additional criticism that disregard of the customary ways of doing things might provoke."[34]

Neither of these two reasons strikes me as completely satisfactory. First, it is difficult to accept that English women would consciously shun the burden of governing a public charity; in fact, we know that they participated actively and publicly in affairs of other charities founded at the same time. Second, the argument about the governors thinking "their new project sufficiently controversial without risking any additional criticism that disregard of the customary ways of doing things might provoke" does not work if we ask, What were the models that the governors presumably had in mind and did not want to disregard? As a matter of fact, in the 1730s and 1740s, the public charity was still a novel institution in England, and the Foundling Hospital had no native models to imitate; in order to find out more about the customary ways of doing things, Coram had to look abroad. Through his friend Thomas Bray, Coram knew that in France "even Princesses and Duchesses, and other Ladies of the Prime Nobility of Paris, to the Number of Two Hundred and above [had] associated themselves, and entered into a Confraternity to manage [L'Hopital des Enfants-Trouves],"[35] and he was eager to follow the continental way of advancing the project. Again, it is difficult to say what would have happened had Coram not become estranged from the affairs of the charity in the early 1740s, but it appears, nonetheless, that the absence of women from the "responsible participation in the government of London Foundling Hospital" did not agree with "the customary ways of doing things":[36] it presented a rupture with both the existing continental tradition and Coram's earlier insistence that Ladies of Quality should constitute the vanguard of the infanticide prevention campaign.

A different explanation is offered by Donna Andrew, who comments upon the "surprising absence of female subscribers among the published subscription lists" (subscriptions being an important source of money for the Hospital) and adds that out of twenty-one women who signed the 1735 petition to the king, not one gave publicly, "that is to say in her own name, to the charity once it became incorporated."[37] The latter information modifies McClure's earlier statement that "over the years many women contributed generously to the Foundling Hospital." Contribute they did, but many of them not in their own names, but rather, as Andrew points out, through "their husbands or other near male relatives."[38] Even more important, we now know that women were absent from the list of governors and guardians *and* from the published subscription lists. If the former could be explained, as McClure suggests, by English women shirking the unfamiliar burden of governing a public charity, what about the latter? Was signing a subscription list also a novel burden singularly unappealing to English women? Not so, Andrew contends: English women were willing to subscribe openly to other charities; a number of them supported the already mentioned City of London Lying-In Hospital and the British Lying-In Hospital, as well as the Lying-In Charity, the Marine Society, and Magdalen House.[39] It was specifically this charity that seemed to scare away potential female philanthropists. Or, as Andrew puts it, "since women were commonly held to be the arbiters and bastions of public morality, they may well have been hesitant to allow their names to appear in support of an institution that could possibly be thought to be 'improper' or conducive to sexual immorality."[40]

Female Philanthropy and the London Foundling Hospital

The most striking evidence of women's hesitation to associate publicly with such an institution comes from John Brownlow's 1858 chronicle of the early days of the London Foundling Hospital. At the end of the volume, Brownlow printed the list of the Hospital's governors and guardians. Running up to the year 1857, it contains close to one hundred names, without a single female name among them.[41] It seems that the pattern of demographic uniformity of the Hospital's governing body, established somewhere in the 1740s, continued to hold well into the nineteenth century, long after the Foundling Hospital had ceased to be a readily available object of titillating accusations.

The *March to Finchley* episode with which I opened this chapter seems to fit the pattern of the double position of women in relation to the Foundling Hospital. On the one hand, the Hospital gratefully accepted the painting, which was a de facto gift from the female donor who drew the lucky number, even though the nominal giver was the artist himself. On the other hand, the female philanthropist remained anonymous and virtually absent from most published accounts of the transaction. The situation was all too typical of the Hospital's interactions with women at mid-century. The work of its inspectresses, as we remember, was received with gratitude and appreciation, but that gratitude and appreciation were for internal consumption, so to speak, for the names that the public associated with the Hospital were not Martha Vansittart, Anna Maria Poyntz, and Juliana Dodd, but Thomas Coram, John Bedford, Jonas Hanway, William Hogarth, Joseph Highmore, George Handel, William Cadogan, Hans Sloane, Richard Brocklesby, Richard Mead, Horace Walpole, Henry Fielding, Samuel Richardson, Charles Burney, and many others—all men who did not fear that their connection with the controversial philanthropic institution would "open [the] Door to Scandal" and who had the luxury of being able to simply shrug off the scurrilous rumors (e.g., of their having presumably sired some of the foundlings) and to continue with their patronage of the charity.

However, some nagging questions still remain. If, as Andrew suggests cogently, women's role as "the arbiters and bastions of public morality" made them "hesitant to allow their names to appear in support of an institution that could possibly be thought to be 'improper' or conducive to sexual immorality,"[42] why was the Foundling Hospital singled out as a charity more injurious to the reputation of aspiring female philanthropists than, for example, Magdalen House, a shelter for "fallen" women? And just what was it that happened in the decade between the Ladies of Quality petition orchestrated by Coram and the *March to Finchley* auction that somehow entrenched the view that the public association of gentlewomen with the Hospital was now less desirable and likely to damage both the cause of the infanticide prevention campaign and such a "delicate . . . beautiful and brittle"[43] thing as female reputation?

One way to address such questions is to correlate them with the cultural phenomenon described by such scholars as Felicity Nussbaum, Nancy Armstrong, and Ruth Perry as the mid-eighteenth-century valorization of domesticity, which presupposed the general retirement of women from the public sphere into the domain of the family. The change in the public attitude toward gentlewomen's participation in the affairs of the Hospital indeed coincided suggestively with what Nussbaum characterizes as the peak of the eighteenth-century "cult of motherhood," or the new cultural conviction that the "domestic woman [had] power to shape the public realm, particularly the nation, through procreation and education."[44] What this development could have meant in practical terms was that a good female citizen was defined as a devoted wife and mother, and not as an aspiring philanthropist offering her unsolicited gifts to the Hospital. Furthermore, as Perry argues, an important condition of the mid-eighteenth-century "colonization" of the female body—the appropriation of women's reproductive services for the "nation and the empire"—was the repression of women's active sexuality. "Maternity," as she writes, "came to be imagined as a counter to sexual feeling, opposing alike individual expression, desire, and agency in favor of a mother-self at the service of the family and the state."[45] We can speculate that since service to the state could be relayed primarily through service to the family, female philanthropy—the activity that benefited the state by bypassing the family—could have been construed as indicative of the woman's indifference toward her "primary" duties of wife and mother, a certain flightiness of character, and perhaps even a certain looseness of morals signaled by her social forwardness.

There is a danger, of course, in smoothing over the immense complexity of what was happening in the domain of public philanthropy at mid-century and claiming that women were withdrawing en masse from the public realm and refocusing their attention on the family. In fact, a number of recent feminist revisions of the Habermasian paradigm of the eighteenth-century bourgeois public sphere have questioned our tradition of rigid gendering of public and private spheres of influence. Susan Staves has argued that a number of historians of the eighteenth-century family "have succumbed to a bourgeois illusion that there can be a clear separation between, on the one hand, a public and economic sphere, and, on the other, a private domestic sphere of true feeling and personal authenticity, [thus accepting] the very ideological formulation created by eighteenth-century advocates of domesticity."[46] Similarly, Dena Goodman has critiqued the oversimplified readings of Habermas's conception of the authentic public sphere and persuasively theorized a "feminist historiography that is not trapped within the public/private opposition."[47]

In the context of this critique, compared to other charities at midcentury the Foundling Hospital was rather exceptional in its total lack of public female support. It could be that as the first institution of its kind in eighteenth-century England, it retained its cultural shock value more tenaciously than did other hospitals, such as the founded shortly thereafter Magdalen House, and that as such, it came to embody—more so than the other charities—anxieties about the role of women in the public sphere. It could also be that the principle of anonymity adopted by the Foundling Hospital (i.e., the mothers could just disappear without a trace after depositing their children at the Hospital, whereas at Magdalen, the physical retention of women somehow implied their greater accountability) appeared to substantiate the continuous harping that the Foundling Hospital made it possible for a certain type of female opportunist to carry on unchecked her "depredations upon mankind,"[48] making this charity thus appear particularly antagonistic to the interests of well-to-do married women.

We recognize the articulation of the latter sentiment in the satiric passage from Tobias Smollett's *Peregrine Pickle* (1751) in which several Ladies of Quality attempt to decide the fate of a young woman who had married for love against the wishes of her family, thus forfeiting her inheritance and provoking her father's implacable enmity, and whose husband died soon after, leaving her a destitute widow with twin infants. One lady recommends placing the infants in the Foundling Hospital; another is convinced that once they enter the Hospital, their mother would be free to seduce rich young men and thus destroy the emotional and financial well-being of good families:

> My lady duchess concluded that she [the young widow] must be a creature void of all feeling and reflection, who could survive such aggravated misery; therefore did not deserve to be relieved, except in the character of a common beggar; and was generous enough to offer a recommendation, by which she would be admitted into an

CHAPTER 5

infirmary, to which her grace was a subscriber; at the same time, advising the solicitor to send the twins to the Foundling-Hospital, where they would be carefully nursed and brought up, so as to become useful members of the commonwealth. Another lady, with all due deference to the opinion of the duchess, was free enough to blame the generosity of her grace, which would only serve to encourage children in their disobedience to their parents, and might be the means not only of prolonging the distress of the wretched creature, but also of ruining the constitution of some young heir, perhaps the hope of a great family; for she did suppose that madam, when her month should be up, and her brats disposed of, would spread her attractions to the public, (provided she could profit by her person) and, in the usual way, make a regular progress from St. James's to Drury-lane. She apprehended, for these reasons, that their compassion would be most effectually shewn, in leaving her to perish in her present necessity; and that the old gentleman would be unpardonable, should he persist in his endeavors to relieve her. A third member of this tenderhearted society [said]: "Let the bantlings . . . be sent to the hospital [and she would take the mother as her servant.]" (429–30)

It hardly matters to the lady duchess and her friends that the young woman in question used to be married and that the children are legitimate:[49] their admission to the Foundling Hospital would automatically activate the scenario of a "fallen" woman now free to continue her depredations upon "great families." And since the second lady either belongs to or ambitiously identifies with "great families," her warning about the threat represented by a "madam" whose "brats" are taken off her hands appears to spell out the reason a woman of quality should not support the Foundling Hospital.

The passage is ambivalent in ways perhaps not consciously intended by Smollett, testifying to the difficulty of deriving any clear-cut ideological "message" from the works of eighteenth-century fiction focusing on illegitimacy. On the one hand, the narrator has no sympathy for the cruel trio and clearly disapproves of their sentiments, including the second speaker's view of the Foundling Hospital as a charity that enables prostitution, ruins the hopes of great families, and thus does not deserve the support of gentlewomen. On the other hand, by letting us know that one of the callous ladies is a "subscriber" to an "infirmary" (which appears from the context to be Magdalen House!), Smollett seems to uphold—whether intentionally or not—the notion that the women who subscribed to charities substituted that kind of ostensible "public" kindness for more valuable and genuine "private" compassion. Indeed, we learn that when "shocked at the nature . . . of this ungenerous consultation," Peregrine rushes to the house of the poor woman with a gift of twenty pounds, he meets there the celebrated Lady V., "who having heard by accident of [the] deplorable situation [of the young widow], had [also] immediately obeyed the dictates of her humanity . . . and come *in person* to relieve her distress" (431; emphasis added). The "private" altruism of Lady V. is thus contrasted to the "public" philanthropy of the lady duchess, leaving the reader in no doubt as to which constitutes true benevolence, but also strengthening the notion that something was seriously amiss with the hearts and minds of ladies who flaunted their support of philanthropic institutions instead of assisting those in need quietly and privately. Note that even the good old argument about raising the children of the Hospital into "useful members of the commonwealth" acquires sarcastic overtones when used by the lady duchess. There is something incongruous, the narrative seems to imply, in a woman's mouthing this ostensibly "male," ostensibly "public" political catchphrase. A woman should express her compassion not by parroting the impersonal slogans of the infanticide prevention campaign but by doing what Lady V.—this "angel ministering to the necessities of mortals"—does: relieve the miserable widow "in person," softening into the "inchanting tenderness of weeping sympathy" while fondling one of the poor babes on her knee, and thanking another kind giver—Peregrine—"with such look of complacency . . . that his whole soul [is] transported with love and veneration" (431). Lady V. seems to be the epitome of the proper domestic woman, "educating," so to speak, young men in noble sentiments, or, in this case, "approving" the young man for following his best impulses.[50]

If we want to complicate even further this already complicated passage, we may remember that Lady V. is not exactly the most "domestic" of women and Peregrine not the most virtuous of young men. She has earlier given birth to an illegitimate daughter (who died in infancy), and he is illegitimate (though he himself does not know about it) and highly promiscuous—a bastard who sires bastards all over Europe and who would not hesitate to rape any current object of his passion. Smollett's novel thus responds subtly to the stale set of accusations regularly raised against the London Foundling Hospital, namely that those who supported the Hospital did it primarily because they hoped that it would save them the expense of caring for their own bastards. Of course, Lady V. would never stoop to leaving her child at the Hospital,

CHAPTER 5

and neither would Peregrine, with his—however warped—notion of "honour," but it is nevertheless significant that the two people who could have—at least hypothetically—benefited from the "services" offered by this institution do not support the Hospital and instead aid the poor woman in person and privately.

The Foundling Hospital thus occupies a double position in *Peregrine Pickle*. On the one hand, supporting a public philanthropy does not automatically render the supporter a good person—and in the case of a woman, it actually seems to indicate her callousness. On the other hand, slandering the Foundling Hospital—by implying that it breeds prostitution or benefits rich fornicators—marks the slanderer as narrow minded and obdurate, her accusations groundless. For a woman, at any rate, to be on the safe side in the world of Smollett's novel, it is better to neither assist nor condemn a public charity, limiting herself to private eleemosynary acts, preferably witnessed—approved and emulated—by a man.

Infanticide, Illegitimacy, and Property in *Sir Charles Grandison*

Broadly speaking, the same advice applies to the women in Richardson's *The History of Sir Charles Grandison* (1753–54), in which the issues of infanticide, illegitimacy, and philanthropy are considered almost exclusively in terms of their potential impact on a middle-class family, or rather on that complicated hybrid of upper-class wealth and titles and middle-class sensibilities that constitutes the Grandison clan. Read in the context of the eighteenth-century infanticide prevention campaign, *Grandison* appears to articulate emotional reasons why an upper-middle-class woman would be wary of supporting a public philanthropy rumored to sponsor illegitimacy and to absolve sexually transgressing females from the consequences of their liaisons. At the same time the novel seems to frown on the private lack of charity and indiscriminate demonizing of bastards and bastard-bearers. This double thrust of *Grandison* frequently makes ambiguous its references to child murder and bastardy, an ambiguity that echoes the incipient discomfort we may detect in the description of the ruthless dispossession of Thomasine's "cubs" in *Clarissa*.

In *Grandison*, the topic of infanticide comes up where it is least expected: in the letter that Sir Charles's sister Charlotte (the newly minted "Lady G.") writes to Aunt Selby and Lucy. Charlotte is pregnant with her first child and mortally afraid of her impending labor, but ever the incorrigible wit, she manages to interlace her dark parturitional forebodings with racy jokes. At the close of her letter, she inserts a note inviting Aunt Selby and Lucy to "come early that [she] can shew [them her] *baby*-things," so that later they "may be able to testify that [she] had no design to overlay [her] little Marmouset."[51] Charlotte alludes here to one of the most popular lines of defense used in infanticide trials—the "benefit-of-linen." If an unmarried mother of a dead infant could prove that she had prepared all the necessary linen well before a baby was born (which showed that she had intended to keep the baby), the case against her would be summarily dismissed.[52] Charlotte, a married, rich, upper-class female, who ostensibly has nothing in common with women typically accused of infanticide[53] or with the ignominious realities of the infanticide courtroom, appropriates the rhetoric of that courtroom with surprising ease. Worse still, she expects that her addressees, the middle-aged dignified lady and the young inexperienced girl, both leading a sheltered existence in provincial Northamptonshire, would also know about the essence of the "benefit-of-linen" defense—otherwise the joke would fall flat. That they do know about it and that they are expected to think that the joke is risqué is obvious from the reaction of Harriet, Charlotte's sister-in-law, who copies Charlotte's letter for her grandmother Shirley (the audience keeps expanding) and observes dryly that the note is in Charlotte's "usual stile" (3:358). So topical a reference to infanticide may seem out of place among characters of refined sensibility (even though everybody gets the joke), and it must have contributed to some of Richardson's contemporaries' dislike for his "patterns of charming pleasantry."[54] Lady Mary Wortley Montagu, for one, thought that "Charlotte's coarse jokes and low expressions [are such] as are only to be heard among the Lowest Class of People" (421).

What does the "benefit-of-linen" joke mean for the pregnant Charlotte? Lois A. Chaber sees Charlotte's witty letter as an exposure of "marriage's institution which disguises the bloody biological ordeal at its center." She is also aware of the "sinister overtones" of Charlotte's allusions to killing her newborn baby and interprets "infanticide [as] the logical culmination of the rebellion against maternity that the prenatal Charlotte (verbally) engages in."[55] My reading of this episode qualifies Chaber's based on the fact that Charlotte refers to a court procedure (the "benefit-of-linen") associated primarily, if not exclusively, with unwed mothers of a certain social class.[56] Chaber's interpretation allows for an attractive subversiveness in Charlotte's playful class-crossing association; the "bloody biological ordeal" of giving birth is the same for Lady G. as it is for, say, Hannah Warwick, a servant who in 1767 was accused of concealing the birth and the death of her illegitimate child.[57] It seems to me, however, that rather than identifying with her big-bellied sister-women across class boundaries, Charlotte is recreating—with a certain degree of schadenfreude—a scenario involving a serving-class woman apprehended and about to be punished for her sexual trespass. This reading is not immediately obvious if we consider Charlotte's remark (as does Chaber) in the context of her frequent expostulations against marriage as a social institution aimed at subjugating women. If, on the other hand, we situate it in the context of the novel's multiple references to illegitimacy, and particularly the references to the ongoing attempt of the Grandison clan to safeguard itself against various illegitimate pretenders to the family fortune, we realize that the pregnant Charlotte has many reasons to brood about the threat represented by bastards and their mothers, and that she may derive a subconscious satisfaction from imagining a bastard-bearer caught and put on trial for her transgression.

The Grandison girls—Charlotte and Caroline—are made aware quite early of the dangers represented by such women and their children. Their father, Sir Thomas Grandison, has several illegitimate children with Mrs. Oldham, formerly a woman of quality who now has to earn her living as a housekeeper. He also supports "another mistress in town, [with] a taste for all its gaieties . . . who even [assumes] his name" (1:320). Mortified by his mounting expenditures, he saves the expense of a dowry for his eldest daughter, Caroline, by preventing her marriage to the virtuous man of her choice, Lord L. Having witnessed Caroline's sufferings, and apprehending "what must be [her] sufferings in turn," Charlotte determines to "take any step, however rash, where virtue [is] not to be wounded, rather than undergo what [her sister] underwent from . . . [Sir Thomas]" (1:404) and nearly throws herself away on an unworthy man, one Captain Anderson. Another sad repercussion of Sir Thomas's illicit liaisons is that, ashamed of his sexually prompted financial indiscretions, he keeps his beloved son, Charles, abroad for many years, thus setting into motion Charles's Italian "entanglement," the source of much grief to the main female character of the story, Harriet Byron.[58] Finally, to make matters worse, Sir Thomas abandons one kept mistress in pursuit of another—a sixteen-year-old Miss Obrien—brought up by her covetous relatives "with a notion that her beauty would make her fortune" (1:353). Sir Thomas dies unexpectedly, just when the young Miss is ready to enter his keeping ("*500l.* a year for her life" [1:354])—and only his death prevents the further disintegration of the family fortune. (Disappointed, but assured that no man can resist a good-looking "young creature" and that he would forget his family and class obligations to satisfy his "vice," Miss Obrien attempts to seduce Sir Charles Grandison in place of his deceased libertine of a father. Sir Charles, however, is of a different mettle. He admires Miss Obrien "as a man would a fine picture" [1:376] and expostulates with her until, confessing her base intentions, she "weeps, and vows that she would be honest." He then marries her off to a "tradesman near *Golden* Square" [1:377; emphasis added]—to let her dig for gold in her proper station!)

Next to one prodigal patriarch is another: Lord W., an uncle on the mother's side of the Grandison family, lives in sin with the "deplorable" Mrs. Giffard—a woman whose lack of "birth" and "education" is compounded by her lack of "moderation" (1:358)—and who thus squanders the estate that Sir Charles, Caroline, and Charlotte are supposed to inherit (provided that Lord W. remains childless). Yet one more Grandison, Sir Thomas's nephew, Everard, finds himself imposed upon by a "cast[off] mistress, experienced in all the arts of such, and acting upon the secret influences of a man of quality [who], wanting to get rid of her, supports her in a prosecution commenced against [Everard] for performance of covenants" (2:442). Another family, the "ancient" and deserving Mansfields, suffers because of the indiscretion of their maternal uncle who, at the age of seventy, married his servant and left his property to her two children, fathered, in fact, by another man (an echo, perhaps, of the story of *Clarissa*'s Thomasine, whose children, according to Belford, were fathered by her clandestine hostler-lover and not by her gentleman-keeper).

Richardson makes a point of portraying the young Grandisons as almost unrealistically vulnerable to the financial damage that could be inflicted by illegitimate children and their mothers. On the one hand, under British law, illegitimate offspring could not inherit property at the expense of legitimate heirs, and being the first-born son seems to ensure Sir Charles's position as the sole inheritor of the parental estate. On the other hand, in practice, there were many ways to divert money and property from legitimate children. First, there were *inter vivos* settlements, that is, "the transmission of property or goods during the lifetime of the bequeather."[59] Sir Thomas engages in *inter vivos* transmissions when he pays for Mrs. Oldham and her children and when he agrees to bestow 500 pounds a year upon Miss Obrien. Second, the whole estate could be whisked away from the first-born son if it were held by his father "in fee simple" rather than in strict settlement. Strict settlement meant that the current owner of the estate was but a life-long tenant keeping the property for his eldest son (who in turn would keep it for *his* eldest son), with no right to will, or lease, or mortgage it except for purposes explicitly discussed in the settlement.[60] Sir Thomas Grandison holds his Irish estate "in fee simple"—Richardson is very particular about this point[61]—which gives him the right to squander it, the right that he, unfortunately, is only too quick to exercise when he borrows money upon this estate to pay his "debt of honour" (1:329), that is, the debt incurred by whoring. That Sir Thomas's borrowing money upon his Irish estate is severely detrimental to his son is clear from the moneylender's insistence—which goes against the set of standard procedures[62]—that Sir Charles should be made aware of the deal and even join his father in the security. Finally, a current owner of the estate could break the entail, as did for example the fifth Duke of Bolton, who had "a very short reign," but still managed before his death to charge his entailed estates "with the payment of his debts, several annuities, and the residue of his legacies," which included 14,000 pounds to his mistress and 12,000 pounds to his daughter.[63]

Richardson does not specify whether Sir Thomas's second estate (back in England) is held in fee simple. One telling detail, however, leads us to suspect that it is. Sir Thomas falls ill just before signing "the releases"—the legal forms guaranteeing Miss Obrien her 500 pounds per year. The person who "posts down, on the first news he [has] of [his master's] being taken ill, hoping to get him to sign the ready-drawn up releases" is one Mr. Bever, his corrupted "English steward" (1:355). We do not know for sure whether the new annual expense of 500 pounds would make Sir Thomas borrow money upon his English estate, but the presence of his "English steward" suggests that the second estate is also held in fee and thus can be spent on the future illegitimate children of Miss Obrien. Significantly, after the mid-seventeenth century, it was rather unusual for a prominent aristocratic family to have all its estates in fee.[64] Besides, the personality of Sir Thomas's "frugal" father strongly suggests that he would take care to tie his "profuse" (1:310) son to the strict settlement. Richardson, meanwhile, was "reasonably well informed about the legal issues"[65] surrounding the strict settlement. Balancing between being explicit on the matter and making his story improbable, he thus hints darkly that, in principle, the younger

Grandisons could meet the same fate as did the nieces and nephews of Lord Mansfield or, indeed, the author's own friend Elizabeth Midwinter, whose father managed to disinherit her altogether, leaving the family property to the illegitimate son he had with his servant. It is likely that what is really going on here is that Richardson projects the familiar economic fear of the middle-class family threatened by illegitimacy onto the upper-class family, although in real life, as McClure and John Habakkuk have argued, the upper-class family would have been protected by its "great wealth"[66] from the danger represented by the bastard pretender to its property.

It is not surprising, then, that Charlotte is uniformly harsh in her judgment upon the designing females of inferior class standing, whom she sees as preying upon well-to-do families. When given a chance to humble their late father's mistress, Mrs. Oldham, Caroline and Charlotte, in particular, do so with a vengeance until their magnanimous brother stops their cruel sport. Later, having made clear what she thinks of this "tribe" of women, Charlotte almost flies at her best friend Harriet, who dares to contradict her and pity the unfortunate Mrs. Oldham and her illegitimate children. "Be quiet, Harriet," snaps Charlotte, "Would you be as tame to a husband's mistress, as you seem favorable to a father's?" (2:305) Because Charlotte's father, and her uncle, and her cousin—virtually every single one of her male relatives, excepting her superman of a brother—have proved susceptible to the charms of designing female interlopers, her marriage and pregnancy make her sharply aware of her own and her future child's vulnerability to illegitimate pretenders to family fortunes. It is in this context that her reference to the infanticide trial could be read as an indirect expression of her desire to see such women apprehended and penalized for their sexual misdeeds.

Richardson did not necessarily agree with Charlotte's uncompromising condemnation of the "tribe" of kept women.[67] As we know, he actively supported both the London Foundling Hospital and Magdalen House and became a governor of both charities in 1754 and 1758, respectively. Much as he detested the practice of keeping mistresses, his narrative strives to differentiate between the custom itself—which he held as evil in principle—and the "unhappy women . . . drawn [into it] . . . by the perfidy of men" (2:356), a fine differentiation not always sustainable in a novel representing so vividly the destructive consequences of illicit love affairs for the legitimate family. Chaber's insightful diagnosis of Charlotte's infanticidal joke as expressing fear of being trapped in the exploitive marriage economy should not thus occlude the larger meaning of this joke within the novel's consistent attempt to safeguard and sanctify this economy. Though replete with the "bloody ordeals" of childbirth and grounded in female conformity, domestic space is figured in *Grandison* as infinitely appealing and warranting a vigilant protection against illegitimate intruders who have the capacity to destabilize it.

The novel's take on female philanthropy is thus grounded in the conflict between its two ways of looking at "fallen" women and their illegitimate offspring: are they "unhappy women" (2:356) and their children "unhappy innocents" (1:366), or are they "creatures" (1:370) of that infamous "tribe," and their children "living proofs" of their "disgrace" (1:366)? Are they to be pitied or castigated? Supported with the services of the London Foundling Hospital and Magdalen House or driven to commit infanticide? And if they are to be pitied and supported, what role, if any, should gentlewomen—legally married wives and mothers, standing to lose from the "creatures'" depredations—play in this charitable endeavor?

The novel does not provide an unambiguous answer to any of these questions. On the one hand, its main heroine, Harriet, consistently expresses her compassion toward the "fallen" women and their children. First, she censures Mr. Greville for abandoning his mistress, whom he "brought with him from the Wales" without giving her "sufficient [means] for a twelvemonth's scanty subsistence" (1:25)—and we can only guess how Charlotte would have responded to this sentiment in her friend. Second, Harriet applauds Sir Charles's behaving generously toward Mrs. Oldham and allowing "her an annuity, for the sake of her sons by his father" and expresses such interest in the fate of the late Sir Thomas's mistress that it prompts Charlotte to observe, in her arch manner, that "our Harriet is strangely taken with Mrs. Oldham's story" (1:375). Finally, it is Harriet who brings up the concept of philanthropy and proceeds to defend a woman's right both to use this trendy neologism and to partake in the activity that it denotes. Insisting that her love for Sir Charles Grandison stems from her desire to "promote and share in [his] glorious philanthropy," she writes an aside directed at her loving but still rather misogynistic uncle Selby: "Yes, my uncle! Why should women, in compliance with the petulance of narrow-minded men, forbear to use words that some seem to think above them . . . ?" (1:389).

On the other hand, Harriet's position as a budding female philanthropist particularly compassionate toward illegitimate children and their mothers is complicated by the possibility of her marrying the only man on Earth who is guaranteed not to keep mistresses and sire bastards. Since Harriet is not to know the fears of an average wife, her generosity of spirit is ultimately worth less than Charlotte's—were Charlotte to be so liberally inclined—and thus cannot be perceived as the official, although unavoidably idealized, "viewpoint" of the novel.

And in any case, Harriet's interest in philanthropy becomes if not less strong then certainly less vocal as she moves closer to being the next Lady Grandison. Although present during the fourth volume's famous exchange concerning public charities, in which Sir Charles describes his scheme for "An Hospital for Female Penitents" (2:356)—the novel's version of Magdalen House—she does not say a word and functions more like the stenographer locked in Sir Hargrave Pollexfen's closet in an earlier episode than as a participant in the conversation. By this time, Harriet, as Jerry Beasley has pointed out, is well on her way to falling completely "under Grandison's influence," being "changed" and "diminished,"[68] and gradually losing "the marks distinguishing her identity from Grandison's: her sharp vocal inflections . . . , her relative independence . . . , and her autonomous personal narrative" (37).[69] Harriet's days of speaking up for kept women and their children and dreaming of glorious philanthropies are over by the end of the third volume.

The History of Sir Charles Grandison thus by no means condemns the philanthropic efforts of its age, nor does it seem to doubt their efficacy and moral outlook. Nor does it say explicitly that upper- and upper-middle-class women should not support the charities directed at easing the lot of illegitimate children and their "unhappy" mothers. At the same time, it makes two points about such support, neither of which is very encouraging. First, it makes us understand why Charlotte, for example, would rather visualize a serving-class woman exposed and punished for her sexual transgression and infanticide than support an institution designed to "preserve" such a woman from her "desperate crime"[70] in hopes of returning her to the path of virtue. Charlotte is fed up with sexually attractive women of inferior class standing and their illegitimate children, the source of the ceaseless drain on her family's emotional and financial well-being. Because of this, she is likely to acquiesce to the view of the Foundling Hospital as an "immoral" charity freeing female opportunists to continue their "depredations upon mankind." Again, Richardson does not say that such a view is correct, but, via Charlotte, his last novel provides tacit emotional validation for the absence of gentlewomen from the lists of public supporters of the Hospital.

The history of Harriet's relationship with Sir Charles Grandison strengthens this validation. Throughout the first and second volume, Harriet feels free to express openly her compassion for illegitimate children and their mothers. In the fourth volume, Sir Charles subsumes her charitable impulses under his own expostulations about the "Hospital for Female Penitents." From that point on, the novel makes clear that whatever philanthropic inclinations Lady Grandison may have, they will have to be articulated in private into the kindly ear of her husband, who then will have the option of making them public and seeking other men's approval of them. To make up for this loss of her independent voice, the novel glorifies the implicit political power presumably exercised by Lady Grandison. As her husband observes, it is virtuous wives who move their men to "purchase and build for them; travel and toil for them; run through, at the call of . . . King and Country, dangers and difficulties; [to] at last, lay all [the] trophies [and] acquirements, at [their wives'] feet; enough rewarded in the conscience of duty done" (3:248).[71] It is virtuous wives, then, who move their men to "purchase" a suitable ground, to "build" a Foundling Hospital, and to support it with their subscriptions and gifts of valuable paintings. *The March to Finchley* will be exhibited in the General Court Room, attesting to the joint effort of British men and women to support "glorious Benefactions,"[72] but the lady must vanish.

- 6 -

THE CHILDREN "OWNED BY NONE"

Divided Bastardy in Frances Burney's Evelina

BAYES: There's a blust'ring verse for you now.
SMITH: Yes, Sir; but why is he so mightily troubled to find he is not a Fishermans Son?
BAYES: Phoo! that is not because he has a mind to be his Son, but for fear that he should be thought to be no bodies Son at all.
—George Villiers, 2nd Duke of Buckingham, *The Rehearsal,* 1671

Though, while legally the son of one Earl, and naturally of another, I am, nominally, nobody's son at all.
—Samuel Johnson, *An Account of the Life of Mr. Richard Savage, Son of the Earl of Rivers,* 1743

The captain . . . said, "Tho' the Law did not positively allow the destroying such base-born children, yet it held them to be the Children of no-body; that the Church considered them as the Children of no-body; and that at the best, they ought to be brought up to the lowest and vilest Offices of the Commonwealth."
—Henry Fielding, *Tom Jones,* 1749

But why do I talk of parentage? alas! I am the son of nobody. I was, indeed, begotten by my valiant father, Gregory Gooby, Esq. upon the body of my chaste mother, Ellen Glen . . . , but it was a clandestine affair, for which my valiant father had no canonical warrant.
—Robert Bage, *Hermsprong; or, Man As He Is Not,* 1796

CHAPTER 6

*I*llegitimacy, infanticide, and, after 1739, the London Foundling Hospital were indelible features of the mental landscape of the eighteenth-century writer. The published fictional impressions of that landscape assumed many forms, both covert and overt, ranging from Richard Steele's reworking of Terence's plot of fornication and exposure into an immaculately polite foundling comedy (*The Conscious Lovers*, 1722); and John Shebbeare's inserting a story of one Miss Standish, forced to send her bastard child to the Foundling Hospital, into his novelized catalogue of seductions and elopements (*The Marriage Act*, 1754); to Samuel Richardson's ambivalent positioning of bastards as both a threat to and a casualty of upper-middle-class familial bliss (*The History of Sir Charles Grandison*, 1753–54). Writers participated in the infanticide prevention campaign and responded to that campaign in their fiction without necessarily framing their actions in terms of "participation" in or a "response" to a phenomenon with identifiable social boundaries; instead, the concern about bastardy and about the abandonment and murder of the illegitimate children of the poor, the debates about the policies of the Foundling Hospital, and the awareness of the titillating new topicality of the old foundling trope constituted an integral part of everyday life for the eighteenth-century British intellectual.

And so the infanticide prevention campaign was part of everyday life for Frances Burney. People in her immediate social circle were either directly involved with the Foundling Hospital or had relatives who were. Dr. Johnson had kept a wary eye on the Hospital since his 1757 spat with Jonas Hanway about the presumed lack of proper religious tutoring for the Hospital's children.[1] Philip Jennings,[2] known as "a great friend of Mrs. Thrale and Miss Burney,"[3] was the brother of Juliana Dodd, a hardworking and influential inspector of the Hospital.[4] In 1774, Frances herself assisted her father, prominent musicologist Charles Burney, in drawing up a plan for turning the Foundling Hospital into a public school of music, an "English Conservatorio," as she called it in her 1832 *Memoirs of Doctor Burney*.[5]

The alumni of the Foundling Hospital were known to complain that its protective atmosphere had left them unprepared for the challenges of the real world outside its walls. For Charles Burney, however, the social encapsulation of the young foundlings—their upbringing "in complete and unsuspicious ignorance of evil" (*Memoirs*, 236)—was the main argument for establishing the first national music school on the basis of the Hospital. Generally, although Dr. Burney felt very strongly the need for fostering native talents instead of importing musicians "from foreign shores," he recoiled at the thought of taking "promiscuously the children of the poor, merely where they had an ear for music, or a voice for song, [because it would mean] running the risk of gathering together a mixed little multitude, which, from intermingling inherent vulgarity, hereditary diseases, or vicious propensities, with the finer qualities requisite for admission, might render the cultivation of their youthful talents, a danger—if not a curse—to the country" (ibid.). What would happen, mused Burney, "should a single one of the tribe go astray"? The "popular cry against teaching the arts to the poor would stain the whole community with a stain indelible.... The institution itself might be branded with infamy" (ibid.), and—a consideration absent from but easily read into Burney's worst-case scenario—the reputation of the instigator of the scheme would suffer a terrible blow. A "conservatorio" opened in the Foundling Hospital, however, would be a very different matter. Its institutional grounding would ensure a comfortable division of labor between Burney and the governors of the Hospital. The former would supervise the teaching of music, and the latter would take it upon themselves to insure that their charges "breathed their infantine lives ... in innocence" (ibid.). In this case, should any of the Hospital's students of music "go astray," nobody would blame Charles Burney and his harebrained scheme of teaching art to the poor because, after all, bastards may turn out badly with or without a musical accompaniment.

This latter consideration remained, of course, unspoken, and when in July 1774 Dr. Burney sounded Sir Charles Whitworth, the governor of the Hospital, about the scheme, Sir Charles "thought it proper, feasible, desirable, and patriotic" (236). Encouraged, Dr. Burney drew up a formal plan for the music school, but to his mortification and Whitworth's disappointment, the next meeting of the Hospital's governors and guardians, convened exclusively to deliberate upon the plan, gave rise to a series of "perplexing" discussions. Frances Burney reported with a measured sarcasm:

> It was objected that music was an art of luxury, by no means requisite to life, or accessory to morality. These children were meant to be educated as plain but essential members of the general community. They were to be trained up to useful purposes, with a singleness that would ward off all ambition for what was higher, and teach them to repay the benefit of their support by cheerful labour. To stimulate them to superior views might mar the religious object of the charity, which was to nullify rather than extinguish all disposition to pride,

CHAPTER 6

vice, or voluptuousness, such as, probably, had demoralized their culpable parents, and thrown these deserted outcasts upon the mercy of the Foundling Hospital. (*Memoirs*, 237–38)

Dr. Burney did not give up his idea without a struggle. He wrote back to the governors that the Foundling Hospital had never been conceived as "a seminary, predestined for menial servitude, and as the only institution of the country where the members were to form a caste, from whose rules and plodden ways no genius could ever emerge" (*Memoirs*, 238). Furthermore, he argued, the Hospital represented a uniquely suitable setting for a social experiment involving the musical pre-professionalization of a large group of children because

> these children are all orphans; they are taken from no family, *for by none are they owned;* they are drawn from no calling, for to none are they specifically bred. . . . Were it not better, then, where there are subjects who are success inviting, to bestow upon them professional improvement, with virtuous education? since, as long as operas, concerts, and theatres are licensed by government, musical performers, vocal and instrumental, will inevitably be wanted, employed and remunerated. . . . And where, if not here, may subjects be found on whom such a national trial may be made with the least danger of injury? (*Memoirs*, 238–39; emphasis added)

Although many of the Hospital's officials seemed persuaded by Dr. Burney's arguments, his plan was ultimately rejected. Frances tells us that her father's "pride was justly hurt" (*Memoirs*, 239) by the petty tenor of the deliberations (the governors gave more weight to the complaints of the Hospital's neighbors, who were afraid of noise issuing from the music school, than to Burney's patriotic exhortations about the wasteful practice of importing musical talents instead of fostering them on native ground), and he dissociated himself from the project. By the late 1780s, a "plan, in many respects similar . . . [was] put into execution," and the Hospital began drawing a steady income from its children's Chapel singing, but, as Frances observes, nobody acknowledged Dr. Burney's role as "the original projector" of this endeavor (234).

Looking back at Charles Burney's debates with the Hospital's administration, it is impossible to reconstruct the exact genesis of the phrase that he used to characterize the unique social position of the foundlings: "for by none are they owned" (ibid.). Did he come up with it himself, or was it Frances who coined it when, as her father's secretary, she assisted him in drawing up the plan for the music school and in devising arguments that should placate the doubts of his opponents? Whichever is the case, it appears that the expression "owned by none" summed up succinctly in the father and daughter's mind and in the public mind the situation of the young inmates of the Hospital. This expression both reflected that, having saved the children from likely death, the Hospital was not accountable to their parents for whatever experimental "professional involvement" it could devise for them, and it evoked the old legal precept that the bastard is *filius nullius*—"the son of nobody." Throughout the eighteenth century such appellations as "nobody," a "child owned by none," and a "son of nobody" were used in a variety of contexts—including works of fiction (see the epigraph to this chapter)—to denote illegitimacy, so it was only fitting that the Burneys adapted one such appellation for their argument.

Published in 1778, four years after the aborted "English Conservatorio" proposal, *Evelina* echoes that proposal's rhetoric of *filius nullius* via frequent references to the title heroine's "nobodiness." "I hardly know myself to whom I most belong," says Evelina sadly to Lord Orville, and she is painfully sensitive to other people's characterizing of her as "nobody"[6] and making remarks that could be construed as pointing to her presumed bastardy. Evelina's "nobodiness" has been a topic of fruitful discussions by such scholars as Margaret Anne Doody, Joanne Cutting-Gray, Kristina Straub, Catherine Gallagher, and, most recently, Susan Greenfield,[7] whose interpretations range from reading Evelina's self-nugatory rhetoric as indicative of her adolescent female angst[8] to exploring Burney's marketing savvy of writing "for, about, and from the point of view of 'Nobody.'"[9]

My position is nearly aligned with Greenfield's, who observes that the language used by William Blackstone in his *Commentaries on the Laws of England*, in which the bastard is defined as "kin to nobody," is "so close to some of the novel's descriptions of Evelina that it almost seems to have influenced them."[10] I suggest that when it comes to Evelina's pained admissions of "belonging to no one" and being "nobody," Burney indeed appropriates her culture's lexicon of illegitimacy, the same lexicon that the father-daughter duo drew upon to defend Dr. Burney's ill-received music school scheme. I further argue that she does so in response to a very particular set of challenges faced by an author writing a *respectable* novel about the supposed illegitimacy of a daughter of a nobleman for a predominantly middle-class audience at the time when aristocratic and middle-class attitudes toward bastardy were quite different.

Evelina's "bastard" troubles are twofold. First, she is in danger of being taken for a natural daughter of a baronet who is not in a hurry to "*properly* own her" (19). As Irene Fizer observes, though an heiress, Evelina "is recognized only as a bastard daughter."[11] Significantly, in her description of this particular aspect of Evelina's predicament, Burney tacitly replaces a typical aristocratic perspective of bastardy with that calculated to appeal to her middle-class readership. As I will demonstrate, the real-life daughter of an eighteenth-century baronet would not discuss her illegitimacy in the debasing terms adopted for this purpose by Evelina and her guardian. If anything, their over-humbled language is more reminiscent of that foisted on the inmates of the Foundling Hospital by benefactors anxious to keep the children aware of their modest social position.

Further complicating Evelina's position as a "bastard heiress"[12] is the possibility that she will lose her inheritance altogether in favor of Polly Green, the daughter of Evelina's wet nurse, a "little usurper," substituted in infancy for Evelina and brought up by her unsuspecting father as his own child. As a variation on the age-old "changeling" motif, the "substituted child" scenario was relatively common in eighteenth-century fiction, responding to a variety of cultural anxieties,[13] one of which had to do with the socioeconomic realities of bastardy. Because Evelina's father is a reformed libertine, a story in which "the lawful child is neglected, [and] another is adopted" (316) functions as a literary stand-in for a familiar real-life situation in which a fitful or guilt-ridden patriarch damages his legal child's prospects by providing for his natural offspring. Again, as in the case of the improbably groveling rhetoric used to denote Evelina's horror of being perceived as illegitimate, the fear that a bastard impostor would siphon her legal sibling's inheritance was much more pertinent to Burney's middle-class readers than to members of the aristocratic class, to which Evelina supposedly belongs.

Burney had to be quite careful in allowing her novel to articulate the familiar anxiety about the distribution of the family resources among legitimate and illegitimate children. Too explicit a concern about the repercussions of bastardy would have rendered her book vulgar, at the very least, or even scandalous, whereas, as Gallagher points out, "Evelina and the novel were both good because they were not scandalous."[14] Still, because of the competing class consciousnesses animating *Evelina*, it remains a doubly haunted novel. Bastardy is both present and absent on its pages as are the shadows of the rejected "English Conservatorio" and its "innocent" (but also dangerous) pupils.

The Children "Owned by None"
Rewriting Class in Evelina

> Could I but say I was descended from honest, tho' mean parents, I would not murmur at my fate, but I have none,—none to own me;—I am a nothing,—a kind of reptile in humanity...
> —Eliza Haywood, The Fortunate Foundlings, 1744

> Joanna: I am nobody; the child of nobody; a branch lopped off and cast away; that might have grown, but that could find no root.
> —Thomas Holcroft, The Deserted Daughter, 1795

Evelina's ambiguous standing as a "bastard heiress" is explained on the first pages of the novel when her guardian, Mr. Villars, invites us to "consider . . . the peculiar cruelty of her situation." Evelina, as he points out, is "[the] only child of a wealthy baronet, whose person she has never seen, whose character she has reason to abhor, and whose name she is forbidden to claim; entitled as she is to lawfully inherit his fortune and estate, is there any probability that he will *properly* own her? And while he continues to persevere in disavowing his marriage with Miss Evelyn [Evelina's mother], she shall never, at the expense of her mother's honour, receive a part of her right, as the donation of his bounty" (19). In other words, a wealthy baronet can acknowledge his illegitimate child and provide for such a child financially—as Sir John Belmont indeed does when he discovers that he has a natural son, one "J. Macartney"—but such a provision alone would not satisfy Evelina's guardian, who demands the acknowledgment "in the face of the world . . . [of] the legitimacy of her birth" (366). Evelina has to be established as a "*lawful* successor" (339; emphasis added) to her father's riches and not as yet another bastard recipient of the repentant libertine's bounty. In the latter case, "the birth of . . . Evelina will receive a stigma, against which honour, truth, and innocence may appeal in vain! a stigma which will eternally blast the fair fame of her virtuous mother, and cast upon her blameless self the odium of a title, which not all her purity can rescue from established shame and dishonour" (337).

Mr. Villars's dark warning about the "stigma" that could be cast upon Evelina by the "odious" title of bastard comes late in the novel, but it is clear that Evelina does not need this warning, having internalized the fear of such a stigma much earlier.[15] How else can we explain that, untutored in the way of the world as she appears at her "first entrance" into London society, she is painfully attuned to any remark that could be interpreted as hinting at her illegitimacy? Witness, for example, Evelina's reporting to her guardian that she was deeply distressed by her grandmother's "gross" (52) way of speaking about the circumstances of her birth: "The manner in which Madame Duval was pleased to introduce me to this family, extremely shocked me. 'Here, my dears,' said she, 'here's a relation you little thought of: but you must know my poor daughter Caroline had this child after she run away from me,—though I never knew nothing of it, not I, for a long time after; for they took care to keep it a secret from me, though the poor child has never a friend in the world besides'" (68). Madame Duval's speech reflects unjustly on Mr. Villars, but it is clear that what shocks Evelina most are the intimations of her illegitimacy contained in that speech, which is borne out by her strong physical reaction—she literally runs out of the room—when Miss Branghton announces, "Lord, Polly, only think! Miss never saw her papa!" (69).

Students of eighteenth-century culture should take issue with the novel's tacit assumption that Evelina's supposed illegitimacy automatically spells her social annihilation—"shame and dishonour," as her guardian puts it. Ruth McClure has pointed out that the period's aristocracy viewed illegitimacy with tolerance, siring and marrying bastards, and advancing them to high office. John Habakkuk describes the situation in more detail:

> The system could also accommodate the illegitimate offspring of landed families so long as paternity was acknowledged and the parent was prepared to pay a portion large enough to compensate. Where there were only illegitimate children and they were well endowed they could make very good marriages. All three daughters of Sir Edward Walpole, Sir Robert's second son, married into the aristocracy with the full panoply of settlements. Ann Newcomen, illegitimate daughter of Sir Francis Wortley, married the second son of the first Earl of Sandwich. Rachel Bayton, illegitimate daughter of John Hall, married the eldest son of the Earl of Kingston. Anne Wellesley, the natural daughter of the Marquess Wellesley, married in 1806 Sir William Abdy, baronet of an ancient family. (153–54)

At the same time, as Habakkuk admits, some marriage treaties might have stalled because of the bride's illegitimacy:

The Children "Owned by None"

In 1769, Edward Mann projected a match between his illegitimate daughter Mary and cousin-german, a promised to give her £20,000, plus another £20,000 if her (illegitimate) brother died. But the projected bridegroom "grew cold," ostensibly because of scruples about marriage to a cousin but more probably, Mann suspected, "from pride and from her being a natural daughter." Horace Walpole commented that Mann "may now be tempted to scrape all he can together, in order to match his daughter more highly." Jean Mary Browne, illegitimate daughter and only child of Charles, fifth Duke of Bolton, and heiress to the greater part of the Bolton's estates, after the failure of the male issue of his brother (which was virtually certain in 1778), despite her prospective wealth, made in 1778 a socially modest match to Thomas Orde, the second son of a Northumbrian gentry family.[16]

We may never be able to establish beyond reasonable doubt that Edward Mann's daughter's bastardy was indeed the reason that her cousin "grew cold." In fact, as Habakkuk observes in his discussion of treaties in which all the parties were legitimate, the disapproval of a prospective bride or groom could arise from many "highly personal causes," such as "religious differences," a family's "bad reputation," "personal disinclinations," and the "disparity of fortune so great that the possibility of an equal bargain was virtually ruled out from the start."[17] The illegitimacy of a young aristocratic woman, in other words, was one of several factors (but by no means the decisive factor) that could, but just as often did not, endanger her marital prospects. With this in mind, both Mr. Villars's passionate conviction that the Baronet's financial generosity could never make up for the everlasting "shame and dishonour" of bastardy and Evelina's corresponding anguish at being perceived as illegitimate appear overstated and in need of further explanation. Villars's choice of terms seems, in fact, to be more reminiscent of the psalms sung by the charges of the Foundling Hospital ("In Guilt I was conceiv'd and born / The Heir of Sin and Shame") than of any sentiment that a real-life daughter of a rich baronet and a wealthy gentlewoman would ever encourage in those around her or express herself.

One possible interpretation of Mr. Villar's language is suggested by Habakkuk's example of the fate of Jean Mary Browne. If the illegitimacy of a rich heiress could indeed confine her to a match more "socially modest" than she could have aspired to otherwise, Evelina's guardian may feel downright hysterical at the mere thought that as a wealthy bastard, Evelina would not make as good a match as she would have made as a legitimate child. Such interpretation, however, would render Mr. Villars profoundly hypocritical, for we learn early on that he apprehends "nothing more than too much raising [Evelina's] hopes and her views," especially because, as he observes melancholically, "a youthful mind is seldom free from ambition" (107). Furthermore, the scenario suggested by Mr. Villars's rhetoric—Evelina's father's acknowledging her as his daughter but not as his legal heiress (his "lawful successor")—is not even applicable to Evelina's actual situation. The singularity of Evelina's position—made possible by the "substituted child" device—is such that as soon as her father recognizes her as his daughter, she automatically becomes his only legitimate child.[18]

But if Mr. Villars's hypertrophied anxiety about Evelina's legal status reflects only very superficially (or not at all) the challenges faced by a real-life natural daughter of a wealthy nobleman and a rich gentlewoman, or even Evelina's actual situation, what *does* it reflect? To begin to answer this question, we should first look at the works of eighteenth-century literature featuring unquestionably illegitimate female protagonists[19] and inquire into the ideological stakes of conceptualizing such protagonists as "unfit" for polite discourse, just as Evelina is conceptualized by her guardian as unfit for any social existence unless her legitimacy is reaffirmed "in the face of the world."

Eliza Haywood's 1744 novel, *The Fortunate Foundlings*, centers on a set of bastard twins, Louisa and Horatio, who, after completing the obligatory route of breathtaking adventures and discovering that although noble and rich, their parents had never been married, settle into happy and prosperous marriages of their own. William Warner has argued that the "sexy and egotistical [novels] of amorous intrigue" (*Licensing Entertainment,* 326) produced by such writers as Aphra Behn, Delariviere Manley, and Haywood, were destined to be driven from the literary market by the newly respectable novels authored by Henry Fielding and Samuel Richardson. Haywood's "formula fiction," as Warner suggests, glorified the "licentious sexuality of the upper class"[20]—precisely the ideological stance that *Pamela* and *Joseph Andrews* insisted on problematizing. And indeed, Louisa's bastardy acquires a certain glamour as the secret of her aristocratic parents' love affair unfolds on the final pages of the novel against a background of French castles and monasteries punctuated by royal name dropping. It is true that unlike her equally illegitimate brother, Louisa is given to passionate outbursts about her origins—"Could I but say that I descended from honest, tho' mean parents, I would not murmur at my fate, but I have none ... I am nothing, ... a kind of reptile in humanity" (178)—but her bastardy by no means hinders her from marrying her devoted aristocratic suitor, Monsieur Plessis. Haywood thus did pay some lip service to the literary tradition correlating the chastity of brides with the chastity of their mothers, but at the same time she remained quite nonchalant about the piece of paper—the parents' marriage certificate or its equivalent—that would obsess the presumably more morally astute authors of other eighteenth-century foundling fictions, such as Frances Burney, Charlotte Smith, and Agnes Maria Bennett.

Here is a detail, however, that complicates our readiness to view Louisa's chic bastardy in the context of Haywood's cowed adulation of the sexual mores of the rich and ranked, an adulation, that, as Warner argues, ultimately rendered her novels problematic for a polite audience. *The Fortunate Foundlings* may be as formulaic and pleasure-driven[21] as the majority of her novels, but its take on the position of the aristocratic female bastard is in part more historically accurate than the one espoused by Burney's *Evelina*. Louisa's story faithfully reflects the fact that in real life, aristocratic female bastards could and did marry well. If at times they felt somewhat handicapped by their family history, that feeling had less to do with the consideration of their personal *unworthiness* (a sentiment blown out of proportion in Louisa's melodramatic "I am a reptile" speech) and more with the awareness of their *expensiveness,* that is, the realization that their parents would have to "scrape" more money "in order to match [them] more highly."[22]

Published shortly after *The Fortunate Foundlings,* Richardson's *Clarissa* touches upon the social disadvantages faced by natural children and appears to counteract precisely the casual view of aristocratic bastardy that *The Fortunate Foundlings* endorses, but in doing so it inevitably reveals its author's biases and anxieties. Trying to talk Lovelace out of his "darling scheme" of cohabiting with Clarissa and getting her pregnant with twins, no less, Jack Belford confesses that he cannot understand why a man of Lovelace's social standing would want to "bastardize" his children, especially if he does plan to eventually marry their mother:

> Why should he wish to expose them to scorn and insults of the rest of the world?—Why should he, whether they are men or women, lay them under the necessity of complying with proposals of marriage, either inferior as to fortune, or unequal as to age?—Why should he deprive the children he loves, and who are themselves guilty of no

fault (if they have regard to morals, and to legal and social sanctions), of the respect they would wish to have and deserve?—and of the opportunity of associating themselves with proper, that is to say with *reputable* company? (614)

Belford's letter is typical for the peculiar mesh of upper- and middle-class sentiments that will come to populate many late-eighteenth-century novels depicting children whose legitimacy can be questioned. His argument does acknowledge that aristocratic parents of bastards sometimes had to bring more money to the table while negotiating their children's marriages than did the parents of legitimate parties, and that if they did not, their children might have to comply with "inferior" proposals of marriage. At the same time, Belford's claim that the bastard children of rich nobleman—or even of well-to-do middle-class parents—though "guilty of no fault" themselves, would be typically barred for life from associating with "reputable" company is highly tendentious. This claim reflects Richardson's position as somebody who has seen enough conflicts about the distribution of resources between legitimate and illegitimate children in middle-class families to be eager to use the affective powers of fiction to condemn extramarital sex. Belford would certainly be aware of the lenience with which aristocrats generally treated bastardy, but, carried away by a good cause, he glosses over important differences between the attitudes and social practices of nobility and those of the middle class.

Similarly, Mr. Villars's and Evelina's conviction that illegitimacy would unquestionably doom Evelina's social aspirations mirrors not so much the heartfelt belief of the hypothetical real-life daughter of a rich baronet, who would almost certainly not think in these self-abasing terms, but rather the subjectivity of the author writing for middle-class audiences and understanding too well their financial worries. The "purchasers of novels [and] the subscribers to circulating libraries," observed an early reviewer of *Evelina*, were "seldom in more elevated situations than the middle ranks of life."[23] These "purchasers" and "subscribers" did not share the nobility's cavalier attitude toward bastardy, indeed could not afford an attitude that implied providing generously for both the legitimate and the illegitimate offspring. This audience would thus be most susceptible to reading the new code of moral respectability into the obligatory legitimacy of the fictional foundling—and to see that code as woefully lacking in Haywood's novel.

We witness here, in other words, the workings of the process by which the eighteenth-century "middling classes [adopted] and then

The Children "Owned by None"

substantially [modified] notions of aristocratic gentility to suit their own middling class agenda."[24] On the one hand, the foundling's alignment with nobility, either by birth or by marriage, continued to afford readers the pleasurable identification with their "betters." (Did the anonymous writer from the 1778 issue of *Critical Review* truly "wish that [Evelina's] husband had not been a lord, and that her father had been less rich"?[25]) On the other hand, although the obligatory legitimacy of the fictional female foundling seemed to express primarily the imperatives of a new polite discourse informed by the old double standard in which the morals of the heroine's mother were supposed to vouch for her own chastity, it also responded to the economic anxieties of middle-class readers.

We can thus say that the foundling narrative's considerations of gender reflected most trenchantly the class-bound concerns of the audience precisely at those times when they seemed to supersede such concerns. Mr. Villars claims that unless Evelina's father acknowledges her as his only legitimate child, "the fair name of her virtuous mother" will be eternally blasted and Evelina herself will have to endure "shame and dishonour." His clamorous avowals, however, smuggle in the economic anxieties of the middling classes under the guise of class-transcending concerns about female chastity.[26]

Tobias Smollett's *Peregrine Pickle* (1751) offers yet another important literary correlative for Mr. Villars's and Evelina's illegitimacy jitters. Smollett's novel includes the "Memoirs of a Lady of Quality," whose protagonist, the "celebrated Lady V.," gives birth to a bastard daughter. The infant dies quickly, leading her mother to observe sadly that the "circumstances of [the child's] birth would have been an insurmountable misfortune to her thro' the whole course of her life, and rendered her absolutely dependent on [Lady V.'s] love and protection" (468). The history of Lady V.'s affair makes clear that the father of the infant, one "Mr. S," would not have been in a position to protect and benefit the child had she lived and reached maturity. As Lady V. observes at one point, "my lover . . . had no fortune to support me; and for that reason I was scrupulously cautious of augmenting his expense" (468). Taking into account Habakkuk's explanation that an aristocratic bastard could marry well "so long as paternity was acknowledged and the parent was prepared to pay a portion large enough to compensate," we can see why Lady V.'s daughter would have indeed been be at a serious disadvantage in the marriage market.

The story of Lady V.'s illegitimate daughter stands in complicated relationship to the rest of *Peregrine Pickle*. With its sympathetic discussion of the titillating details of Lady V.'s love affair, "Memoirs of a Lady of Quality" is carefully bracketed off as a report of social mores and mentality alien to that of the novel's middle-class lovers, Peregrine and Emily. Had Emily Gauntlet fallen for Peregrine's artful seduction and gotten pregnant, she would have disqualified herself from being a heroine of a respectable narrative and Peregrine's future wife. Lady V., by contrast, is portrayed as deeply admired both by Peregrine and by her sophisticated company and is commended for the "thousand acts of uncommon charity" (538) that she modestly glosses over in her Memoirs. In other words, what Smollett attempts to do in his novel is combine a breathless Haywood-style account of the illicit adventures of aristocrats, such as Lady V. and her lovers, with an assiduous, near-Richardsonian panegyric to the upright morals of middle-class women, such as Emily Gauntlet. The upper-class romance, bastardy and all, continued to sell books (indeed, several readers confessed to buying Smollett's novel "merely for the sake of reading" the Memoirs[27]), while the middle-class romance provided the moral grounds for the critique of Peregrine's promiscuity and for his future reformation, and thus could have been hoped to redeem the novel as a whole.

The eighteenth-century readers' reaction to such representational two-timing was often suggestively aligned with class. Richardson called the Memoirs "the very bad Story of a wicked woman," which was hardly surprising given his passionate sermonizing on illegitimacy in *Clarissa*, and his friend Mrs. Delany considered it "wretched stuff." Thomas Gray went even further in his sarcastic claim that Peregrine was simply used as a "vehicle," and a "very poor one with a few exceptions" for "that miracle of tenderness and sensibility . . . Lady Vane." By contrast, Lady Mary Wortley Montagu thought that the "memoirs contained more Truth and less malice than any I ever read in my life."[28]

Burney's *Evelina* thus inherited a rather contradictory literary tradition that both titillated its readers with the stories of unrepressed sexuality of aristocratic women and increasingly coded female bastards as nonexistent—literally dying out, as in the case of Lady V.'s infant daughter. If the story of Evelina's virtuous mother is a class-adjusted revision of the story of Lady V., then Evelina's legitimacy is truly the only guarantee of her social and physical survival, as the desperate language used by her guardian has seemed to imply all along. Reflecting the economic and social concerns of an eighteenth-century middle-class audience, concerns that directly shaped the period's "polite" discourse, fictional female bastards, even those born to aristocratic parents, were obligated either to die or to abandon any hopes for marital happiness and social fulfillment.

"Innocence" and the Plot of Divided Bastardy

Burney's correspondence highlights her attention to the legitimacy (i.e., birth circumstances) of people around her. In a 1776 letter (two years before the publication of *Evelina*), she describes to her good friend Samuel Crisp the visit of a celebrated operatic soprano from Italy, and she casually informs him about the singer's illegitimate origins. "La Signora Agujari," writes Frances, "has been nicknamed, my father says, in Italy, from some misfortune attendant upon her birth—but of which she, at least, is innocent—La Bastardella. She is now come over to England, in the prime of her life and her fame, upon an engagement with the proprietors of the Pantheon, to sing two songs at their concert, at one hundred pounds a night!" (*Memoirs of Dr. Burney*, 2:21). Signora Agujari's bastardy is really irrelevant for both Frances and Mr. Crisp, and yet, in a culture obsessed with illegitimacy—and particularly within a social class as sensitive to the economic repercussions of illegitimacy as the eighteenth-century middle class—the implicit reckoning of bastards goes on in the thick of everyday interaction, even when there seems to be no observable payoff to such vigilance.

Signora Agujari, as Burney notes offhandedly, is "at least . . . innocent" of the "misfortune" to which she owes her fascinating nickname. The term *innocent* comes up frequently in eighteenth-century references to bastard children, connoting a particular set of implicit beliefs and anxieties. It evokes a representational system that fluctuates between condemning illegitimate children as evil outsiders poised to wreak havoc on legal families and pitying them as innocent (or "at least innocent") victims of their parents' indiscretion, first disenfranchised by society and then demonized for trying to redress their socioeconomic disadvantages. If we attempt to articulate the psychological motivation behind such a fluctuation, it could be as follows: The bastard pays a high price for the obligation she herself did not incur (i.e., she is innocent), and so she must be bitter and angry, seeking to vent her anger on her more fortunate legitimate siblings and to take by force or stealth what has been unjustly denied to her. And for that, she is to be condemned, her own usurping actions—no longer her parents' sins—now are to be the foundation for punishing and excluding her. What happens then is that within a socioeconomic system grounded in the disenfranchisement of illegitimately born children, every such child—even in infancy—could be perceived, however unselfconsciously, by those around her, as bound to rebel at some time in the future against paying somebody else's sexual debts, and by rebelling to incur her own social debts. And if so (the psychosocial reasoning informing illegitimacy is inevitably circular), it becomes so much easier to demonize her even as a newborn (hence, the perpetuation of the myth of the inherently evil bastard) and thus to make her pay for her future debts now.

Though unspoken, this kind of reasoning informs the polemics surrounding the Foundling Hospital (including Charles Burney's plea for an "English Conservatorio") and the fictional writings of such authors as Richardson (who tacitly takes for granted the nasty nature of Thomasine's "cubs" in *Clarissa*). It is in the context of this vexed double view of illegitimate children that the very appellation of "innocence" acquires ominous overtones in Burney's first novel. Evelina is "shocked" by her grandmother's "gross" expostulation on the circumstances of her birth, but her shock mounts to agony when her well-meaning cousin, Miss Polly Branghton, attempts to soften the impact of Madame Duval's tactlessness by observing that Evelina "to be sure, . . . is not to blame for her mama's undutifulness, for she couldn't help it" (68). Evelina is not to blame just as the Italian Bastardella is "at least innocent" of the "misfortune attendant upon her birth"—the very terms on which Evelina is acquitted of "blame" could imply her illegitimacy and propensity for deviance in the eyes of eighteenth-century readers. Evelina's reaction to her tenderhearted cousin's remark (and to her grandmother's subsequent tirade on Caroline Evelyn's having gone "astray") is literally inexpressible. We get only a faint reflection of Evelina's feelings via Mr. Branghton's proposal to "talk o' something else, for Miss looks very uneasy-like" (69), but the pitch of her discomfort is forcefully underscored by the fact that even the obtuse and callous Mr. Branghton is aware of it and takes pity on her.

Innocence is thus a loaded term in the context of the culture of illegitimacy—the young charges of the Foundling Hospital are "innocent" and so is La Bastardella—and Burney responds subtly to this ambiguous meaning by transposing, at a crucial moment, the appellation of innocence from Evelina to one of her "bastard" doubles, Polly Green. Throughout the novel—and while her position as the legitimate daughter of a baronet remains in question—Evelina's innocence is repeatedly invoked by Mr. Villars, Lady Howard, Lord Orville, Evelina's late

The Children "Owned by None"

mother, Mrs. Selwyn, Evelina herself, her cousin Polly, and Madame Duval. The moment, however, that Evelina is pronounced a "lawful successor" to her father's estate, the proclamations of her innocence cease altogether and give way to similar avowals about Polly Green. Echoing the earlier sentiment of Lady Howard, who notes that Evelina's upbringing was conducive to "inexperience and innocency" (21), Evelina observes that Polly was "brought up in as much retirement as myself," and immediately goes on to inquire if "this *innocent* daughter" of Dame Green "was yet acquainted" with the story of her origins (375; emphasis added).

Once the dubious privilege of "innocence" is transferred from Evelina to Polly, the novel begins to retroactively bastardize this lower-class pretender to the Belmont family's property. Polly Green is portrayed as simultaneously innocent and evil, a casebook scenario of the conventionally conflicting conceptualization of bastards. Evelina's sympathetic exclamations, such as "Poor unfortunate girl! how hard is her fate!" (376) peter out in the wake of Mrs. Selwyn's harsh harangues on the most expedient method of getting the "fictitious daughter" (377) out of everybody's way. Sir John Belmont, as Mrs. Selwyn informs Evelina,

> is willing to save the *little impostor* as much of the mortification of her *disgrace* as is in his power: now if you immediately take her place, according to your right, as Miss Belmont, why not all that either of you can do for her, will prevent her being *eternally stigmatized*, as the *bantling* of Dame Green, wash-woman and wet nurse of Berry Hill, Dorsetshire. Now such a genealogy will not be very flattering, even to Mr. Macartney [infatuated by the spurious Miss Belmont], who, all-dismal, as he is, you will find by no means wanting in pride and self-consequence.... Though compassion may make us wish to save the poor girl the confusion of an *immediate and public fall,* yet justice demands that you should appear, henceforward, in no other light than that of Sir John Belmont's daughter. Besides, between friends, I, who know the world, can see that half this *prodigious delicacy for the little usurper,* is the mere result of self-interest; for while *her* affairs are husht up, Sir John's, you know, are kept from being brought further to light. (378; emphasis added)

Mrs. Selwyn's speech is remarkable on several counts. First, it accomplishes the transposition of Evelina's former anxiety about illegitimacy onto Polly.[29] Mr. Villars used to worry about the "stigma" threatening

Evelina if her father did not publicly acknowledge his marriage to her mother (337); now Sir John Belmont wants to move quickly to save *Polly* from being "eternally stigmatized, as the bantling of Dame Green." Second, as far as the readers of Burney's novel are concerned, this stigmatization is already a fait accompli. Not many would bother to check whether or not Polly's mother was married to Polly's father (in fact, it appears that she was[30]), and so Polly registers as indeed the "bantling"—the bastard—of Dame Green, the true "nobody" of the story despite being actually legitimate. Third—and most important—Polly is actually blamed for having taken Evelina's place. Called "the little impostor" and then, in case we missed it the first time, "the little usurper," Polly is implicitly made responsible for having been brought to Sir John Belmont as an infant. So the "immediate and public fall" is about the right punishment for the presumptuous "bantling," and the only reason she is "spared" that richly deserved "disgrace" is the "prodigious"—and, as Mrs. Selwyn implies, self-interested—"delicacy" of her adoptive father.[31] Polly is as innocent of Dame Green's crime as the typical bastard is of her mother's sexual trespass; neither is "to blame for her mama's undutifulness" (68), but since both are made to bear the social cost they themselves did not incur, they become fair game for demonizing.

And, as it turns out, the ground for portraying Polly as an evil lower-class impostor is laid down quite early in the novel via the figure of Evelina's vulgar grandmother, Madame Duval, and her déclassé relatives. A long time before we learn that the presumed daughter of Sir John Belmont has been educated in a French convent and, "though English at birth, [can] scarcely speak her native language" (227), we are introduced to Madame Duval, whose native English is hopelessly corrupted by her long sojourn in France. Similarly, the revelation that the false Miss Belmont's mother is a Berry Hill "wash-woman" echoes Captain Mirvan's earlier claim that Madame Duval could be easily "taken for [Lady Howard's] wash-woman." Madame Duval's exulting response to the Captain's insult—"Her wash-woman, indeed!—Ha, ha, ha!—why you han't no eyes; did you ever see a wash-woman in such a gown as this?" (51)—foreshadows the novel's forthcoming intimation that, in the absence of the right pedigree, all that stands between Polly Green and the washbasin is a rich "gown" purchased for her by Sir John Belmont. Her very name signals Polly's dubious social standing since she shares it with Madame Duval's good-natured silly niece, Polly Branghton. In other words, in the doublespeak of the novel, Polly could be "innocent" (375) and "pretty," and look "mild and good-humoured" (316)—this is Evelina describing her first impression of the false Miss Belmont—but she is also an "impostor" and "usurper," aligned, ominously, not just with one but with several presumptuous "wash-women."

Calibrated to respond to the psychosocial particularities of the eighteenth-century culture of illegitimacy, the novel's ambiguous view of Polly still shapes our reading of *Evelina* today. Literary critics tend to acquiesce to Burney's implicit elevation of Evelina as *the* foundling of the story without realizing that this elevation is necessarily achieved by ignoring her lower-class double. Consider Margaret Anne Doody's argument about *Evelina*'s indebtedness to the romance of antiquity, particularly to *Ethiopian Romance*. Doody argues that "Burney [was] enabled to write *Evelina* because . . . a novelistic tradition [had conveyed] a strong and serviceable myth to her,"[32] and she outlines the similarities between the adventures of Charicleia, the foundling from *Ethiopian Romance*, and Evelina:

> Charicleia . . . grew up in ignorance of her parentage—her very *name* is wrong, the name of her adoptive, not her true father. . . . Charicleia, like Evelina, has the guardianship of a good priest, her spiritual "father," to rely upon, though Burney's heroine, unlike her predecessor, does not have to endure the bereavement of this "father." In Heliodorus's novel, as in Burney's, the heroine has to wait for recognition until the end of the novel. . . . Evelina has to rely on her father's perception and intuition as well as the mother's words that speak for her; like Charicleia she keeps her history and identification in the secret private writing that is also the mother's story.[33]

Similarly, Martha Brown situates the story of Evelina in the context of the "typical romance plot, beginning with the Greek prose romances of Heliodorus, Longus, and Tatius." She points out that, like the hero of such a story, "abandoned . . . or 'exposed' . . . by his parents, rescued and reared by a kindly shepherd, . . . Evelina [is] forced on [her] journey or [quest] by the dubious circumstances of [her] birth and by [her] right to inherit."[34]

It is time to ask on what grounds Polly Green is left out of the influential critical exploration of the "genetic inheritance" of Burney's novel.[35] After all, Polly's qualifications for the title of foundling are stronger than Evelina's. In a striking reprise of the myth of Moses, the infant Polly is brought to a powerful man (Sir John Belmont) by her mother, who pretends to be her nurse, and is raised under his name, with no intimation of her real identity whatsoever. Evelina, by contrast, knows well who her parents are—the level of informedness going well beyond anything we encounter in the ancient foundling narrative. Brown points out that in the "typical romance plot" of antiquity, when the "child reaches maturity [and] falls in love, the romance . . . is blocked, often by the mystery surrounding the hero's birth."[36] No insuperable obstacles block Evelina's romance with Lord Orville (in fact, Burney ensures that he proposes to Evelina before the mystery of her birth is cleared up[37]); Polly, on the other hand, is indeed prevented from marrying Mr. Macartney because of their supposed consanguinity, and it is not until the truth of her birth is revealed that she can be reunited with him. It appears, then, that in establishing the heroine's literary-historical lineage critics implicitly rely on factors other than immediate parallels between her adventures and those of the protagonists of the ancient romance. That Polly has, so far, remained beyond the pale of scholarly inquiry into the ancient origins of Burney's novel shows how easily we buy into the class-bound sensibility attendant upon the eighteenth-century focus on legitimately born foundlings as the true protagonists of a saga of landed property. As a daughter of a washwoman, the legitimately born Polly is stigmatized as the "bantling" of the novel and continues to serve as a pale foil for its properly pedigreed *real* foundling, Evelina.

It would not do, however, to simply grant Polly her hitherto denied membership in the club of the eighteenth-century female foundlings who embody the continuity between the ancient and early modern literary traditions. We should also ask why Burney needs to bastardize Polly when the novel already features one unquestionable bastard, Mr. Macartney. Doody has observed in a different context that Evelina has a "male counterpart" in Mr. Macartney: "both are apparently illegitimate, both adolescent, both without fixed social identity."[38] How many bastards or almost-bastards does a novel require in order to reassure us of the protagonist's unquestionable position as the only legitimate child, the sole "lawful successor" to her father's name and estate?

I suggest that Burney deploys the repetitive transposition of Evelina's illegitimacy—onto the "bad" foundling Polly and onto the bastard Mr. Macartney—to weaken the unavoidable association of Evelina with a real-life natural child, appearing as if out of nowhere (from the point of view, that is, of the legal family) and positioning herself, in her dangerous innocence, as completely dependent on her father's bounty. On the one hand, Evelina does literally force herself into her father's sight, and, subsequently, his will; on the other, by doing so, she turns out to have displaced the illegitimate usurper, Polly Green, and thus reasserts the privileged socioeconomic standing of legal children. Furthermore, unlike the indigent Mr. Macartney or any real-life illegitimate child, Evelina does not really need her father's money (even though she gets it anyway) because of her marriage to Lord Orville.

The rhetoric accompanying this double dissociation of Evelina from the dark figure of the real-life bastard is both coy and revealing. Could it be possible, asks the shocked!—shocked!—Evelina, upon first encountering the pretended Miss Belmont in Bristol, "that, while the lawful child [i.e., Evelina] is neglected, another is adopted?" (316). Yes, Evelina, one feels compelled to intone, had it not been possible and had the eighteenth-century middle-class reading public been less apprehensive about just this exact scenario, the story of Evelina-as-a-foundling would not have been written in the first place. Little Polly Green becomes the token "bantling" of the novel, thus allowing the better-born, better-connected, more eloquent in her "native language" Evelina to put aside her initial worries about being perceived as illegitimate, and, furthermore, allowing eighteenth-century readers to relive, in the safe setting of a novel, their anxieties about the moral and socioeconomic repercussions of bastardy as an institution. By carefully distinguishing among several different pretenders to a family fortune, such as the innocent "natural son," who can also be quite dangerous (Mr. Macartney nearly murders his father in a duel); the truly innocent legitimate "foundling," Evelina; and the usurping, dangerous, lower-class, practically foreign, yet also tantalizingly innocent, "bantling," Polly, Burney's novel functions as a compensatory fantasy for a culture groping for, but not necessarily finding, a moral justification for a deeply troubled status quo according to which the unhallowed sexuality of parents (excluding aristocrats) led to the socioeconomic exclusion of children.

Now, perhaps, we can also understand why the novel's sprawling list of the capital's sightseeing attractions—featuring Drury Lane, Covent Garden, and Samuel Foote's play-houses, the Haymarket Opera-House, Ranelagh, the Pantheon, Portland Chapel, Buckingham House, Kensington Gardens and Palace, Pall-Mall, Vauxhall, the Cox Museum, Bedlam, Hampstead, the Tower of London, the Monument to the Great Fire of London, Paul's Church, the White-Conduit House, Bagnigge Wells, etc.—does not include the London Foundling Hospital. This is a significant omission, considering that the Hospital remained a must-see for tourists through the second half of the century. One possible reason for its absence from the pages of *Evelina* is that, writing in the immediate aftermath of Dr. Burney's frustrating failure to talk the Hospital's governors into converting their institution into the "English Conservatorio," Frances did not want to remind the dedicatee of her novel of his recent disappointment. Moreover, a visit to the charity whose mission, according to its charter, was to save the "exposed and deserted children," the children "owned by none" (*Memoirs of Dr. Burney*, 238)—or even a thought of such a visit—would have inevitably prompted Evelina to reflect upon her own status as a "deserted child" (19) hardly knowing to whom she belongs (353), thus giving free rein to the association of the novel's token foundling with real-life illegitimate children, precisely the association that Burney wanted to keep under control via her plot of repeatedly divided bastardy.[39]

Multiplying Foundlings of Late-Eighteenth-Century Novels

Burney appears to have inaugurated a tradition of using a plot of divided bastardy to sever a foundling heroine's association with her real-life illegitimate counterparts. Ten years after the appearance of *Evelina*, Charlotte Smith published her novel *Emmeline, The Orphan of the Castle*, featuring a young woman who is thought to be illegitimate for most of the story only to be established at the end as the legal heir to a large estate. This discovery spells a significant financial drawback for her uncle/guardian. He now has to give up the estate (which he inherited by default, as his brother, Emmeline's father, was thought to have died without legitimate children) and has to pay Emmeline the arrears for the years the property has been in his possession. As a typical eighteenth-century foundling, Emmeline, of course, does not really need her newly found wealth because not one but several well-off suitors, undeterred by her humble status, have been vying for her hand in marriage. Still, to diffuse any potential embarrassment over the similarities between the story of Emmeline and that of a real-life bastard, Smith shifts the loci of illegitimacy and introduces, in the middle of the novel, a *real* natural child, the son of Emmeline's "unfortunate" friend, Lady Adelina (283).

To make the little boy function as the legitimately born Emmeline's bastard double, the novel simultaneously fosters and undercuts the identification between the two characters. Thus at the time when Emmeline still thinks that she is illegitimate, she is shown to "give vent to her full heart by weeping over the little infant, whose birth, so similar to her own, seemed to render it to her a more interesting and affecting object. She lamented the evils to which it might be exposed; tho' of a sex which would prevent it's encountering the same species of sorrow as that which had embittered her own life. Of her friendless and desolate situation, she was never more sensible than now" (273).

Of course, as Emmeline will discover soon, the boy's birth is not at all "similar to her own." Moreover, her laments about the "evils" to which as a female bastard she is liable to be "exposed" have not been borne out by the events of the novel. Her presumed illegitimacy did not stop any of her ardent suitors from wishing to marry her; if anything, it might have saved her from heartless fortune hunters (for, as in other such narratives, legitimacy confers wealth). The parallels between the boy and Emmeline are further complicated by their shared surname, Godolphin. Emmeline becomes "Mrs. Godolphin" upon marrying the boy's uncle, her happy marriage crowning the discovery of her legitimate origins. By contrast, the boy's emergence as "William Godolphin, Jr." only underscores his mother's transgression (had she forbore having sex out of wedlock, her son would not have had to assume the name of her brother) and reaffirms his status as the designated bastard of the story.

The tradition of providing the foundling heroine with one or several bastard doubles or else contrasting her—a "good," proper foundling—with a "bad" foundling (e.g., Polly in *Evelina*) continued with a vengeance in Agnes Maria Bennett's novel *The Beggar Girl and Her Benefactors* (1797). With a plot liable to confound any reader who lets her attention flag even for a moment, Bennett's novel features two legitimately born foundlings, Horace and Rosa, routinely described as "base" or "bastards" by different characters. At the end, of course, Horace turns out to be a peer of realm and the heir to several splendid estates, but in the process of establishing his parentage, he has to displace and dispossess several bastard claimants to his fortune, such as the illegitimate children of the former steward–turned–Member of Parliament, Solomon Mushroom.

Rosa's situation is even more complicated. The legitimate child of a countess, Lady Denningcourt, she is switched as an infant with the daughter of her wet nurse, Mrs. Wilkins, and thus begins her life as a "little beggar," abused by the alcoholic caretaker who cannot see her without feeling guilty about the fraud she had committed. Meanwhile, Mrs. Wilkins's own daughter, called Elinor Bawsky (the novel's Polly Green figure) is raised in the household of Dr. Croak and his mistress

CHAPTER 6

Mrs. Bawsky, who are generously paid for their efforts by one of the countess's relatives, who, for a reason of his own, wants to persuade Lady Denningcourt that her daughter had died in infancy.

Rosa is saved from her inevitable demise by Colonel Buhanun, who adopts her shortly before going back to the army, thus setting in motion Rosa's peregrinations from one benefactor to another, a journey that ends only when, by accident, Rosa finally reaches the house of Lady Denningcourt. Shortly before Rosa's arrival, Lady Denningcourt is told that her daughter is alive, and she retrieves Elinor (her supposed child) from Dr. Croak, only to become increasingly heartbroken over the girl's inferior mental capacities, which appear even more lacking as the countess compares the hopelessly common Elinor to the accomplished Rosa.

Elinor is miserable to the point of going mad amidst the riches and sophistication that she is supposed to inherit and is never so happy as when she is allowed to wait on Rosa, assuring this indigent object of her mother's charity that she "would be content to play [Rosa's maid her] whole life" (5:178). The blood will out, Bennett quietly assures her readers. The clearly undeserving Elinor finally elopes with her old flame, the son of Dr. Croak, a low-bred, if kind, young man, leading the countess to observe sadly that even though "nothing . . . can ennoble a plebeian soul, [her] child is the only instance [she] ever knew of real good principles and integrity of heart, on which confidence and indulgence could make no impression" (5:266). A series of startling discoveries follow, revealing that Rosa is the real daughter of Lady Denningcourt and her former husband, Colonel Buhanun, and that Elinor is an "innocent . . . impostor" (5:313). As in *Evelina*, the loaded appellation of "innocence" is transferred from the long-suffering real heiress to the fake one the moment their respective true identities are established.

Predictably, Rosa's transformation from a beggar girl to the daughter of a countess is accompanied by a drastic reshuffling of wills. Thus both of the novel's foundlings, Rosa and Horace, though appearing out of nowhere as illegitimate pretenders to family wealth typically would, are, in fact, shown to displace a whole panoply of wrong heirs, such as the "bad" foundling Elinor and the bastard Mushrooms. The legitimate foundlings thus become both the symbols and the agents of the status quo, keeping out unworthy claimants to rank and fortune.

To return, then, to the important critical project inaugurated by scholars, such as Doody and Brown, of reconstructing the distinguished literary pedigree of such heroines as Evelina, Emmeline, and Rosa and

The Children "Owned by None"

thus acknowledging the indebtedness of Burney's, Smith's, and Bennett's stories to the foundling romances of antiquity, we should also remember that all those writers relied on the novelistic presence of bastard doubles to shield their heroines from the topical indignities of the Enlightenment's culture of illegitimacy. We may profitably compare Evelina Belmont with Heliodorus's Charicleia because Burney conveniently offers up Polly Green as the personage most readily associated with that real-life anonymous illegitimate correspondent of the *Universal Spectator*, whose relatives considered him as "a Robber who . . . unjustly deprived them of a small Estate [his father] settled upon [him]."[40] The writer who disrupted this tradition of contrasting "bantlings" with "good" foundlings and who daringly elevated a bantling into a romantic heroine in her own right is the subject of the concluding chapter of this book.

-7-

HARRIET SMITH IN BRUNSWICK SQUARE

"Common Sense" Bastardy in Austen's Emma

As she walks hurriedly to Randalls, summoned there by some bad news that only her best friend, Mrs. Weston, would know how to break to her, Emma Woodhouse tries to guess what might be the matter. Her "friends... in Brunswick Square" (361) appear to be fine—the suddenly uncommunicative Mr. Weston at least assured her of that; it must be then that something "of a disagreeable nature, in the circumstances of the family" has befallen Mr. Weston's son and Emma's projected beau, Frank Churchill. What can it be? Emma lets her "active... fancy" roam: "Half a dozen natural children, perhaps, and poor Frank cut off." This would be "very undesirable" indeed, although—Emma runs a quick check of her feelings to make sure that she is still not in love with and does not intend to marry Frank—"it would be no matter of agony to her." An "animating curiosity" (362) it could inspire, no doubt, but certainly no agony.

The disagreeable news turns out to be completely different from Emma's conjectures. As Emma learns about Frank Churchill and Jane Fairfax's engagement, her "very undesirable" but also somewhat titillating vision of "half a dozen natural children" metamorphoses into a plainly "tormenting" (369) image of just one natural child, Harriet Smith, bitterly disappointed—once again!—in her matrimonial hopes. Mr. Weston's earlier assurance that Emma's "dear friends... in Brunswick Square" are well adds a curious prequel to this metamorphosis because Brunswick Square, where Isabella Knightley resides, is actually "one of the posher areas of the newly developed Foundling Hospital estate."[1] Emma's edification thus unfolds against a succession of images exemplifying different aspects of the eighteenth-century culture of illegitimacy: from the peripheral glance at the controversial charity that renegotiated the cultural categories of "bastard" and "foundling," to the tragicomic vision of Frank Churchill's uncle's fending off the demands of his former mistresses and their bastard children, to the disappointed fantasy about the foundling poised to make a brilliant marriage in spite of her obscure origins.[2]

The connection between Emma's personal enlightenment and the culture of illegitimacy that we can thus tease out of Austen's description of the morning at Randalls is not incidental. Because Austen wanted her readers to see the world of Highbury largely through Emma's eyes, even when they knew that her perspective was incomplete or mistaken,[3] they had to learn ostensibly *with* Emma as a character but actually *through Emma* as a novel that there could be ways of representing female bastards other than reimagining them as fabulous legitimate foundlings or simply writing them off as having "neither [the] sense nor principles" (*The Beggar Girl*, 4:37) requisite for respectable matrimony. Shortly after the eye-opening conversation at Randalls, Emma will have to completely give up her darling scheme—so fit for a novel teeming with surrogate children and parents[4]—of "adopting" Harriet, educating her in her own image, and marrying her to a man who can appreciate the combination of her natural beauty with her newly engrafted social "elegance."[5] Harriet will have to go away, to the area of London associated, importantly, with the Foundling Hospital, to form a family of her own with a worthy man who will keep her happy and engaged in productive labor—a solid, "common sense" (57) destiny, not unlike the one envisioned by the champions of the Hospital for their young charges.

It is easy for modern readers to underestimate the importance of this particular resolution of Harriet Smith's story. By forcing Emma to give up Harriet and by letting Harriet marry Robert Martin, Austen radically challenged the tradition, perpetuated by the writings of Frances Burney, Charlotte Smith, Maria Edgeworth, Agnes Maria Bennett, and others, of treating the legitimacy of the female foundling as the absolute condition of her marital eligibility. Furthermore, whereas in several of those novels, including Edgeworth's *Belinda*, Bennett's *The Beggar Girl*, and the anonymous *Fatherless Fanny*, the adoption of a lost child by an upper-class patron constituted the crucial step leading to the discovery of the child's genteel origins, in *Emma*, Austen encouraged those expectations only to quash them. Unlike Clarence Hervey in *Belinda* and Lord and Lady Ellincourt in *Fatherless Fanny*,

Emma cannot rewrite her protégé's bastardy, but, as Austen's novel seems to suggest, such a rewriting no longer constitutes a sine qua non of a respectable narrative.

"Common Sense" Reading of Female Bastardy in Emma

Since critics have aligned Harriet's "precarious social position" with that of Henry Fielding's Tom Jones and Frances Burney's Evelina,[6] it is important to clarify the relationship between her story and the eighteenth-century foundling narrative. On the one hand, given Austen's "intense interest in probing and manipulating the conventional import of fiction, announced as early as the juvenilia,"[7] one can focus on the parodic aspect of Harriet's "foundling" career and observe, for example, that it is constituted by a series of conspicuous absences. There are no scars, rings, strawberry-shaped moles, or other crucial tokens generating a dramatic anagnorisis (and indeed no recognition scenes featuring a tearful biological parent), no aristocratic fiancés, no inherited riches, no dangerous adventures (unless we count the threat represented by "half a dozen [gypsy] children, headed by a stout woman, and a great boy, all clamorous, and impertinent in look, though not absolutely in word" [305]), and no central billing. What we have instead is Emma's touching conviction that sooner or later Harriet will be "found" by her gentleman parent(s) and that in preparation for that moment, she should procure herself a gentleman husband—a scenario familiar to eighteenth-century readers of Richard Steele, Burney, and Smith.

Checking off the conventions of the foundling narrative that *Emma* lacks is easy and perhaps even somewhat detrimental to our valuation of Austen's literary taste; as Clifford Siskin has pointed out, it has become a habit in Austen criticism to articulate her "virtues . . . in terms of what she lacks."[8] Indeed, given that Steele used his scatterbrained Biddy Tipkin to make a travesty of the foundling romance as early as 1705 (*The Tender Husband*), Emma's amusing commitment to imagining her friend as a heroine of such a romance could be seen as Austen's poking fun at too obvious a target. On the other hand, if we consider the eighteenth-century foundling narrative as a cultural code for both expressing and deflecting the period's anxiety about a host of difficult social issues bound up with illegitimacy, Austen's engagement with this narrative—and her rejection of its conventions—acquires a markedly different tenor.

This study has argued that what sets the eighteenth-century foundling narrative apart from its ancient or twentieth-century counterparts (for, from the story of Exodus to Steven Martin's "Jerk" and Peter Carey's Jack Maggs, the image of a child of ambiguous origins seems to have a timeless appeal) is its fixation on the legitimacy of the foundling, and, tied up with legitimacy, the issue of his/her gender. The eighteenth-century fictional female foundling had to be legitimate in order to qualify for the role of a romantic heroine, particularly if the author had any "higher claims to moral truth or beauty."[9] On the one hand, the heroine's legitimacy, especially if doubted at the outset of the story, functioned as a wish-fulfilling fantasy for readers who were increasingly aware of the injustice of the economic system that demonized illegitimate children by denying them legal right to inherit any part of their parents' property, yet were invested in many ways in the perpetuation of that system. On the other hand, the reaffirmed morals of the heroine's mother—who turned out, after all, *not* to have had sex out of wedlock—seemed to guarantee her own wedded integrity, a sentiment reflected in the anguished refusal of Mary, an illegitimate daughter of a prostitute in Mary Hays's 1799 *The Victim of Prejudice*, to "bring dishonour as [her] only dowry to the arms of the man" she loves (75). Concern about the distribution of property and the sexual double standard were the two key impulses generating scores of legally conceived though temporarily misplaced Indianas, Evelinas, Emmelines, Fannies, and Rosas.

Austen's early novel, *Sense and Sensibility*, offers a curious illustration of the literary mindset conditioned by the proliferation of such heroines. Hoping to ease Marianne's anguish at being abandoned by Willoughby, Colonel Brandon relates the story of Willoughby's villainous treatment of Brandon's seventeen-year-old ward, Eliza. A natural daughter of Brandon's late sister-in-law, also named Eliza, she had been seduced by Willoughby and left pregnant "with no creditable home, no help, no friends, ignorant of his address!" (182). Given Willoughby's exploitive tendencies, Marianne thus should count her blessings in having escaped him with her honor unsullied, for one sexual lapse would have relegated her forever to social and textual obscurity—the fate of both Elizas. A remarkable feature of "the tales of the two Elizas," as Claudia Johnson points out, is "their insistent redundancy. One Eliza would have sufficed as far as the immediate narrative

CHAPTER 7

purpose is concerned, which is to discredit Willoughby with a prior attachment."[10] Johnson sees the multiplying narratives of seduction as evidence of "the sinister possibility that plights such as [Eliza's are proliferating] throughout the kingdom"[11]—a compelling explanation, particularly if we correlate it with the statistics documenting the continuing increase in the number of illegitimate births.

To Johnson's analysis of the "insistent redundancy" of Brandon's tale may be added that the sexual lapse of the second Eliza has been tacitly predetermined by the earlier sexual trespass of her own mother, contributing to what now appears to be a family history of female illegitimacy. Twentieth-century sociologists have a special term, "bastardy-prone sub-society," to denote a hypothesis that bastard children or children exposed to illegitimacy in the family "would [themselves] be candidates for sexual irregularity."[12] Whereas the validity of this hypothesis remains debated by scholars dealing with socialization processes, the "like mother, like daughter" reasoning that underlies it is certainly not a twentieth-century invention. In other words, Austen's story of multigenerational illegitimacy is indebted to the eighteenth-century literary tradition of signaling the virtue of daughters via the virtue of their mothers, thus ensuring readers that the brave lords who marry the forlorn foundling heroines are making the right decision because, the earlier adventures of these temporarily "lost" girls notwithstanding, they will faithfully carry their noble husbands' genes into the next generation. In the context of this tradition, the second Eliza simply cannot turn out well, no more than can Hays's Mary, whose terrible fate—she is raped by the predatory Sir Peter Osborne—has been predetermined by the "stigma" of her birth.

If in *Sense and Sensibility,* one of her earliest novels, Austen still adheres to the unspoken rule that the illegitimate female character should end badly and can by no means be trusted with the property and genes of a good man, her *Emma* represents a radical break with this rule. Remarkably, it is Emma herself who provides an eloquent justification for dispensing with that rule without realizing that she is doing so. She is, in fact, secretly convinced of that precept's efficacy—yet another instance of what Wayne Booth has characterized as the double perspective of *Emma*[13] and Susan Greenfield has recently described as Austen's deft balancing of "ironic distance with interior insight."[14]

At first glance, Emma appears to be willing to discuss Harriet's bastardy in admirably frank terms devoid of dramatic posturing or simpering coyness. For example, when the inevitable appellation of "nobody" comes up, the tone is very different from both Louisa's hysterical "I have . . . none to own me . . . I am a nothing,—a kind of reptile in humanity" (Haywood, *The Fortunate Foundlings*, 128) and Evelina's pathetic, "I hardly know myself to whom I most belong" (Burney, *Evelina*, 289). In response to Mr. Knightley's heated remark that, as an illegitimate and ignorant girl, Harriet would be lucky to marry "a respectable, intelligent, gentleman-farmer," Emma notes coolly that although, because of "the circumstances of her birth, . . . in a legal sense [Harriet] may be called Nobody, it will not hold in common sense," and she further insists that Harriet "is not to pay for the offence of others" (57).[15]

We have, of course, heard similar reasoning before, although in each case it turned out to be compromised either by the speaker's own vested interests or by the author's lack of nerve in backing up such enlightened sentiments with action. In Henry Fielding's *Tom Jones*, Mrs. Miller's late husband used to say that "the words 'dishonorable birth' are nonsense . . . unless the word 'dishonorable' be applied to the parents; for the children can derive no real dishonour from an act of which they are entirely innocent" (665). Of course, buried in the depth of *Tom Jones* are certain hints that Mr. Miller cohabited with his future wife before marriage, and their firstborn might, therefore, be illegitimate. Less charitable readers may imagine Mr. Miller making this speech in an effort to talk his future wife into cohabitation and thus suspect him of being not an altogether disinterested party in dismissing as "nonsense" the words "dishonourable birth."

In Edward Moore's *The Foundling*, Colonel Raymond counters the young Belmont's assertion that he cannot marry Fidelia because she might be "but the Out-case of a Beggar . . . oblig'd to Chance for a little Education" by promptly observing that "then [Fidelia's] mind is . . . dignified by her Obscurity; and [that Belmont] will have the Merit of raising her to a Rank which she was meant to adorn." The Colonel further reminds his friend that he wants "no Addition to [his] Fortune, and [has] only to sacrifice a little necessary Pride to necessary Happiness" (144–45). Noble sentiments all, but toothless in the context of the play since Fidelia turns out to be well-born, rich, and the Colonel's own sister.

In a similar vein, in Bennett's *The Beggar Girl*, the personal charm and remarkable accomplishments of little Rosa Buhanun prompt the author to remind her readers that many a "miserable outcast . . . rescued from the dunghill" would be similarly transformed were charity "to make the trial" (1:224). The remaining four volumes of Bennett's novel, however, flatly contradict this egalitarian outburst. Rosa, a presumed "bastard" (1:39) "taken from the lowest order of deplorable mendicants, her mother an abandoned wretch, whose evil propensities she had imbibed" (1:184), turns out to be the daughter of two highly accomplished aristocratic parents, illustrating not the transformative potential of charity but the retentive powers of "good blood" (2:257). By the same token, the "abandoned wretch's" *real* daughter, Elinor Bawsky, remains base in both her taste and intellect in spite of her careful education and genteel upbringing. When Countess Denningcourt bemoans Elinor's lack of sophistication, blaming her early caregivers for not providing their charge with correct principles, Rosa thinks to herself that "Elinor's deficiencies were not the consequence of neglect" (5:168). According to the inexorable logic of the novel, Elinor's low origins determined her inclinations just as surely as Rosa's exalted parentage determined hers.

Finally, in the anonymous *Fatherless Fanny*, the title heroine offers an eloquent critique of a system that allows the rich and legitimately descended social players to denigrate those less fortunately born. Admitting that she is a "poor outcast Orphan . . . dependant on the bounty of strangers, and unblest even with a *name*," Fanny nevertheless insists that her "nature assimilates not with such degrading circumstances" and that she feels "no innate symptoms of baseness." Why, then, asks Fanny, should she "be trampled upon by those whose fortunes are better, although their sentiments may be inferior to [hers]?" (129–30). Again, as in other such stories, the "Fatherless" Fanny turns out to be legitimate and have both a mother and a father belonging to the highest ranks of nobility.

In other words, although eighteenth-century writers dealing with bastards and suspected bastards were quick to offer high-minded pronouncements about such characters' noble potential, their actual plots never put such pronouncements to the test. In *Emma*, however, Austen does substantiate Emma's conviction that Harriet should not be made to pay for the offenses of others—for Harriet stays a tradesman's illegitimate daughter yet marries well and achieves happiness—even if, in the end, Austen and Emma turn out to have very different ideas about what could constitute a "common sense" resolution of Harriet's fate.

Emma's version of such a common sense outcome is clearly influenced by her not-too-selective reading list. She imagines Harriet as the heroine of a late-eighteenth-century foundling romance, dwelling with particular delight on her friend's fairy-tale appearance ("a fine bloom, blue eyes, light hair" [20]), finding herself "on fire with speculation" about Harriet's "extraordinary . . . adventure" involving the gypsies (306), and, above all, continuing to match Miss Smith with men above her social level. Emma's reasoning on those occasions is clearly informed by such stories as *Fatherless Fanny,* in which the foundling heroine's eyes are described as of the "softest blue" (32); "every visitor" to her boarding school is "told, with a significant nod, that time would prove the child to be *somebody*" (13); and the foundling's aristocratic admirer "fervently" pays her his address before being "informed with the secret of her birth," for it is "her mind and her angelic person that he [courts], not her fortune or her rank" (382).[16]

Something else is going on, however, amidst Emma's envisioning Harriet as a stereotypical foundling heroine. By thinking of Harriet as a new Rosa or Fanny, a child of unknown parentage brought up in a boarding school who catches the benevolent attention of an elegant upper-class lady capable of radically improving the foundling's standing in the world, Emma can imagine herself in the role of an influential benefactress, such as Lady Denningcourt, who shelters Rosa, or Lady Ellincourt, who "adopts" Fanny. Such high-class patronages allow the poor "nameless" fictional foundlings to be "introduced . . . in parties," where they can meet "persons of a superior rank" and eventually enter a "union" with a man from "a noble family" (*Fatherless Fanny,* 153, 155). So too Emma hopes that by "introducing [Harriet] into good company . . . [she will give] her the opportunity of pleasing someone worth having" (126). No wonder that she is particularly vexed when Mrs. Elton tries to usurp the role of a social lioness patronizing beautiful and virtuous female orphans such as Jane Fairfax. If, as Greenfield has compellingly argued, Emma is profoundly anxious about her social position, wishing to stand "at the crossroads of the Highbury world"[17] as an acknowledged and beloved leader and arbiter of that world, then the exclusive identification with such powerful and benevolent personages of the late eighteenth–early nineteenth century "foundling" novels as Lady Ellincourt and Lady Dennincourt must supply her with a particularly pleasurable fantasy.

What this means is that by the end of the novel, Austen has to make a point of introducing her own "common sense" interpretation of Harriet's situation, thus overriding Emma's complicated emotional dependence on the trappings of the foundling romance.[18] This deliberately presented alternative interpretation draws on the geopolitics of late-eighteenth-century London. When Emma finally gives up her plan of arranging Harriet's fortune, she sends her away to the house of her brother-in-law, Mr. John Knightley, whose family lives in Brunswick Square—one of the recently developed parts of the estate of the London Foundling Hospital[19]—and it is in the house at Brunswick Square that Harriet finally is engaged to her truly "common sense" suitor, a "gentleman-farmer," Robert Martin.

In fact, the reader is first invited to think of the Hospital much earlier in the novel, when Isabella Knightley praises the "neighborhood of Brunswick Square as so different from almost all the rest . . . , so remarkably airy, [the only place] that she could be satisfied to have her children in" (95). From the early days of the eighteenth-century infanticide prevention campaign, its champions spoke about the importance of housing the rescued children "in the suburbs of the city, in a wholesome dry area,"[20] and one of Captain Coram's inducements for buying the four plots of land in Lambs Conduit Fields was the reported healthfulness of the neighborhood. Of course, Austen's choice of address for the London Knightleys could be accidental, but it seems that such a coincidence would be highly unlikely for a novel centering as relentlessly as *Emma* does on illegitimate children, orphans, and adoptions. Instead, I suggest that Austen settles the Knightleys in Brunswick Square precisely in order to be able to send Harriet there at the opportune moment when Emma's romantic imaginings have become inadequate to the point of being destructive, and Harriet has to be "coded" via a different set of cultural associations.

Here, the ideological iconography of the Foundling Hospital comes in particularly handy. From its inception in 1739, it was the credo of the Hospital that its children should be aware of their humble social station and yet acquit themselves well in the world by using wisely the educational and social resources, however modest, provided to them by their adopted home. The associative trajectory of Harriet's career under Emma's wing—from a fairy tale to the social politics of the Foundling Hospital—thus highlights the novel's rejection of a foundling romance for a story of a female bastard who "makes good" (to adopt Michael McKeon's characterization of Tom Jones) in the truly "common sense" of the word: by marrying into a situation of "security, stability, and improvement" (443), in which "retired enough for safety, and occupied enough for her cheerfulness, . . . [she] would never be led into temptation, nor left for it to find her out" (444). Sir Jonas Hanway himself would not have been able to put it better if asked to describe what kind of future he and his colleagues at the Hospital envisioned for their young charges.

Harriet Smith in Brunswick Square

In having Harriet actually go to stay in the area of London directly associated with the Foundling Hospital to signal her novel's developing commitment to the truly common sense version of Harriet's social prospects, Austen echoes, at least in part, the rhetorical strategy used by Maria Edgeworth in her 1801 novel, *Belinda*. There, the reference to the Hospital also provides a quiet rhetorical counterpoint to the romantic aspirations of the male protagonist, Clarence Hervey. Mr. Hervey adopts a beautiful foundling girl, Rachel—whom he promptly renames Virginia, as a tribute to de Saint-Pierre's *Paul et Virginie*—to groom her into a perfect future wife for himself. The story is modeled on the ill-fated scheme of Thomas Day, a close friend of the writer's father. As Marilyn Butler tells in her biography of Edgeworth, Day's plan was to

> train a foundling girl in a perfect seclusion after the example of Rousseau's Sophie, in the hope that she would make an ideal wife. Day took two girls to France but retired to Lichfield only with the one he preferred, Sabrina Sidney. As his behavior at Lichfield indicates, he was never single-minded about marrying Sabrina; she finally offended him over a trivial matter in 1773 and was sent away to eight years of genteel retirement. In 1781 she married Day's friend John Bicknell, who died, leaving her unprovided for, in 1784. During her long widowhood, she was housekeeper to Dr. Charles Burney the younger at Greenwich.[21]

In *Belinda*, Clarence Hervey is also "never single-minded about marrying" his young protégé, who is raised (a nod to Rousseau's *Emile*) in an almost perfect innocence. Comparing Virginia with Belinda Portman, whom he meets through his friend, the brilliant lady Delacour, Clarence begins to think Virginia "an insipid, though innocent child. . . . [Belinda] he found was his equal; [Virginia] his inferior; the one he saw could be a companion, a friend to him for life, the other would merely be his pupil or his plaything" (344). To avoid the ugly denouement of the original story—Clarence cannot simply send Virginia away as Thomas Day did his Sabrina—Edgeworth conjures up a rich "West Indian . . . gentleman" (368), one Mr. Hartley, arriving in London in search of his long-lost child, "his poor Rachel" (358). The father and daughter are soon reunited, Rachel/Virginia confesses her passion for a young man who turns out to have saved Mr. Hartley's life several years ago, and Clarence Hervey is free to marry Belinda.[22]

Standing out in this hurried series of improbable coincidences is the reference to the London Foundling Hospital. Upon first arriving in

London to search for his daughter, Mr. Hartley goes to the Hospital hoping that one of its "oldest girls" would turn out to be his Rachel. Rachel's mother, we have learned earlier in the story, "was carried from a boarding-school, when she was scarcely sixteen, by a wretch [i.e., Mr. Hartley] who, after privately marrying her, would not own his marriage, stayed with her but two years, then went abroad, left his wife and his infant, and has [not] been heard of since" (332–33)—until now. Here, the potentially ambiguous circumstances of Rachel's birth, on the one hand, and her father's subsequent inquiry about her at a charity dedicated to saving the lives of illegitimate children, on the other, imply at least the possibility of an alternative reading of her story. Rachel could have been an indigent bastard (would have been, very likely, in real life), and, though not necessarily brought up at the Foundling Hospital, would have had rather limited social prospects and hardly qualified for marrying a man of the world such as Clarence Hervey.

In other words, Edgeworth tentatively introduces—and Austen consciously develops—the theme of the Foundling Hospital as a "reality check" for the foundling narrative at the turn of the century. Both *Belinda* and *Emma* feature characters wishing to adopt a foundling and mold her into a perfect wife for an appreciative husband (a plan, as Elizabeth Kowaleski-Wallace has argued, that is bound to misfire because it "seeks to make women creditable partners for their husbands by denying them the opportunity to exercise their own judgment"[23]). When Frank Churchill asks Emma to "find somebody" (i.e., a wife), for him, to "adopt her, educate her," and "make her just like" herself (342), Emma feels certain that he is talking about Harriet.[24] But as in *Belinda*, in which the reference to the Foundling Hospital functions as a prelude for freeing Clarence Hervey from his fatuous commitment to educating a foundling into a wife, so too in *Emma*, the introduction of Brunswick Square (and through it, the Foundling Hospital) as the place where Harriet should go in order to be reunited with her common sense sweetheart signals the end of Emma's interpretation of Harriet's story as well as her own along the lines of *Fatherless Fanny* and *The Beggar Girl*.

Somewhat paradoxically, it is the essential conservatism of Harriet's story, its levelheaded class consciousness, that renders Austen's novel more "progressive" (if we still want to use this loaded term) in its view of illegitimacy than are other works of fiction discussed throughout this study. On the one hand, when Harriet's true—and truly inconspicuous—parentage comes to light, Emma's shrewd assessment of her own former folly and her protégé's real social prospects acquires a tenor somewhat grating to our sensibilities:[25]

> [Harriet] proved to be the daughter of a tradesman, rich enough to afford her comfortable maintenance which had ever been hers, and decent enough to have always wished for concealment. Such was the blood of gentility which Emma had formerly been so ready to vouch for. It was likely to be as untainted, perhaps, as the blood of many a gentleman: but what a connection had she been preparing for Mr. Knightley, or for the Churchills, or even for Mr. Elton! The stain of illegitimacy, unbleached by nobility or wealth, would have been a stain indeed. (443)

On the other hand, socially handicapped as she is by her illegitimacy, Harriet is still a heroine of a respectable middle-class romance crowned by a marriage, the first such heroine within the literary tradition that either coded female bastards as foundlings (*Evelina, Emmeline, Fatherless Fanny, The Beggar Girl*), or made them suffer seduction (*Sense and Sensibility*), or infamy (*The Beggar Girl*), or rape (*The Victim of Prejudice*), or killed them off altogether (*Peregrine Pickle*). It is true that the outcome of Harriet's adventures on the marriage market vindicates Mr. Elton's smug earlier assertion that "everybody has his [social] level," but it is also true that for most of the eighteenth century, fictional female bastards could not aspire to *any* level in the social hierarchy, lurking as silent, embarrassing half-presences on the margins of the narrative. Harriet may be ever so "sheep-like" (in Marvin Mudrick's uncharitable characterization), but she is certainly not doomed—in spite of her incorrigible illegitimacy—to a tragic fate or textual marginalization.

But putting aside for a minute the inauspicious fate reserved for female bastards in the Enlightenment's belles lettres, the dénouement of Harriet's story compares favorably even with that of her eighteenth-century male counterparts. Fielding's male bastard's "making good" is predicated upon a rather fantastic reversal of fortune that will put him in possession of two great estates, but Austen's female bastard's making good is defined more poignantly by her *being there* for more than 300 pages and making a good common sense marriage. Similarly, when Richardson's Sir Charles Grandison behaves in an enlightened way toward the illegitimate sons of his late father and Mrs. Oldham by giving them enough money to be educated for an "honest" line of employment, the readers are given to understand that the boys are destined to remain the beggarly beneficiaries of their stepbrother's good will, dependent on him (if not forever, then for some significant length of time) for their aspirations to respectable existence. In contrast, Harriet is shown to slip from under the ultimately oppressive care of her benefactress, hardly needing her in the first place and certainly not dependent on her for her future well-being.

Beyond Emma: *Changes in Fictional Representations of Illegitimacy*

In allowing her bastard heroine to do well within the satisfying confines of common sense, Austen's personal inclination to literary iconoclasm dovetailed ongoing transformations in socioeconomic realities of illegitimacy. By the early 1800s, the number of "legitimate and quasi-legitimate births (in which the parents marry after conception but before birth) . . . [had] jumped to an astonishing fifty percent, half of which [were] fully illegitimate,"[26] which meant that illegitimate children constituted an ever growing social presence and had to be integrated into the economic order on a scale unprecedented in previous English history.[27]

The rules of such integration had been slowly changing over the course of the eighteenth century. As argued in the earlier chapters, even in the midst of a series of complicated socioeconomic transformations known today as the Industrial Revolution, inherited money and property continued to constitute the crucial source of livelihood for most people. In such circumstances, it was hardly surprising that both readers and writers remained obsessed by a plot featuring a suddenly materialized protagonist laying an emotionally compelling claim to precious family resources. Grounded in a real-life scenario in which an illegitimate child has had to be supported at the expense of her legitimate siblings or else be cruelly penalized for crimes that she herself did not commit (that is, for the sexual sins of her parents), the foundling narrative reflected painful socioeconomic and moral dilemmas faced by more people than today's students of the eighteenth century, not yet in the habit of automatically considering illegitimacy as a crucial factor in the period's life, are generally aware of.[28] At the same time, that narrative politely elided those dilemmas by revealing, at the end of the story, the legitimacy of the foundling.

It is difficult to pinpoint the exact moment in British economic history when the absolute importance of inherited capital diminished in comparison to the earning potential of the middle-class individual (and we can never speak about the complete separation between the two since inherited capital continues to provide a desirable resource for any economic initiative).[29] Still, we must hypothesize a slowly developing awareness on the part of the eighteenth-century reading public that, first, the partial loss of one's inheritance to an illegitimate sibling could be made up for by future economic entrepreneurship, and, second, that a bastard could also find employment that would make it less necessary for him/her to act as "a Robber" who "unjustly" deprives his/her legitimate siblings of their much-needed inheritance.[30]

Such awareness must have contributed to the gradual acceptance of the bastard, and particularly of the female bastard as a literary character whose illicit origins did not absolutely determine her own sexual depravity and ultimate doom. In other words, whereas for most of the eighteenth century, works of fiction centering on female protagonists of unknown origins routinely reimagined the economic threat represented by real-life bastards as the threat of sexual deviance that could only be alleviated by the discovery of the presumed bastard's legitimacy, by the early 1800s, a different scenario, such as that played out in *Emma*, in which a female bastard is able to support herself financially within respectable marriage, becomes a viable representational alternative. Hence Austen's final emphasis on Harriet's future life of useful occupation (444). Married to a "gentleman-farmer," whose industry is sure to advance him in the world, Harriet has no vital necessity to interfere with the financial prospects of any extant legal siblings.[31]

Emma's articulation of the connection between the female bastard's economic self-sufficiency and her upright morals ultimately paved the way for such characters as Bernard Shaw's Vivian Warren (*Mrs. Warren's Profession*, 1893). Vivie Warren is the Cambridge-educated illegitimate daughter of a prostitute–turned–brothel keeper, and because she is able to support herself as an accountant in Chancery Lane, she does not need her inheritance. One reason Vivie would not want to take her mother's money is that it is derived from the exploitation of young women in an international chain of brothels—and Shaw finds a particular satisfaction in rendering wobbly the moral ground on which we stand when we condemn this source of family fortune—but what is interesting for our present argument is the meaning of Vivie's bastardy in the context of her earning capability. Technically speaking, Mrs. Warren's sexual promiscuity could impact our view of her daughter's morals, which is the perspective animating Austen's story of the two Elizas and the whole centuries-long tradition of insisting on the legitimacy of fictional female foundlings, but in Shaw's play, genealogy-based morality takes a back seat to economics. Because Vivie can earn her own living, she can separate both her finances and her sexual morals from her family history.

It seems, then, that if we situate Richard Steele's Indiana (*The Conscious Lovers*, 1722) and Shaw's Vivie on the far ends of the continuum representing the full spectrum of eighteenth- and nineteenth-century representations of foundlings, we are able to see how the dependence on inherited income or the lack of such a dependence renders the legitimacy of the heroine either absolutely imperative or relatively unimportant. Harriet Smith's place on this hypothetical continuum is roughly halfway between Indiana and Vivie: unlike the former, she is allowed to be illegitimate and marry the man she loves, but, unlike the latter, she is not yet allowed to earn a respectable living outside of the confines of the family.

Note that economics had always had the power to supersede genealogy in the figuration of the female bastard's morals. Both male and female illegitimacy was often overlooked among the nobility (except when it was used to negotiate a more advantageous financial deal for the parents of the legitimate party). Because the generous support of a natural daughter (or a natural son) represented much less of a problem for a rich upper-class family than it did for a middle-class family, many an eighteenth-century aristocratic female bastard made a brilliant marriage in spite of her mother's former sexual transgression. The eighteenth-century foundling narrative, of course, did not represent the view of this minority of England's population. Paradoxical as it may sound, then, the expanding earning potential of the middling classes meant that more and more people could afford the "aristocratic," so to speak, that is, a more casual, view of illegitimacy. Note again how this complicates the notion (which may strike us as intuitively true) that an eighteenth-century bastard protagonist embodied the most trenchant challenge to the period's aristocratic ideology. The problem with this notion is that it does not take into consideration that bastardy historically represented much less of a threat to aristocracy than to the middling classes.

Emma thus adopts an older, more traditional stance on bastardy when she asserts that Harriet's "stain of illegitimacy" could be bleached only "by nobility or [inherited] wealth" (443)—the laundering recipe also used by Fielding in his *Tom Jones*—but Austen already knows better. By allowing a female bastard such a prominent position in her story and by marrying her "up" but still very much within the confines of common sense, Austen testifies that factors other than "nobility"—specifically, the incipient cultural realization that a bastard now represented less of an economic threat to the well-being of a middle-class family—could "bleach" the stain of illegitimacy almost as effectively.

By positing a cause-and-effect relationship between the growing cultural awareness that inherited capital did not absolutely define the person's future economic prospects, on the one hand, and the relative relaxation of the rule that fictional foundlings, especially female foundlings, *had* to be legitimate, on the other, this study does not claim that *Emma* has inaugurated the culture-wide lessening of interest in the question of the legitimacy of the literary foundling. Indeed, the development of the nineteenth- and twentieth-century lore of the romantic bastard, from Emily Brontë's Heathcliff to Jean-Paul Sartre's "Nobody's son," strongly suggests otherwise.[32] What I instead propose is that Austen's portrayal of Harriet Smith marked an important turning point in the history of English belles lettres, at which the content and the meaning of information conveyed by the fact of a character's illegitimacy became distinctly ambiguous. The protagonist's bastardy could still denote, and thus make sense of, his or her tendency toward economic aggressiveness, social subversion, or untamed sexuality, but it could also be "wasted" on a rather insipid personage, such as Harriet. Bastardy could signify everything, or nothing, or something open to endlessly conflicting interpretations (think, for example, of the broad spectrum of the possible meanings of Esther Summerson's illegitimacy in Charles Dickens's *Bleak House*[33]). Bastards and foundlings continued to populate fiction—and they still do—but the literary tradition of the obligatory transformation of bastards into foundlings, particularly in the case of female characters, as a function of a primarily economic concern about the (re)distribution of family resources came to its end by the early nineteenth century.

Postscript

BBC REWRITES TOM JONES'S ILLEGITIMACY

Although the tradition of the obligatory transformation of female bastards into foundlings may have ebbed by the 1810s, representations informed by that tradition still resonate with us today in unexpected and subtle ways. Consider the flashback at the end of the BBC 1998 production of *Tom Jones*, which shows Tom's late parents, Miss Bridget Allworthy and Mr. Summer, smiling at each other and very much in love. The next shot is a mercifully brief close-up of Mr. Summer's face disfigured by disease as he lies dead in the parish church with Bridget crying over his body. We learn from a voice-over supplied by Tom's presumed mother, Jenny Jones, that on the very day Mr. Summer was to ask for Bridget's hand from her brother, Mr. Allworthy, "he was taken with a small-pox and passed away by the following morning," leaving Miss Allworthy pregnant with his child and terrified at the impending loss of her reputation.

The revelation that Tom's parents would have married had it not been for Mr. Summer's untimely death is the invention of this particular movie. In the book, Bridget is not at all inclined to wed her lover, who is handsome and genteel but poor. As the thunderstruck Allworthy reminisces at the end of the story, "I confess I recollect some passages relating to that Summer, which have formerly gave me a Conceit that my Sister had some Liking to him. I mentioned it to her: For I had such a regard for the young Man, as well on his own account, as on his Father's, that I should willingly have consented to a Match between them; but she expressed the highest Disdain of my unkind Suspicion, as she called it, so that I never spoke more on the Subject" (833).

POSTSCRIPT

Henry Fielding's Bridget, vehemently disclaiming any tenderness for an indigent son of a clergyman, is very different from the BBC Bridget, crying over Mr. Summer's body on the very day when he would have revealed their mutual attraction to Mr. Allworthy. More is at stake here, however, than simply transforming a hypocritical stuck-up character into a sympathetic suffering one. What Fielding has emphatically refused to do and the movie sheepishly does is mitigate Tom's illegitimacy and his mother's sexual trespass by implying that his parents were almost as good as married because they planned to get married. In fact, sociologists studying early modern illegitimacy put such "courtship pregnancies" in a class by themselves, implying that the charge of promiscuity could not be leveled against a couple whose marriage plans were disrupted through no fault of their own.[1]

The introduction of the "courtship pregnancy" motif into the narrative can lead to certain misunderstandings. The picture closes with a moving tribute to Fielding, which includes the mention of a "scandal" surrounding the first publication of *Tom Jones*. Based on what they have just seen, some viewers account for that controversial reception by the sexual explicitness of the novel, amplified by several nude scenes in the BBC production.[2] In reality, however, the scandal was precipitated not only by the characters' sexual escapades but also by Fielding's audacity in leaving his hero a bastard. Jacobite critics claimed "that an earthquake that threatened London and other cosmic disorders were God's punishment for this indecency," and, generally, the offended first readers of the novel wished that Fielding had "revealed a secret marriage between Bridget and her illicit lover, who had died anyway."[3] The BBC producers' tampering with Tom's irredeemable illegitimacy caves in to that old wish, but the only apparent benefit of this "improvement" is that Bridget comes off as more virtuous—a curious instance of prudishness on the BBC's part. Why not leave the foundling hero a bastard, since Fielding himself did?

It seems that removed as we are from the anxieties surrounding the issue of illegitimacy in the days of Fielding, we could still be made to respond to representations engendered by those anxieties. It mattered then whether Tom was legally conceived or not, and, judging by the movie's tiptoeing around the issue, it may still matter now. The twentieth- and twenty-first-century audiences may be unaware of the socio-economic conditions (i.e., the importance of inheritance for one's economic survival and the grave threat represented by a bastard sibling's claim on that inheritance) that fueled the demonization of bastards for many centuries, but the echoes of that demonization still haunt our cultural imagination. Tom's considerable personal charms apparently acquire a different slant if he is perceived as a bit less of a "bastard" and a bit more of a love child deprived by a fluke of fate of a loving two-parent family.

The final scene of the movie amplifies the stakes of this tacit shift in perception. We see Tom riding up to his house in a carriage together with Allworthy, the older man snuggly dozing off now and then, the younger man gazing at him with tenderness. The carriage stops, and Tom's family—Sophia and their two children, Tom and Bridget—joyfully welcome him at the door. Amidst their happy domestics, there is another married couple, Honour and Partridge, and as they turn around to enter the house behind their masters, we see their hands sliding quietly toward each other's bottoms. Tom is thus firmly ensconced in his role as paterfamilias; Allworthy does not have to keep an eye on him and can afford to nod off; Bridget Allworthy's memory is sanctified by her grandchild being named after her (note that the novel itself does not specify the name of Tom's daughter); and sex, particularly of a playful, non-procreative kind, is displaced onto the comic couple of a lower social standing.

Tom, the movie implies, has shaken off rakishness (and some of his libido?) together with his bastardy, or is it that his former rakishness was an expression of his bastardy? BBC's *Tom Jones* seems to be implicitly playing off the old association of bastardy with unruly sexual appetite, which is deeply ironic because this is an association that Fielding himself sought to subvert by populating his novel with numerous bastards and refusing to see their bastardy as a meaningful common denominator explaining their behavior. The BBC's Tom is the virtuous son of the virtuous mother, his new respectability guaranteed through the use of the same representational strategy that the eighteenth-century writers relied on to guarantee the respectability of their female protagonists. The old transformation of female bastards into foundlings becomes an equal opportunity endeavor.

The "rewriting" of early modern bastardy thus goes on, even in a culture that has lost most, if not all, of the former socioeconomic incentives for monitoring the legitimacy of its citizens. To me it indicates that one of the key endeavors of my study—to uncover the mundane and thus poignant existence of eighteenth-century illegitimate men and women from under the agglomeration of cultural fantasies about "bastards" and "foundlings"—remains a project in progress. Although we may never be able—and, in fact, would not even want—to postulate a certain cutoff point at which the "real" experience of bastardy ends and its cultural reimagining begins, we should at least be aware of our enduring tendency to ignore the former and to overprivilege the latter in our ongoing reconstruction of early modern cultural history.

Notes

Notes to Introduction

1. Twinam, *Public Lives, Private Secrets*, 7.
2. Shorter, "Illegitimacy, Sexual Revolution, and Social Change," 251.
3. Gillis, *For Better, For Worse*, 110. For a statistical analysis of eighteenth-century illegitimacy, see Shorter, 237–72; Laslett, Oosterveen, and Smith, *Bastardy and Its Comparative History*, 71–249; Trumbach, *Sex and Gender Revolution*, 229–334; Ehmer, "Marriage," 317–19.
4. For the analysis of the declarations of bastardy available from the Greater London Record Office, see Trumbach, 273–75.
5. Wycherley, *The Plain Dealer*, 267. Similarly, Pinchwife observes in *The Country Wife* that "Cuckolds and Bastards . . . are generally makers of their own fortune" (189).
6. Quoted in McClure, *Coram's Children*, 11.
7. Lawrence Stone qualifies Gillis's assertion by arguing that prior to the 1690s, the rates of common-marriage illegitimacy among the rural poor were relatively negligible, but that between 1690 and 1790, there was a rise in bastardy "from 6 to 20 percent of all first birth, and the even more startling explosion of prenuptial conceptions" (*The Road to Divorce*, 65).
8. Gillis, *For Better, For Worse*, 111. For a discussion, see pp. 110–14.
9. Similar class dynamics characterized illegitimacy in other European countries. In Germany, for example, "in rural communities illegitimacy was seen as less of a problem than in middle-class circles" (Geyer-Kordesch, "Infanticide and the Erotic Plot," 114). For a related analysis of illegitimacy and class in eighteenth-century colonial Spanish America, see Twinam, 59–242.
10. McClure, *Coram's Children*, 10. The aristocratic tolerance for bastardy goes back to the Middle Ages, when as Jeffrey R. Watt points out, "men of elite often kept mistresses and raised the illegitimate children of these affairs alongside their legitimate offspring" ("The Impact of the Reformation," 148).
11. For further discussion, see Staves, "Resentment of Resignation," 210.
12. Habakkuk, *Marriage, Debt, and the Estates System*, 214.
13. Ibid.
14. Ibid. The most famous case involving the claims of an illegitimate successor in the absence of any legitimate children is, of course, that of Duke of Monmouth.

NOTES

15. As Trumbach has argued, the bastardy examinations in the eighteenth-century London show that "illegitimate sexual relations . . . usually occurred between fellow servants and must frequently have had marriage as their eventual aim" (232). For the discussion of specific occupations of those men, see p. 234.

16. As Richard Adair suggests, "[T]here may possibly . . . have been semi-institutionalized networks of infanticidal wet-nurses, although it is difficult to distinguish neglect from deliberate killing" (*Courtship, Illegitimacy and Marriage*, 44). Laslett, Oosterveen, and Smith point out that the illegitimate infant mortality in early modern England was "often twice as high" as the legitimate (52). Valerie Fildes estimates that in the late seventeenth century, as many as "1,000 foundlings a year were possibly abandoned on the streets of London" ("Maternal Feelings Re-assessed," 143).

17. Trumbach, 233.

18. Quoted in Langer, "Infanticide," 358.

19. Quoted in McClure, 232.

20. Fielding, *Tom Jones*, 663.

21. Boswell, *The Kindness of Strangers*, 9.

22. For a discussion on the eighteenth-century distinction of "'good breeding' from its sexual and necessarily lineal connotations and limitations," see Freeman, *Character's Theater*, 198–99, 204.

23. As Michael McKeon points out, "what 'happens' at the end of . . . *Tom Jones* . . . is less a social than an epistemological event; not upward mobility but—as in the invoked model of Oedipus . . .—the *acquisition of knowledge*" (*The Origins of the English Novel*, 408; emphasis added).

24. For a different view of the significance of the gender of hypothetical Lovelace's sons, see Hopkins, "Mr. Darcy's Body," 117.

25. For a discussion of the Marriage Act, see Stone, *The Road to Divorce*, 121–28; Bonfield, "European Family Law," 113–44; Trumbach, 267–68; and Habbakkuk, 18–20.

26. As Stone observes, by "the end of the eighteenth century, it was clear that most of the arguments by the original opponents of the 1753 Marriage Bill were fallacious. There had been no striking concentration of wealth in the aristocracy, nor any gigantic explosion (so far as we can tell) of fornication and concubinage" (*The Road to Divorce*, 131). Although "the bastardy rate certainly rose sharply in the late eighteenth century, . . . so did the rate of pre-nuptial conceptions. If consensual unions in fact grew in the late eighteenth and early nineteenth centuries, they seem to have been associated with the social traumas of mass migration, urbanization, and industrialization, or with economic and social backwardness, rather than with the working of the 1753 act" (129–30).

27. For a discussion of a "truly enormous" increase in rates of illegitimacy in eighteenth-century France, see Viazzo, "Mortality, Fertility, and Family," 177.

28. Setzer, "Introduction," 29.

29. Ibid., 28.

30. Findlay, *Illegitimate Power*, 5.

31. London, *Women and Property in the Eighteenth-Century English Novel*, 25. For discussions of the centrality of women in eighteenth-century fiction, see Doody's *The True Story of the Novel*, 279–80, and Laura Brown, *Ends of Empire*, 89–90. For a

related discussion of the "repeated appearances" of the "long-lost daughter" in sentimental comedies, see Freeman, 219–20.

32. Doody, "Beyond *Evelina*," 483. See also Doody, *The True Story of the Novel*, 298, and Martha G. Brown, "Fanny Burney's 'Feminism': Gender or Genre?," 395–96. For a further discussion of the classical foundling narrative, see Robert, *Origins of the Novel*, 21–46, and Greenfield, *Mothering Daughters*, 36–37.

33. McKeon, *The Origins of the English Novel*, 159.

34. Ibid., 406.

35. Hunt, *The Family Romance*, 175.

36. Schmidgen, "Illegitimacy and Social Observation," 139–42.

37. Ibid., 149.

38. Ibid., 134, 151, 153.

39. Alryyes, *Original Subjects*, 24.

40. Ibid., 25.

41. Ibid., 116; emphasis added.

42. Ibid., 26; emphasis added.

43. Robert, *Origins of the Novel*, 30.

44. Van Boheemen, 48–49.

45. Note that for the purpose of this introductory discussion, I have deliberately placed both plays and novels that depict foundlings, such as *The Conscious Lovers* and *Tom Jones*, under the umbrella headings of "foundling fiction" or "foundling narrative."

46. As Akira Hayami, Jenny Teichman, and Daniel Ogden have separately demonstrated, illegitimacy is *not* a universal social institution. See Teichman, *Illegitimacy: An Examination of Bastardy*. See also Hayami, "Illegitimacy in Japan," where he argues that "in Japan before its 'modernization,' illegitimacy was absent. . . . There was not even an expression for bastardy in the whole huge Japanese vocabulary (sets of character combination). The concept of illegitimacy was introduced along with the rest of European package at the outset of 'modernization' and showed 'illegitimacy' to be high, though tending to fall to vanishing point as industrialization proceeded" (6). See also Ogden's argument that there was no bastardy in Sparta because the land was allocated by the State and not inherited (*Greek Bastardy in Classical and Hellenistic Periods*, 246).

47. Pocock, *Virtue, Commerce, and History*, 103.

48. Ibid., 104.

49. Ibid., 110.

50. Findlay, *Illegitimate Power*, 78. For a related analysis of abandoned children in literature of the Renaissance, see Estrin, *The Raven and the Lark*.

51. Pocock, *Virtue, Commerce, and History*, 119.

52. Barker-Benfield, *The Culture of Sensibility*, xix. Barker-Benfield here quotes Perkin, *The Origins of Modern British Society*, 99.

53. See Teichman, 153, 162–64, on the history of British pressure groups such as the National Council for the Unmarried Mother and Her Child, which has been fighting for the equal rights of illegitimate children since 1918 (it is currently known as the National Council for One-Parent Families).

54. Shakespeare's *King John* and Brome's *A Jovial Crew* constitute notable exceptions to this rule.

55. See McKeon. For a related analysis, see Parker, *The Authors' Inheritance*, 87.
56. Richetti, *The English Novel in History*, 4.

Notes to Chapter 1

1. Loftis, *Steele at Drury Lane*, 196.
2. Folkenflik, "Introduction," 18.
3. For discussion, see Williams, *The Long Revolution*, 621.
4. Dennis, "Remarks on the Conscious Lovers," 530. As a "tragic" comedy featuring a distressed female, *The Conscious Lovers* is suggestively related to the late-seventeenth/early-eighteenth-century tradition represented by the "she-tragedy." See Laura Brown's *Ends of Empire* for an analysis of the "pleasure of the she-tragedy—that misogynist pleasure to be found in the pain of the female victim" (99).
5. Steele, *The Conscious Lovers*, 323. All subsequent quotations from *The Conscious Lovers* are from this edition. Page numbers are supplied, not line numbers.
6. Freeman, *Character's Theater*, 204.
7. Kenny, "Richard Steele and the 'Pattern of Genteel Comedy,'" 34.
8. See, for example, Dryden's 1690 *Amphitryon*, in which Mercury and Phoebus discuss Jupiter's "prerogative" to father bastards (1736). Note though that the political valence of such references remained ambiguous. For a discussion of *Amphitryon's* complicated attitude toward "Jupiter's philandering," especially in the possible context of Dryden's relationship with the court, see Milhous and Hume, *Producible Interpretation*, 219–20, and Hume, *Reconstructing Contexts*, 185.
9. Freeman, *Character's Theater*, 216.
10. Here is the relevant excerpt from the essay in *The Theatre*:

> This Gentleman was formerly what is call'd a Man of Pleasure about the Town; and having, when young, lavish'd a small Estate, retir'd to India, where by Marriage, and falling into the Knowledge of Trade, he laid the Foundation of the great Fortune, of which he is now Master. . . . He is a true Pattern of that kind of third Gentry, which arose in the World this last Century: I mean the great, and rich Families of Merchants, and eminent Traders, who in their Furniture, their Equipage, their Manner of Living, and especially their Oeconomy . . . deserve the Imitation of the modern Nobility. (Quoted in Freeman, 216)

Indiana must have been conceived just at the moment of Mr. Sealand's reformation from a Man of Pleasure into the "true Pattern" of a new gentry, and she thus narrowly avoided the fate of a "natural" child.

11. In referring to "post-Collier England," I do not intend to overestimate the significance of Collier's notorious tract. I rather use it a as shorthand designation for the period's general tendency toward censuring sexual explicitness of its theatrical productions—for, as Hume reminds us, we cannot claim with any certainty that "Jeremy Collier succeeded in cleaning up 'Restoration Comedy' in the years

after his diatribe of 1698. . . . . New plays unquestionably did become a lot less smutty, but this process started long before Collier, the evidence for his influence is at best doubtful, and Collier himself regarded his campaign for reform as dismal failure" ("The Aims and Limits of Historical Scholarship," 407).

12. *Terence's Comedies: Made English* (1694), 13. Echard's name was omitted from several first editions. It was finally reinstalled in the sixth edition of 1726.

13. As H. Grant Sampson points out, Terence's plays were "universally taught" throughout the eighteenth century ("Terence, Comic Patterns, and the Augustan Stage," 90). See also Malcolm Kelsall on Terence's status as one of the most important classical dramatists "shaping neo-classic theory and sensibility" ("Terence and Steele," 11).

14. Echard's critique of Roman customs and manners could also be read in the context of what Howard Weinbrot sees as the late-seventeenth-century critique of Roman decadence and paganism (chap. 7). For a recent discussion of theatrical representations of "Romans and Britons" at the end of the century, see Orr, *Empire on the English Stage*, chap. 8.

15. Ogden, *Greek Bastardy*, 105.

16. Jumping one hundred years ahead, we hear a curious if unintended echo of Echard's reasoning in Elizabeth Inchbald's explanation of why "no person of talents and literary knowledge" had undertaken translating August von Kotzebue's *Das Kind der Liebe* [*Love Child*] into English before she did, in 1798. The potential translators, wrote Inchbald, must have been deterred "by the consideration of [the play's] original unfitness for an English stage, and the difficulty of making it otherwise" (von Kotzebue, *Lovers' Vows, A play, In five acts. Performing at the Theatre Royal, Covent-Garden*, ii–iii). It is interesting that Inchbald lists among the reasons for the play's "unfitness" the "indelicately blunt" (iii) behavior of the young aristocratic woman who proposes marriage to the man she loves, as well as the "dangerous insignificance" (ii) of one of the secondary characters; but she does not mention as objectionable the play's frank discussion of bastardy even though she significantly modifies that discussion in her translation, thus making us suspect that she herself considered that aspect of the play quite risqué. Not only is the play now called *Lovers' Vows* instead of a more forthright *Love Child*, but also the original's discussion of an army career as the only one open to the bastards is dropped altogether from the end of act 4. Furthermore, unlike Stephen Porter, Inchbald never uses the word *bastard* in her translation. Inchbald was wrong, of course, in claiming that no other translators had undertaken the play. Stephen Porter's version appeared the same year, is much more faithful to the original, and contains a vitriolic preface, in which Porter asserts that he "was engaged" on translating the play "before she was" and wonders at Inchbald's "very invidious advertisement" (von Kotzebue, *Lovers' Vows, or, the Child of Love. A Play, in Five Acts. Translated from the German of Augustus von Kotzebue*, i).

17. See Petty, *An Essay Concerning the Multiplication of Mankind*. For a discussion of Petty's proposal, see Andrew, *Philanthropy and Police*, 58.

18. Scholars disagree on whether infanticide had actually increased by the early decades of the eighteenth century. Some have argued that "in eighteenth-century England the incidence of infanticide was lower than it had been in the mid-sixteenth century" and that its frequent denunciations by writers (such as

NOTES

Defoe), painters (such as Hogarth), and other public figures was the "result of increased social conscience rather than ... the reflection of an increase in crime." This view is supported primarily by the scant number of cases prosecuted at the court of law. Others have pointed out that abandonment of infants should count as infanticide because the abandoned child had practically no chances for survival, and they assert that "it is undoubtedly true that there was an enormous rise in the number of children abandoned, all over Europe, in the eighteenth-century" (Viazzo, 176).

19. England, of course, was not the only European country afflicted by infanticide and abandonment. For discussion, see Boswell, 15–16.

20. Bowers, *The Politics of Motherhood*, 4. For a comparative analysis of the patterns of abandonment of illegitimate children in urban and rural areas, see Ehmer, 319.

21. Adair suggests that "there may possibly . . . have been semi-institutionalized networks of infanticidal wet-nurses, although it is difficult to distinguish neglect from deliberate killing" (44).

22. Wrightson, "Infanticide in Earlier Seventeenth-Century England," 19.

23. Recent examinations of fictional depictions of victimized children and their deviant parents in conjunction with transformations in political, economic, aesthetic, and reproductive landscapes of early modern Europe range from Thomas Laqueur's radical assertion of an ontological linkage between eighteenth-century forensic descriptions of dead infants and the developing British novel (176–204) to Deborah A. Symonds's analysis of a careful repositioning of the figure of the "unnatural" (murderous) mother in fictional and legal discourses of the time (*Weep Not for Me*, especially 191–210). For a response to Laqueur's argument and a useful overview of publications on eighteenth- and nineteenth-century infanticide, see Thorn, "Introduction." Among other recent explorations of the theme of infanticide in early modern literature, see Dolan, *Dangerous Familiars*; Travitsky, "Child Murder in English Renaissance Life and Drama"; Bowers, *The Politics of Motherhood*; and Findlay, *Illegitimate Power*. Dolan extends her analysis of depictions of domestic crime in England, 1550–1700, to include some of the seventeenth-century pamphlets describing infanticidal parents and stepparents, and she examines the infanticide-through-exposure motif in Shakespeare's *The Winter's Tale*. Travitsky explores the unsympathetic portrayal of infanticidal mothers in Renaissance drama. Bowers considers infanticide an important constituent of an Augustan "mythology that at once exploits and denies explicitly maternal agencies and subjectivities" (4). Within early modern cultural studies, infanticide studies thus pursue an important double project of uncovering the historical emergence of the "accepted" cultural readings of dead infant—and silenced maternal—bodies and of showing how these readings informed the early modern "construction and containment of maternity" and female agency (Francus, "Monstrous Mothers, Monstrous Societies," 135).

24. Boswell, *The Kindness of Strangers*, 76–79.

25. Bakhtin, *The Dialogic Imagination*, 417.

26. Coram, quoted in Langer, "Infanticide: A Historical Survey," 358.

27. On the increase of illegitimacy throughout the eighteenth century, see Laslett, "Introduction," 14, 18, and 52. For a suggestive related discussion of the

Notes

difference between the perceived and the actual increase in infanticide in early-eighteenth-century England, see Viazzo, 176.

28. I wish I could sound less tentative on this issue, although I am also reminded of Hume's recent observation that when it comes to historical scholarship, literary critics are seldom "prepared simply to say that the evidence . . . will justify only a very tentative hypothesis" ("The Aims and Limits of Historical Scholarship," 418). Hume insists that "the scholar must understand (and make clear to others) exactly what is being claimed, and where those claims slide across the boundary between fact and speculative interpretation" (415). Although any aspiration to a distinction between the "matters of fact" and "speculative analysis" (403) may appear particularly suspect in a study dealing with representations of illegitimacy, I have endeavored, whenever possible, to retain some critical distance from my historical explications and to alert my readers to the differing degrees of certainty with which I myself treat different claims that I make.

29. Loftis, *Steele at Drury Lane*, 200.
30. Freeman, *Character's Theater*, 204.
31. Addison, *The Guardian*, No. 105, July 11, 1713.
32. Freeman, *Character's Theater*, 2–3.
33. Kenny, "Richard Steele," 34.
34. Connely, *Sir Richard Steele*, 380.
35. Ibid., 371.
36. Quoted by Tracy, the editor of Samuel Johnson, *Life of Savage*, 17.
37. Savage, *An Author To be Lett*, A3, A4. As Lawrence Lipking observes, *An Author To be Lett* is "remarkably vicious . . . even by the standard of the War of the Dunces" (*Samuel Johnson*, 75). For a suggestive recent analysis of Savage's controversial personality, see Blakey Vermeule, *The Party of Humanity*, 119–53.
38. In 1728, fresh from receiving the royal pardon for his murder of James Sinclair, Savage published one of his most famous poems, "The Bastard." Samuel Johnson characterizes the time of "The Bastard" composition, in the house of Lord Tyrconnel, as "the Golden Part of Mr. Savage's Life, [when] he had no Reason to complain of Fortune: his Appearance was splendid, his Expenses large, and his Acquaintance extensive. He was courted by all who endeavored to be thought Men of Genius, and caressed by all who valued themselves upon a refined Taste" (*Life of Savage*, 44).
39. Johnson, *Life of Savage*, 16.
40. See Loftis, *Steele at Drury Lane*, 184.
41. Canfield, "Shifting Tropes of Ideology in English Serious Drama," 220.
42. James Thompson, "Sure I have seen that face before," 295. See also Nandini Bhattacharya's argument that "from the very beginning . . . Indiana's entry into respectably society is negotiated by means of her virtue, even had her birth as a commoner been an obstacle otherwise" (*Reading the Splendid Body*, 106).
43. Ironically, the role of Indiana in the Drury Lane performances of *The Conscious Lovers* was played by Anne Oldfield, an object of Savage's perennial (if not necessarily erotic) attachment and herself a mother of two illegitimate children.
44. Connely, *Sir Richard Steele*, 381.
45. Lynch, *The Economy of Character*, 26.
46. Cave, *Recognitions*, 120.

47. Note that the subject of "tokens" will assume a renewed prominence in eighteenth-century cultural imagination after the opening of the London Foundling Hospital in 1739. At the time of Steele's writing, however, fictional tokens did not have many real-life resonances, for indigent mothers who murdered their infants or abandoned them to a certain death did not leave tokens with them. For a discussion of tokens left with the young charges of the foundling hospital by their mothers later in the century, see Laura Schattschneider, "The Infant's Petitions."

48. As discussed earlier (in my analysis of *Andria*), the meaning of the term *illegitimate*, when used in the texts of the antiquity, is different from the one generally used in this study and common in the eighteenth century.

49. Robert Markley, personal communication.

50. Goux, *Oedipus*, 19.

51. Ibid., 115.

Notes to Chapter 2

1. Defoe, *The Fortunes and Misfortunes of the Famous Moll Flanders*, 1. Subsequent references to *Moll Flanders*, unless otherwise noted, will be from this edition and placed in parentheses.

2. In arguing that *Moll Flanders* should be read in the context of the eighteenth-century infanticide prevention campaign, I follow the long-standing scholarly tradition of historicizing Defoe's novel, represented by Paula Backsheider's *Daniel Defoe: Ambition and Innovation* and *Daniel Defoe: His Life;* Ian Watt's *The Rise of the Novel;* Maximilian E. Novak's "Some Notes Toward a History of Fictional Forms"; John Bender's *Imagining the Penitentiary;* Lincoln Faller's *Crime and Defoe;* Gregory Durston's *Moll Flanders;* and Robert Mayer's *History and the Early English Novel*. As William Warner observes in *Licensing Entertainment*, "[T]he very coarseness of Defoe's narrative filter allows his writings to conduct a more ample and complex documentation of eighteenth-century realities" (150).

3. McDowell, *The Women of Grub Street*, 6.

4. Although I use the word *infanticide* as interchangeable with *child murder* throughout this study, the former term was not widely used in the eighteenth century. For a discussion of terminology associated with child murder during this period, see Jackson, *New-Born Child Murder,* 6, and Dickinson and Sharpe, "Infanticide in Early Modern England," 36.

5. For information on the British legal system's dealings with infanticide, see Hoffer and Hull, *Murdering Mothers;* Jackson, *New-Born Child Murder;* Wrightson, "Infanticide in Earlier Seventeenth-Century England" and "Infanticide in European History"; Damme, "Infanticide"; May, "'She at first denied it'"; and Francus, "Monstrous Mothers, Monstrous Societies."

6. Richard Burn, in his 1763 *Ecclesiastical Law,* states that "every lewd woman who shall have any bastard which may be chargeable to the parish, the justices of the peace shall commit such woman to the house of correction to be punished and set to work, during the term of one whole year" (I:120). Adair points out that corporal punishments for the "parents of illegitimate children, especially the mothers—

Notes

have been noted for Somerset, Nottinghamshire, Sussex and the West Riding of Yorkshire. In the Isle of Man persistent female sexual offenders were dragged into the sea behind a boat in the seventeenth and eighteenth centuries" (152). Wrightson reports the intervention of manorial courts as in the case of the "Jury of one Lancashire Manor, [that] fined the father of a pregnant girl until he was forced to turn her out" ("Infanticide in Earlier Seventeenth-Century England," 66).

7. The 1624 Statute (21 Jac. I c. 27) focused on unwed mothers and stated that "[If] any Woman . . . be delivered of . . . Male or Female, which . . . should by the Lawes of this Realm be a bastard, and . . . she endeavour to conceal the Death thereof, as it may not come to light, whether it be borne alive or not, but be concealed, in every such Case the Mother so offending shall suffer Death as in the case of Murther. . . ." (Pickering, *Statutes at Large*, 298). Consequently, as Jackson points out, the assumption that only mothers of bastard children had motives for murder "served to justify the complementary belief that the murder of a newborn child by a married woman, because motiveless, could only be explained in terms of some evident disease." So in the 1668 case when "'a married woman of good reputation' was indicted for murdering her newly born child, [she was judged to be possessed by] the 'temporary phrenzy' [and] found not guilty to the 'satisfaction of all that heard it'" (*New-Born Child Murder*, 40). Similar laws were passed in France (1156, 1586, 1708), Sweden (1627), Württemberg (1658), Scotland (1690), Bavaria (1751), Canada (1758), and the United States (1855) (Schwartz and Isser, *Endangered Children*, 36–37). In England, the Lord Ellenborough's Act of 1803 restored the presumption of stillbirth and introduced an alternative verdict: if an illegitimate mother were acquitted on a charge of murder, she could still be punished with a two-year imprisonment. Interestingly, this act still centered on unwed mothers and their bastard children; it took the next piece of legislation dealing with infanticide, the 1828 Offences against the Person Act, to dispatch with the distinction between illegitimate and legitimate children.

8. Similar arguments have recently been made about Victorian England. As Schwartz and Isser have pointed out, in the second part of the nineteenth century, it was thought that "the punitive bastardy legislation embodied in the Poor Law with its refusal of 'outdoor' relief, the difficulty of getting fathers to support their children, and the inability of women to find work . . . forced more neonaticide and abandonment" (31).

9. Wrightson, "Infanticide in European History," 7. Also, for an important recent discussion of the comparative effects of Protestant and Catholic measures against bastardy, see Watt, "The Impact of the Reformation and Counter-Reformation."

10. As Alan Macfarlane observes, the "hint that the bastard's religious status was extremely dubious occurs in Thomas Becon's works, where he cites the old law that bastards should not be allowed to enter the congregation of the faithful." Macfarlane also cites a case of "a man of Great Totham [who] was presented at the archdeaconry court in 1612 'for inconsistency and bastardy for which cause he hath not beene [*sic*] admitted the holy communion this last Easter'" ("Illegitimacy and Illegitimates in English History," 78–79).

11. Dickinson and Sharpe point out that although the capacity "to keep their pregnancy secret until a very last stage" may appear "remarkable to the modern

NOTES

observer," unmarried women in the early modern era regularly managed "to maintain such secrecy." By exhibiting exceptional "physical and psychological resilience," they ensured that even a birth would "pass unnoticed by other members of an infanticidal mother's household" (45).

12. Wrightson, "Infanticide in European History," 5.

13. Sometimes such sermons warned parishioners about the mortal sin of killing an infant before baptism. To kill the unbaptized newborn was to detract from the community of Christian souls in heaven, because "a child before he is baptized is not a child of God but a child of the Devil" (Stone, *The Family, Sex and Marriage in England*, 472–74. For further discussion of the evolution of ecclesiastical views on infanticide, see Kellum, "Infanticide in England in the Later Middle Ages," and Walker, *Crime and Insanity in England*.

14. On the practice of neighborly snooping after women suspected of being pregnant out of wedlock, see Jackson, *New-Born Child Murder*, especially chap. 2.

15. See Bradley, "An Inquiry into Seasonality in Baptisms, Marriages, and Burials," and Mills, "The Christening Custom at Melbourn, Cambridgeshire."

16. Once the child had been introduced to the community through the baptismal ceremony, his parent(s) became publicly accountable for him and were much less likely to attempt to murder or expose him. Interestingly, according to the nineteenth-century Napoleonic Code, the murder of a child prior to registration was considered a much heavier offense than the murder of a registered child. Stripped of all religious connotations, the code explicitly addressed the fact that "until registration the child enjoyed less protection than the ordinary citizen from the normal deterrents of the law" (Walker, 126).

17. For a related discussion of religious practices possibly adapted to forestall infanticide, see Vom Saal, "The Role of Social, Religious, and Medical Practices in the Neglect, Abuse, Abandonment, and Killing of Infants," 43–71.

18. Quoted in Langer, "Infanticide," 358.

19. See Wrightson, "Infanticide in Earlier Seventeenth-Century England," 12; Hoffer and Hull, 7, 39, 78, 97, 100–102; and Jackson, *New-Born Child Murder*, 29.

20. Dickinson and Sharpe, 38.

21. Addison, *The Guardian*, No. 105, July 11, 1713.

22. Defoe, *The Generous Projector*, 10.

23. Brownlow, *The History and Design of the Foundling Hospital with a Memoir of the Founder*, 2–3. As Susan Chaplin suggests, by the first decades of the eighteenth century, the image of an infanticidal mother as an object of compassion begins to replace the image of such mother as a monster (*Speaking of Dread*, especially the chapter "The Discipline of Sensibility: Infanticide, Sensibility, and Femininity in *The Memoirs of Miss Sidney Biddulph*").

24. Addison, *The Guardian*, No. 105, July 11, 1713.

25. Habermas, *The Structural Transformation of the Public Sphere*, 36.

26. Recent research of Luc Racaut offers an unexpected additional context for Addison's concerns about England's lagging behind the Catholic countries in preventing infanticide. As Racaut demonstrates, from the outset of the Reformation, Protestants had been the subject of a "blood libel" by Catholics, routinely accused of sacrificing their own children during their religious orgies. In the eyes of the early modern Catholic polemicists, especially those in France, this blood

Notes

libel "served to justify further persecutions of [heretics, i.e., of Protestants], in the same way that it had been used against Jews across the ages" ("Accusations of Infanticide on the Eve of the French Wars of Religion," 34).

27. For a suggestive recent discussion of *A Modest Proposal* and cultural representations of child murder, see McDonagh, *Child Murder and British Culture*, 18–23.

28. See also Defoe, *Augusta Triumphans*.

29. Quoted in Nichols and Wray, 16. Interestingly, the issue of "public benefit" in conjunction with infanticide was raised once again later in the century, even though the "public" was now defined on a very different scale. In the famous 1798 *An Essay on the Principle of Population*, Malthus lists the primary "checks" on population growth, such as war, famine, and disease. Thus alluding to the late-eighteenth-century visitations of smallpox, he notes that "small-pox is certainly one of the channels, and a broad one, which nature has opened for the last thousand years, to keep down the population to the level of the means of subsistence." He also mentions that in addition to three major checks, there are other "active and able ministers of depopulation," such as abortion and infanticide, though he does not discuss in detail the workings of these lesser "ministers," except by informing his readers that infanticide had been historically practiced in Australia, the Pacific, North and South America, Central Asia, India, China, and ancient Rome and Greece (32). The teleological implications of the Malthusian theory of population checks do not fare well with economists and historians today; indeed, it is often viewed as inspired in its conception but still an oversimplified account of complex mechanisms involved in the dynamics of population growth (see Fogel, *The Relevance of Malthus for the Study of Mortality Today;* Hollander, *The Economics of Thomas Robert Malthus;* and Dupaquier, Fauve-Chamoux, and Grebenik [eds.], *Malthus Past and Present*). Historian Rudolph Binion points out that Malthus "reduces human behavior to laws of nature expressible in mathematical terms, [thus following] a common ambition of the *philosophes* throughout the Enlightenment, overawed as they were by the example of the natural scientists of the seventeenth century who had seemingly reduced all physical phenomena to a few simple and elegant mathematical formulae—or rather who had purportedly detected those simple and elegant formulae encoded in nature" ("'More Men Than Corn,'" 565). For a suggestive recent analysis of the implications of Malthusian "world of surplus population" for late-eighteenth-century politics, see Lamb, *Preserving the Self in the South Seas*, 286.

30. Jackson, *New-Born Child Murder*, 48.

31. Quoted in May, 35–36.

32. For an analysis of "The Cruel Mother; being a True Relation of the Bloody Murther Committed by M. Cook" and a series of other pamphlets depicting child murder, see Francus. Another recent study of eighteenth-century ballads dealing with infanticide is Symonds's *Weep Not for Me*. See also John Richetti on the popularity of early-eighteenth-century pamphlets about "sensational crimes and domestic violence" ("Popular Narrative in the Early Eighteenth Century," 5–6).

33. Similarly, as Dickinson and Sharpe observe, "[M]en figured very rarely as principals in infanticide prosecutions. . . . [They] were very rarely thought to be involved in the deaths of . . . illegitimate children, and were extremely unlikely to be convicted" (41).

34. Adair, 79.

35. Complicating Adair's assertion is Jeffrey R. Watt's recent reminder that unlike their Catholic counterparts, early modern Protestant magistrates were generally more active in at least "trying to establish the paternity of illegitimate children" (150).

36. The French Foundling Hospital was opened in 1670. Bray, Coram, and Defoe often refer to it as an example that British "Men of Sense" should emulate. See, for example, McClure, *Coram's Children*, 3–15.

37. Quoted in Solkin, *Painting for Money*, 162.

38. On "gypsies" in *Moll Flanders*, see Benedict, *Curiosity*, 168, and Durston, 48. Compare to Robert A. Erickson's discussion of one "Jenny Hackabout," a real-life bawd and procuress, who, "after leaving off the trade of bawd because, of the expense of keeping off Indictments, bribing the Informers, and other Accidents" became so successful a midwife "that there was scarce a Whore about Town but was her Customer"; Jane was also expert at disposing children, as soon as they were born, to "Gypsies" for "forty shillings" (*Mother Midnight*, 269).

39. The case is described in Macfarlane, 76–77.

40. Rogers, "Notes," in Daniel Defoe, *The Fortunes and Misfortunes of the Famous Moll Flanders*, 274.

41. Ibid.

42. For a detailed analysis of Mother Midnight's relationship with Moll, see Erickson, "Moll's Fate."

43. As Warner observes, Defoe's "narratives indulge what they censure, repeat what they proscribe" (*Licensing Entertainment*, 151).

44. As P. Hudson and W. R. Lee have argued, "As long as male wages remained precariously low or male employment was casual or seasonal, most married women were obliged to seek work in the non-formal economy. Wives were forced to supplement family income because of the persistent and serious economic need. Women were able to find supplementary income in childminding, casual cleaning and taking in lodgers ... laundry work and trading in consumables. Much activity of this kind drew on women's neighbourhood and kinship networks and involved reciprocity and payment in kind as well as monetised transactions" (*Women's Work and the Family Economy in Historical Perspective*, 30).

45. Clark, *Correspondence of the Foundling Hospital Inspectors*, xxxvi.

46. Ibid., xxxvi–xxxvii.

47. Solkin, 159.

48. Quoted in Nichols and Wray, 27.

49. For a related discussion of Moll's "immunity from the fruits of her miscellaneous unions," see Flynn, *The Body in Swift and Defoe*, 70.

50. As Amy L. Masciola observes, there "appears to have been as much concern among commentators about "single women's sexuality going 'wholly undiscovered' as there was for the lives of innocent children" ("'The Unfortunate Maid Exemplified,'" 64).

51. Bakhtin, *The Dialogic Imagination*, 320.

52. As Francus puts it, Moll's "abandonment of her children is a ... displaced infanticide" (156). In discussing infanticide from the perspective of the mother,

Notes

Moll Flanders prefigures the much later novel, Elizabeth Inchbald's *Nature and Art*.

53. Compare to Novak's argument about the "cycle of necessity" in Defoe's fiction—his tendency to excuse (if partially) and explain the faults of his characters, including Moll (*Defoe and the Nature of Man*, 76, 78–82). See also George A. Starr on the comparison between Moll's reasoning about "doing away with the child" and the passage dealing with child abandonment in his 1728 *Street-Robberies* (*Defoe: Spiritual Autobiography*, 147, n. 22), and Alryyes's discussion of "marriage and fertility" as "decidedly superceded by the hero's freedom" (154).

54. Moll's matter-of-fact reasoning about the difficulties of her situation could be seen in light of what J. Paul Hunter characterizes as Defoe's "accomplishment—an accomplishment repeated in times in novels ever since—in making Moll's life seem ordinary even though it violates community standards in ways unthinkable to most readers" (*Before Novels*, 36). On the other hand, Moll's descriptions of her "perplexity" and "apprehensions" echo in suggestive ways what Dana Rabin has recently described as an increased use of "the language of the mind" in the Old Bailey infanticide trial transcripts from the 1720s and the 1730s: "By claiming that they were 'not sensible,' 'agitated in mind,' 'almost distracted,' 'stupefied,' 'confused' and 'delirious,' defendants and witnesses explained a wide range of emotional states from confusion to delusion and insanity. . . . This language and the larger interest in sensibility convinced those participating in the courtroom dialogue—from the defendants and witnesses to the judges and prosecutors—that the women accused of infanticide had no criminal intention of murdering or hurting their children and that they should not be held responsible for the crime" ("Bodies of Evidence, States of Mind," 81).

55. Bowers, *The Politics of Motherhood*, 123. Similarly, as Novak points out, in Moll's case, "[S]elf-preservation [is] allowed to take precedence over parental love" ("Conscious Irony in *Moll Flanders*," 51). For a related discussion, see Chaber, "Matriarchal Mirror" and Pollak, "Moll Flanders, Incest, and the Structure of Exchange."

56. Richetti, "The Portrayal of Women in Restoration and Eighteenth-Century English Literature," 75.

57. Ibid., 75.

58. On Defoe's general tendency to cut his characters' "description of significant and potentially interesting events" in their lives, see Faller, 100.

59. For a related discussion of the apparent lack of coherence in Moll's account of her birth, see Alkon, *Defoe and the Fictional Time*, 143.

60. Nancy K. Miller is convinced that Moll is illegitimate (*The Heroine's Text*, 5), although, strictly speaking, we have no conclusive evidence for it in the text.

61. In one of the funniest mother-son exchanges of early modern English literature, Humphrey asks Moll to bring him "a wife from London" (267). Both Humphrey and Moll are happily oblivious of the fact that her brother/husband had also brought himself a "wife from London" and that the number of Moll's children scattered through London should make her worry about history repeating itself.

62. Pocock, *Virtue, Commerce, and History*, 104. For a different reading of the "watch" episode, see James Thompson, *Models of Virtue*, 142.

63. See Starr for a different reading of Moll's tendency to place the responsibility for her misdeeds on external evil agents (*Defoe and Casuistry*, 153–54).

64. Miller, 10. For a different reading of the invocations of "fate or Providence" in Defoe, see Warner, *Licensing Entertainment*, 151.

65. As David Morse observes in his discussion of Burney's Evelina, "[T]he contradiction involved in her social progress and in the whole trajectory of the novel, is that she must gain both knowledge and experience of the fashionable world in order to preserve and protect the virtue that she has, yet at the same time she has to stay as unspoiled as she was at the outset" (*The Age of Virtue*, 149).

66. Of course, as Richetti has observed, "[T]he facts are that [Moll] could have as easily come to her criminal career through any number of alternative sets of circumstances which are not related to the lack of state provisions for orphans and deserted children" (*Defoe's Narratives*, 97).

67. Rogers, "Introduction," xv.

Notes to Chapter 3

1. Richardson, *Clarissa*, 53. All subsequent page references will be to this edition and noted parenthetically in the text.

2. London, 15. See also Hill, "Clarissa Harlowe and Her Times"; Barrell, *The Political Theory of Painting from Reynolds to Hazlitt;* and Zomchick, *Family and the Law in Eighteenth-Century Fiction.*

3. Theodore Albert, quoted in Zomchick, 61.

4. Zomchick, 60.

5. Ibid., 62.

6. Terence, *The Comedies,* 65.

7. Moore's biographer, John Homer Caskey, considers Rosetta an invention of Moore's, not corresponding to any particular character in Steele's play, except perhaps Indiana's Aunt Isabella, since like Isabella, Rosetta takes Fidelia under her protection (*The Life and Works of Edward Moore,* 41). I think that Rosetta in her vivacity also bears some resemblance to Steele's Lucinda. Also in *The Conscious Lovers,* Lucinda and Indiana turn out to be sisters, and one important consequence of this discovery is the halving of Lucinda's fortune. In the case of Moore's Fidelia, she is the sister of Colonel Raymond, Rosetta's suitor, and by being readmitted into her family, she makes Rosetta's fortune smaller indirectly—via diminishing the portion of Colonel Raymond.

8. Quoted in Caskey, 39.

9. The name of the young lady remained unknown. The meeting is reported in Anthony Amberg's "Introduction," 49. All subsequent page references will be to this edition and noted parenthetically in the text.

10. Quoted in T. C. Eaves and Ben D. Kimpel, *Samuel Richardson,* 286.

11. Richardson, *Selected Letters,* 188–92.

12. Moore abandoned the plan of turning *Clarissa* into a play by 1751.

13. Quoted in McKillop, *Samuel Richardson, Printer and Novelist,* 162.

14. See McKillop, 184.

15. Fielding wrote to Lyttelton on August 29, 1749, "I never wished for Power

more than a few Days ago for the Sake of a Man whom I love, and that more perhaps from the Esteem I know he bears toward you than from any other Reason. The man is in love with a young Creature of the most apparent worth, who returns his Affections [Jenny Hamilton, whom Moore would marry in May 1750]. Nothing is wanting to make two very miserable People extremely blessed but a moderate Portion of the greatest of human Evils" (quoted in Battestin and Battestin, *Henry Fielding*, 482).

16. Ibid.

17. Fielding's letter to Lyttelton was written in May 1749—*after* Richardson inserted the reference to *The Foundling* in his *Clarissa*—so I cannot argue that Fielding's support of Moore's matrimonial plans played any role in Richardson's decision to use that reference (besides, it is not clear that Richardson would even know of the letter to Lyttelton at the time it was written). My point, however, is that Moore and Fielding were friends before the publication of *The Trial of Selim* (1748), and there must have been other instances of their friendship that Richardson was aware of. After all, he did group Moore and Fielding together in his humorous response to Moore's letter of praise for *Clarissa* (this happening shortly after Fielding's own admiring comments on *Clarissa*), observing that "the poor Clarissa may be admitted to fill a gap in the Reading World; while Mr. Moore and Mr. Fielding are . . . reposing their Undestandings" [*sic*] (quoted in McKillop, 169).

18. Warner, *Reading Clarissa*, 75.

19. See, for example, London on Clarissa's "making of herself into a saint" (34); Richetti on Clarissa's "passion play of holy dying" (*The English Novel in History*, 117, but also 115); Castle on Richardson's rendering of Clarissa "into a decomposing emblem of martyred Christian womanhood" (*Clarissa's Ciphers*, 173); Leo Braudy on Clarissa as an "anti-physical saint" ("Penetration and Impenetrability in *Clarissa*," 189); and Doody on Clarissa's being "martyr for her faith . . . without knowing it" (*Natural Passion*, 105).

20. Compare to Doody's argument that "Lovelace has concluded that tragedy is feminine (and therefore inferior), comedy masculine (and therefore superior). Unconsciously he deeply believes that since the male must always be the superior force, the tragic in life never takes precedence over the comic unless a weak male permits the usurpation" (*Natural Passion*, 115). For a related argument, see also Doody, "Saying 'No,' Saying 'Yes,'" 89. See also Ronald Paulson, who suggests that by ultimately rendering Clarissa's story tragic, Richardson implicitly contrasts it "with comedy, Fielding's genre" (*The Beautiful, Novel, and Strange*, 132–33). Similarly, Miller observes that "entrapped by the logic gender, Lovelace makes a mistake of genre: he fails to perceive that Clarissa is not made for comedy" (89). Finally, see Richetti's recent further development of his earlier argument that Lovelace's "subversive and specifically aristocratic comedy of seduction and stratagem replaces the essentially novelistic sense of reality that characterizes Clarissa's good faith negotiations with her family in the opening volumes of the novel, when she seeks to evade the marital and economic destiny planned for her and to develop her own sense of integrity and self-determination" (in his "Richardson's Revisions in the Third Edition of *Clarissa*," forthcoming).

21. Quoted in Van Marter, "Richardson's Revisions of *Clarissa* in the Third and Fourth Editions," 139.

22. In fact, the opposite argument has been made, which is that *The Foundling* "may have been colored by *Clarissa* as it certainly was by *Pamela*" (McKillop, 70). However, we have no reason to assume that the influence could not have been mutual, given *Clarissa*'s and *The Foundling*'s history of continuous revisions and their respective authors' friendship at the time.

23. See Eaves and Kimpel, "The Composition of Clarissa and its Revision before Publication."

24. That I haven't been able so far to discover any other such scenes in the literature of the period does not mean that they don't exist.

25. Warner, *Licensing Entertainment*, 202–3. Richardson's relationship with romance remains debated by eighteenth-century scholars. Richetti sees *Clarissa* as "a massive rejection of romance, a transformation of the clichés of the amatory pattern into a monumental novel without parallel in English or in European fiction" (*The English Novel in History*, 99). Doody argues that in *Clarissa*, Richardson appropriates the "conventions of the 'inflaming Novels' and 'idle Romances' which he condemns" (*A Natural Passion*, 128). Albert J. Rivero suggests that in *The History of Sir Charles Grandison*, Richardson lets "Mrs. Shirley and Lady G. mount their attack on romance . . . to expel the 'foreign,' the 'romantic,' from Richardson's own narrative" ("Representing Clementina," 211). Warner points out that for Richardson, "producing a 'new species of writing' [pivoted] upon a shift of style—from decadent ornamentation to 'an easy and natural manner,' from aristocratic ostentation to 'simplicity.' Richardson will reform the novel by redressing it" (*Licensing Entertainment*, 202).

26. For a different reading of Lovelace's demand of Clarissa's heart, see Zomchick's argument that having treated Clarissa as a thing throughout the novel, Lovelace cannot "free himself from the compulsion [of doing so] even after Clarissa's death, when he wishes to possess her stilled heart" (88).

27. Compare to Terry Eagleton's view that what "'circulates' in the novel, what unifies its great circuits of textual exchange, is simply Clarissa herself, whether as daughter or lover, rival or confidante, protégée or property-owner" (*The Rape of Clarissa*, 56).

28. For a suggestive related discussion of the relationship between Clarissa's estate and her "self," see Schor, "Notes of a Libertine Daughter," 107.

29. Theodore G. Albert, 2, 8, quoted in Zomchick, 61.

30. Zomchick, 61–63.

31. Belford's condemnations of bastardy grew even louder in the third edition, prompting Mark Kinkead-Weekes to observe that Belford's "sermon on Belton's love of the bastards" represents a didactic imposition rather than a "genuine improvement" ("Clarissa Restored?" 170–71).

32. Chandler, "Moving Accidents," 158.

33. Colman, *The English Merchant*, 7. All subsequent page references will be to this edition and noted parenthetically in the text.

34. As Freeman reminds us, "[W]hile each genre offers a particular cultural logic with which to engage particular social issues and categories of identity, form itself is not intransigent but rather transformed and rearticulated in relation to the cultural work it is asked to perform" (235).

Notes

Notes to Chapter 4

1. The sentiment belongs to Mrs. Deborah Wilkins, who declares that she cannot "touch" any of "these misbegotten wretches" and further claims that Tom "stinks" and "doth not smell like a Christian" (35).
2. For a discussion of Blifil's illegitimacy, see Alter, *Fielding and the Nature of the Novel*, 41–42.
3. For an analysis of Nancy Miller's illegitimacy, see Amory, "Law and the Structure of Fielding's Novels," 344–47.
4. Teichman underscores the difficulty of coming up with a "universal definition [of illegitimacy], a single set of necessary and sufficient conditions" that could help us to classify a child as a bastard, when she points out that the definition of bastardy depends on the definition of marriage and "that the status (or statuses) recognized as marriage varies considerably from one . . . community to another" (23).
5. McKeon, *The Origins of the English Novel*, 159.
6. Castle, *Masquerade and Civilization*, 197, 198.
7. Castle, "'Matters Not Fit to Be Mentioned,'" 75.
8. Shakespeare, *King Lear*, in *Shakespeare: The Complete Works*, I. ii.12–16.
9. The full quotation is as follows:

> *Posthumus:* . . . We are all bastards,
> And that most venerable man which I
> Did call my father was I know not where
> When I was stamped. Some coiner with his tools
> Made me a counterfeit . . .
> (*Cymbeline*, in *Shakespeare: The Complete Works*, II.v.2–6)

10. For contemporary critical analysis of Savage's relationship with his mother, see Nussbaum, "'Savage' Mothers"; and Bowers, "Critical Complicities." Nussbaum argues that Savage and Johnson succeed in presenting Mrs. Brett as "a bizarre instance of the Other, the marginal human, a monstrosity" (174), and Bowers analyzes Savage's and Johnson's suggestive linkage of virtuous motherhood and financial largesse. See also Holmes, *Dr. Johnson and Mr. Savage*, particularly 53–82.
11. MacLean, *The Name of the Mother*, 62
12. Translated by and quoted in ibid., 159.
13. Douglas, *Uneasy Sensations*, 91.
14. Collins, "The Hidden Bastard."
15. As Novak observes, commenting on Peregrine's cruel practical jokes, "Peregrine is probably a 'hero' admired only by Smollett" (*Eighteenth-Century English Literature*, 134). For a related discussion of Peregrine's pranks, see Beasley, "Smollett's Art," 160.
16. Douglas, *Uneasy Sensations*, 94.
17. Ibid., 78.
18. See Findlay, 238–48.

19. For a related discussion, see Schmidgen, "Illegitimacy and Social Observation," 147–48. Speaking of Smollett's Ferdinand Count Fathom, Schmidgen points out that his "rapid accommodation to new surroundings and situations belongs to the cultural repertoire by which bastards were constructed in the eighteenth-century" (147). Schmidgen also analyzes Chesterfield's letter to his illegitimate son, in which the father seems to advise the young man to cultivate his "chameleonic gifts." Tom Jones, in Schmidgen's analysis, demonstrates a milder version of such "gifts," by being "remarkably willing to be guided by circumstances" and possessing a "dramatic responsiveness to his immediate surroundings" (148).

20. Rawson, *Henry Fielding and the Augustan Ideal under Stress*, 7. See also Campbell, "'The Exact Picture of his Mother,'" for a discussion of Joseph Andrews's status as a foundling.

21. Richardson, of course, agreed eagerly that it was "truly coarse"; quoted in Paulson and Lockwood, *Henry Fielding*, 172.

22. This particular response belonged to an anonymous critic writing under the pen name of "Aretine" (quoted in ibid., 68). It is remarkable how consistently those disliking *Tom Jones* focused on its treatment of illegitimacy. "What Reason," Richardson fumed famously, "has [Fielding] to make his Tom illegitimate, in an Age where Keeping is become a fashion?" (quoted in ibid., 174). The anonymous author of *An Examen of the History of Tom Jones* wrote that he could not believe that Allworthy did not have "the Prudence to instill into his vicious Foster-Son a Remembrance of his disadvantageous Birth" (quoted in ibid., 190).

23. Ibid., 173. For a recent analysis of Astraea and Minerva's exchange with Richardson concerning Fielding, see Michie, *Richardson and Fielding*, 43–44 and 81–82.

24. For a discussion of the conventions of the "foundling" motif in *Tom Jones*, see J. Paul Hunter, *Before Novels*, and Damrosh, Jr., *God's Plots and Man's Stories*. For a discussion of Fielding's parodying the conventions of the classical foundling narrative, see the argument advanced by James Thompson, who observes that the scene in which Allworthy recognizes his bank bills "is one in a long series of recognitions, of Mrs. Waters, Partridge, Tom's ancestry, his essential goodness, each in its own way, a classic anagnorisis" (*Models of Virtue*, 133).

25. Compare it to Zimmerman's observation that Tom Jones abounds in "plausible but false narratives" (*The Boundaries of Fiction*, 142).

26. Shakespeare, *The Life and Death of King John*, in *Shakespeare: The Complete Works*, I,1.85.

27. Lennard Davis sees its intersection of "news"—the reportage of the ongoing Jacobite uprising—with the action of the novel proper as indicative of Fielding's commitment to journalism and symptomatic of his larger project of evolving a new "factual" style of writing fiction (*Factual Fictions*, 204). Homer Obed Brown offers an interpretation of the same episode based on the structural similarities between the politics of succession that prompted the uprising and the genealogical instability shaping the history of Allworthy's family ("*Tom Jones*," 211). These arguments participate in the discussion of the social and economic referentiality of Fielding's fiction started by Ian Watt in his 1957 *The Rise of the Novel* and continued by such scholars as Paulson in 1967 (*Satire and the Novel in*

Notes

Eighteenth-Century England); Alter in 1968 (*Fielding and the Nature of the Novel*); and Andrew Wright in 1975 (*Henry Fielding: Mask and Feast*).

28. Compare to Braudy's discussion of Fielding's depiction "of situations in which human sympathy is thwarted by the stereotyped ideas of character—Tom's bastardy, for instance" (*Narrative Form in History and Fiction*, 171).

29. Compare to Hunter's observation that "Tom is not a military hero, a great warrior who can save the nation singlehandedly at a moment of crisis" ("Fielding and the Disappearance of Heroes," 139).

30. Compare to Richetti's argument that the presence of history in *Tom Jones* should be read as an indication of an *absence*—a sign of what this novel is *not* about. As he points out, Tom's "personal preoccupations (his pursuit of Sophia) prevent him from participating in the historic battle of Culloden and the defeat of Prince Charles." The main characters are thus "abstracted from such areas of historical and potentially troublesome experience to be more or less appropriated by comic pattern and plot. The sociohistorical is a backdrop from whose involvements characters are snatched by the benevolent hand of a narrative system with its own aesthetic and didactic purposes" (*The English Novel in History*, 170).

31. Parker, *The Author's Inheritance*, 78.

32. We know that Ralph Allen, on whom Allworthy was presumably modeled, actively contributed to several charitable foundations, including the London Foundling Hospital. See Martin Battestin's notes to the Battestin/Bowers edition of *Tom Jones*.

33. McClure, *Coram's Children*, 55.

34. See, for example, Fielding's praise of the Foundling Hospital in *The Champion* 21 (February 1739/40).

35. Note that whether intentionally or not, Bennett echoes Thomas Coram's old complaint about the abandoned infants thrown on the "dust heaps" of London.

Notes to Chapter 5

1. Quoted in Nichols and Wray, 255.
2. Quoted in ibid., 255.
3. Quoted in Paulson, *Hogarth: His Life, Art, and Times*, 2:93.
4. Brownlow, *The History and Design*, 61.
5. See Nichols and Wray, 16.
6. See McClure, *Coram's Children*, 21, 44–46.
7. Coram wrote that "Noblemen and Gentlemen highly approving the said Ladys Charitable inclinations [had] by another Instrument in Writing Declared their hearty Concurrence" (quoted in Nichols and Wray, 16).
8. Quoted in ibid., 20; emphasis added.
9. Fielding, *The Covent Garden Journal*. Quoted in Andrew, *Philanthropy and Police*, 57.
10. Linda Colley points out that before the introduction of a census in 1800, it was widely believed that "Britain's population was in decline" (*Britons: Forging*

NOTES

the Nation 1707–1837, 240). See also Andrew, 55; Solkin, 158; and Ramsey, "'A mad intemperance . . . of building,'" 211–16, for an analysis of the fears of depopulation as one of the leading factors in the public support for the Foundling Hospital. Compare to Lieutenant Lismahago's characterization of Scotland as a "nation, whose people had been for many years decreasing in number, and whose lands and manufactures were actually suffering for want of hands" (Smollett, *The Expedition of Humphry Clinker*, 256–57).

11. Solkin 2, 179, 19.
12. For an important analysis of the hospital's location and outlook, see Ramsey, 225–34.
13. Brownlow, 60.
14. Solkin, 159–60.
15. Foucault, *Madness and Civilization*, 251.
16. Quoted in McClure, "Johnson's Criticism of the Foundling Hospital and Its Consequences," 105, 17–26.
17. See McClure, *Coram's Children*, 72.
18. For Dr. Johnson's rather idiosyncratic critique of the hospital and the governors' subsequent reaction to it, see McClure's "Johnson's Criticism."
19. Brownlow, 136.
20. Adair, 213. See also Adair, 204, and Fildes, 147–49, for the figures comparing the number of foundlings to the number of illegitimate children in London.
21. Brownlow, 60.
22. Ibid., 28.
23. Ramsey, "A Mad Intemperance," 230.
24. Quoted in McClure, 232.
25. Ibid., 233.
26. Solkin, 159.
27. Quoted in Nichols and Wray, 21.
28. Clark, xxii–xxiii.
29. Ibid.
30. Ibid.
31. Ibid.
32. Coram became estranged from the Foundling Hospital in the early 1740s. As McClure observes, "from May 1742 to the end of his life, Coram had little official contact with the Founding Hospital" (*Coram's Children*, 55).
33. McClure, *Coram's Children*, 46.
34. Ibid.
35. Bray, *A Memorial Concerning the Erecting in the City of London or the Suburbs thereof of an Orphanotrophy or Hospital for the Reception of Poor Cast Off Children or Foundlings*, 28.
36. McClure, *Coram's Children*, 46.
37. Andrew, *Philanthropy and Police*, 62.
38. Ibid., 63.
39. Ibid., 88.
40. Ibid., 64.
41. For the full list, see Brownlow, 141–44. Note that the list is prefaced by the

Notes

name of one perfunctory "patron" who happens to be a female—"Her Most Gracious Majesty Queen Victoria."

42. Andrew, *Philanthropy and Police,* 64.

43. Burney, *Evelina, or The History of a Young Lady's Entrance into the World,* 136.

44. Nussbaum, 165. As Nancy Armstrong points out, by contrast with the "old agrarian" days when a private "household [had been] a largely self-contained social unit," the whole colonial/imperialist project of England was now perceived as hinging upon the stability of each individual family, a perception duly reflected, as Armstrong points out, in the increasing popularity of the conduct books legitimizing the "new domestic economy" grounded in "interest-bearing investments" (*Desire and Domestic Fiction,* 75).

45. Perry, "Colonizing the Breast: Sexuality and Maternity in Eighteenth-Century England," 209.

46. Staves, *Married Women's Separate Property,* 223.

47. Goodman, "Public Sphere and Private Life," 15. For a useful critical reassessment of the notion of a separate private sphere for the eighteenth-century woman, see also McDowell, 8. Elizabeth J. MacArthur complicates the division between the private (female) and public (male) spheres by proposing the notion of the "embodied" public sphere. She argues that men and women become "public-sphere subjects through a process of assuming their corporality, especially their sexuality" ("Embodying the Public Sphere: Censorship and the Reading Subject in Beaumarchais's *Mariage de Figaro,*" 68).

48. Defoe, *The Fortunes and Misfortunes of the Famous Moll Flanders,* 7.

49. For a related discussion, see Rachel G. Fuchs's analysis of the encouragement of "domestic motherhood" for "poverty-stricken married mothers," who might be tempted to abandon their babies (160).

50. In addition, Smollett could be using this example to imply that Lady V. is truly if unostentatiously religious. Fuchs observes that all eighteenth-century European religions "advocated private, voluntary charity to the deserving poor among their co-religionists, and strongly urged individualized personal contact between charitable donors and recipients" (165).

51. Richardson, *The History of Sir Charles Grandison,* 3:358. Subsequent references to *Grandison,* unless otherwise noted, are from this edition and are noted in parentheses.

52. See Jackson, *New-Born Child Murder,* 34, 142–43; Hoffer and Hull, 68–69; and Rabin, 77.

53. On the whole, infanticide was associated in the eighteenth century with unmarried women (Rabin, 76) "drawn from the lower classes" (Dickinson and Sharpe, 49).

54. Montagu, 421.

55. Chaber, "'This Affecting Subject': An 'Interested' Reading of Childbearing in Two Novels by Samuel Richardson," 234.

56. See Jackson, *New-Born Child Murder,* 42, 77; Hoffer and Hull, 23–25, 127–28, 166–68.

57. See Jackson, *New-Born Child Murder,* 48.

58. At one point, Harriet explicitly laments Sir Thomas's insistence on keeping Sir Charles abroad because it has brought him together with Clementina.

59. Adair, 116. See also Laslett, *Family Life and Illicit Love in Earlier Generations*. For a further discussion, see Bonfield, "'Affective Families,' 'Open Elites' and Strict Family Settlements in Early Modern England."

60. On the evolution of the British strict settlement, see Habakkuk, 1–76.

61. Explaining to Lord L. why he cannot provide a proper dowry for his daughter Caroline, Sir Thomas mentions that he holds his Irish "estate in fee" (1:329). The ostensible purpose of this remark is to introduce the dutiful letter written to Sir Thomas by his son; its real purpose, as I argue, is to illustrate the precariousness of Sir Charles's and his sisters' financial situation.

62. Under the conditions of the strict settlement, the older son should be consulted about all actions concerning the estate. This rule does not apply if the estate is held in fee simple.

63. Habakkuk, 374.

64. Historians connect the widespread adaptation of the strict settlement with royalist families' attempts to prevent confiscation and selling of their estates under the Commonwealth. As Habakkuk points out, if "the royalist was a tenant for life, only his life interest was for sale—an interest not very attractive to purchasers in general, and therefore easily bought in cheaply by some member of the royalist family. But if the royalist were tenant in tail—an interest which could easily be enlarged—the confiscated estate when put up for sale could well pass by purchase into the hands of a stranger" (11).

65. Based on a manuscript that records Richardson's "private thoughts concerning the marriage settlement to be made for his oldest daughter and a Bath surgeon," Staves infers that he was quite well informed about the legal repercussions of the various settlement arrangements (60).

66. McClure, *Coram's Children*, 10. See also Habakkuk, 214.

67. Charming as Richardson made his Charlotte, her views differ from his on many occasions. For example, it is unlikely that he, a successful printer coming up in the world, approved of her repeated snubbing of "cits" (2:322; 3:267)—the well-to-do representatives of London City.

68. Beasley, "Richardson's Girls: The Daughters of Patriarchy in *Pamela, Clarissa*, and *Sir Charles Grandison*," 45.

69. Ibid., 37.

70. Brownlow, 28.

71. Richardson here foreshadows the argument that Rousseau would make in his 1762 *Emile*, namely that woman's "dignity depends on remaining unknown; her glory lies in her husband's esteem, her greatest pleasure in the happiness of her family" (quoted in Colley, 240).

72. Fielding, *The Covent Garden Journal*, vol. 1. Quoted in Andrew, 57.

Notes to Chapter 6

1. Dr. Johnson claimed in the 15 April–15 May 1757 issue of the *Literary Magazine* that when he "wandered through the Hospital, [he] found not a child that seemed to have heard of his creed, or the commandments"—an accusation that prompted the governors of the Hospital to threaten the *Literary Magazine* with a

Notes

libel lawsuit. For the full story of Dr. Johnson's rather heavy-handed critique of the hospital, see McClure, "Johnson's Criticism of the Foundling Hospital and Its Consequences."

2. This is Philip Jennings of Coley, not his father, Peter Jennings of Stratfield Saye.

3. See Clark, xxiii.

4. See the previous chapter for a discussion of Juliana Dodd's role in the 1759 scheme to pay the nurses an extra three pence a week to enable them to buy the children's clothing themselves instead of receiving it from the Hospital.

5. Burney, *Memoirs of Doctor Burney, arranged from his own Manuscripts, from Family Papers, and from Personal Recollections, by his daughter, Madame d'Arblay*, 1:233. All subsequent quotations from the novel refer to this edition and are marked parenthetically in the text.

6. Burney, *Evelina*, 35, 289. All subsequent quotations from the novel refer to this edition and are marked parenthetically in the text.

7. See Doody, *Frances Burney: The Life in the Works;* Cutting-Gray, *Woman as "Nobody" in the Novels of Fanny Burney*, 109–130; Straub, *Divided Fictions: Fanny Burney and Feminine Strategy*, 160–61; Gallagher, *Nobody's Story: The Vanishing Acts of Women Writers in the Marketplace, 1670–1820*, 203–256; and Greenfield, 40–41.

8. Doody, *Frances Burney*, 41.

9. Gallagher, 214.

10. Greenfield, 46.

11. Fizer, "The Name of the Daughter: Identity and Incest in *Evelina*," 79.

12. Ibid. See also Schmidgen's consistent reference to Evelina as a "bastard" (151–56).

13. See, for example, the story of a spectacular infant swapping in Bennett's *The Beggar Girl and Her Benefactors*—right down to the copying of the tattoo on the heiress's side that was supposed to establish her identity beyond doubts. Such tales responded, among other things, to the fear of well-to-do parents, who left their infants with wet nurses immediately after birth, that by sucking their nurses' milk, the children would also imbibe these women's hidden vices and thus undergo subtle personality changes.

14. Gallagher, 233.

15. As Patricia Meyer Spacks observes about Evelina's attempt to "understand her own [story, a] depressed sense of possibility governs [her. She] interprets on the basis of fear rather than desire" (*Desire and Truth: Functions of Plot in Eighteenth-Century English Novels*, 161.

16. Habakkuk, 154.

17. Ibid., 115.

18. For a related discussion, see Greenfield, 42.

19. When I use the term *unquestionably*, I do it to contrast such heroines with Defoe's Moll Flanders—a quasi-bastard/quasi-foundling, whose bastardy is never stated unequivocally. Fielding's Nancy Miller could be considered another example of a quasi-bastard because one has to read between the lines to realize that Nancy was born prior to her parents' marriage.

20. Warner, *Licensing Entertainment*, 115.

21. Ibid., 115.

22. Horace Walpole; quoted in Habakkuk, 154.

23. *Critical Review* 46 (September 1778): 202–4. Quoted in Susan Kubika Howard. All subsequent references to *Critical Review* come from this edition.

24. Freeman, 203. Interestingly, as Geyer-Kordesch has demonstrated, the class-related modification of a fictional story of seduction, illegitimacy, and infanticide can also move in a different direction. Goethe's adaptation in his *Faust* of a ballad called "The Three Riders," featuring the abduction and rape of an innkeeper's daughter, results in the loss of the original ballad's "warning on rape and lack of protection for women in public places.... The cautionary power of the ballad is recast in a sugary sentiment of middle-class distancing as 'folklore'" (111).

25. *Critical Review*, 561.

26. Note that an alternative reading could be suggested by Greenfield's discussion of the complicated relationship between Evelina and her guardian, who, as Greenfield argues, is "deeply attached" to her and may thus "harbor sexual feelings" for her (42–43).

27. Quoted in James L. Clifford, "Introduction," in Smollett, *The Adventures of Peregrine Pickle, in which are included Memoirs of a Lady of Quality*, xvii.

28. Quoted in Clifford, xvii.

29. As Fizer observes, "when Evelina is acknowledged as Belmont's true daughter, her own criminality shifts to Polly Green" (88).

30. As Evelina tells Mr. Villars, at the time that Dame Green came up with her scheme, "her husband was dead, and she had little regard for any body but her child" (375).

31. Burney's interest in what Barbara Darby sees as the "plot of usurpation and constitution" (*Frances Burney Dramatist: Gender, Performance, and the Late-Eighteenth-Century Stage*, 146–47) is not limited to *Evelina*. Darby notes that it is also present in *The Woman-Hater* (1801), about which Doody observes, "[it] is as if Burney rewrote Evelina from the view of 'the little usurper,' 'poor Polly Green'" (*Frances Burney: The Life in the Works*, 308).

32. Doody, *Beyond Evelina*, 483.

33. Ibid.

34. Martha Brown, 395–96.

35. Doody, *The True Story*, 298.

36. Martha Brown, 30.

37. For a different reading see James Thompson's *Models of Virtue*, 153.

38. Doody, *Frances Burney*, 62.

39. For a further analysis of Evelina's "fear of abandonment" and "exposure," see Ruth Bernard Yeazell, *Fictions of Modesty: Women and Courtship in the English Novel*, 134–35.

40. Quoted in McClure, *Coram's Children*, 11.

Notes to Chapter 7

1. Rachel Ramsey, personal communication. I am indebted to Ramsey for her observation that Brunswick square would be associated in Austen's readers' mind with the London Foundling Hospital.

Notes

2. My discussion here grows out of the established critical tradition of speaking about *Emma* as a chronicle of Emma's education. See, for example, Belsey, *Critical Practice*, 79; Booth, *The Rhetoric of Fiction*, 265; Neill, *The Politics of Jane Austen*, chap. 6.

3. See Greenfield for a discussion of *Emma*'s "unique capacity to render Emma's thoughts and their inaccuracy simultaneously" (150).

4. As Claudia L. Johnson points out, in Highbury, "the orphaned offspring . . . appear to comprise a rather large proportion of the community" (*Jane Austen: Women, Politics, and the Novel*, 134). Similarly, Greenfield comments on the "abundance of . . . motherless children in the novel" (153).

5. For different critical readings of Harriet's relationship with Emma, for instance, on Emma's possibly lesbian attraction to Harriet, see Mudrick, *Jane Austen: Irony as Defense and Discovery*, 192, and Wilson, "A Long Talk about Jane Austen," 69. See also Johnson (*Jane Austen*, 123) for a response to Mudrick's and Wilson's interpretation. On Emma's Pygmalion-like "shaping" of Harriet, see Sabor, "'Staring in Astonishment': Portraits and Prints in Persuasion"; Dwyer, *Jane Austen*, 97; Harris, *Jane Austen's Art of Memory*, 170; and Neill, 24. On Austen's hostility toward "female ties outside the family," as exemplified by Emma's relationship with Harriet, see Todd, *Feminist Literary History*, 101. Finally, see Greenfield for an interpretation of "Emma's apparently inappropriate attachment to Harriet Smith" in terms of Emma's desire to compensate "for the marriage and thus loss of Miss Taylor" (150).

6. Seber, *General Consent in Jane Austen*, 38–39. James Thompson, however, aligns Harriet with another Burney character, Henrietta Belfield from *Cecilia* (*Between Self and World: The Novels of Jane Austen*, 167). On a tale of "a deserted orphan" published in the *Lady's Magazine* in November 1802 as an important source of Emma's fantasy of Harriet as a gentleman's daughter, see Copeland, "Money," 142–43.

7. Johnson, *Jane Austen*, 91. See also Seber on the parody of the traditional foundling narrative in Austen's *Love and Friendship* (39).

8. Siskin, *The Work of Writing: Literature and Social Change in Britain, 1700–1830*, 201. Also, see Greenfield for an alternative argument that in *Emma*, "Austen seems less fearful of formulaic implications . . . maybe because she is more confident of her own originality" (145).

9. Warner, *Licensing Entertainment*, 115.

10. Johnson, *Jane Austen*, 57.

11. Ibid., 58.

12. Laslett, "The bastardy-prone sub-society," 221.

13. For Booth's analysis of the double perspective of the heroine provided by the simultaneous inside and outside view, see *The Rhetoric of Fiction*, 243–70.

14. Greenfield, 151.

15. Interestingly, Mudrick has characterized Emma's attempt to "talk away . . . Harriet's parentless illegitimacy" as "nonsense" (190).

16. For a seminal analysis of Austen's indebtedness to the novels of contemporary women writers, see Doody, "Jane Austen's Reading." For a recent elaboration of Doody's argument, see Udden, "Veils of Irony: The Development of Narrative Technique in Women's Novels of the 1790s," 160–77.

17. Greenfield, 162.

18. But see Johnson for a suggestive complication of our ready tendency to critique Emma's habit of romanticizing her reality (*Jane Austen*, 134–36)

19. As Ramsey observes, by the late eighteenth century, "as the city continued to spread, the Governors [of the Hospital] found themselves in possession of some of London's most valuable development property" (233). For more information about Brunswick Square as a part of the developed foundling hospital's estate, see Nichols and Wray, 279–84.

20. Bray, 1.

21. Butler, *Maria Edgeworth: A Literary Biography*, 39, n. 2.

22. For an important analysis of the colonial overtones of Clarence Hervey's treatment of Rachel/Virginia, see Greenfield 119–21.

23. Kowaleski-Wallace, *Hannah More, Maria Edgeworth, and Patriarchal Complicity*, 100.

24. The theme of Emma's "education" of Harriet mirrors in suggestive ways the theme of Emma's own education and particularly her relationship with her multiple guardians—from Ms. Taylor to Mr. Knightley. See, for example, Margaret Kirkham's discussion of Emma's upbringing by her "hero-guardian" (*Jane Austen: Feminism and Fiction*, 138).

25. Though we can also read it, of course, as Neill does, as "a joke at Emma's expense" (108).

26. McKeon, 158.

27. Interestingly, the year 1875 is considered "the turning point" in the overall history of European illegitimacy. After that, the rates of illegitimacy began to decline. For a discussion, see Ehmer, 320.

28. As James Thompson points out in a different context, "inheritance, as the crux of courtship plots is gradually repressed (it lies at the center of *Clarissa* and *Tom Jones*, but already by *Pride and Prejudice* and *Emma* it has been pushed to the margins) because it is the site of contradiction and confusion" (*Models of Virtue*, 153).

29. For an argument about the "strong" linkage between "the economic success of children" and "inheritance patterns" in early modern Europe, see Bonfield, "Developments in European Family Law," 114.

30. Quoted in McClure, *Coram's Children*, 11.

31. We never hear of such siblings, but there is no reason to think that they don't exist. Of course, Harriet's anonymous father still is known to help her out financially, but his help is clearly considered a supplemental source of Harriet's income, since the primary source is provided by her husband's industry.

32. As Robert has demonstrated, the psychosocial opposition between the archetypes of "bastard" and "foundling" has continued to animate nineteenth- and twentieth-century literature. For an analysis of Sartre's self-characterization as "bastard" and "Nobody's son," see also Maclean, 157–63.

33. For a discussion of Esther's illegitimacy, see Schor, *Dickens and the Daughter of the House*, 101–123.

Notes

Notes to Postscript

1. See Levine and Wrightson, "The Social Context of Illegitimacy in Early Modern England," 161.
2. After watching the movie, students in my eighteenth-century course (Spring 2001, University of Kentucky) unanimously agreed that Fielding's novel must have caused a scandal upon its first publication because of its sexual explicitness.
3. Homer Brown, 211.

Bibliography

Primary Sources

Addison, Joseph. *The Guardian*, No. 105, July 11, 1713.

Anonymous. *Fatherless Fanny, or A Young Lady's first Entrance into Life, being the Memoirs of a Little Mendicant and her Benefactors*. London: G. Virtue, 26 Ivy Lane, and Bathe Street, Bristol, 1811.

Anonymous. *Joyful News to Batchelors and Maids: Being a Song, in Praise of the Fondling Hospital, and the London Hospital in Aldersgate-Street*. London, 1760.

Anonymous. *The Life of Mr. Richard Savage* (1727). Edited with introduction by Timothy Erwin. Los Angeles: William Andrews Clark Memorial Library, 1988.

Anonymous. *Some Objections to the Foundling Hospital Considered by a Person in the Country to Whom They Were Sent*. London: T. Pasham, 1761.

Austen, Jane. *Emma* (1816). New York: Bantam Books, 1981.

———. *Sense and Sensibility* (1811). Edited by James Kinsley. Oxford: Oxford University Press, 1990.

Bage, Robert. *Hermsprong; or, Man As He Is Not* (1796). Edited by Stuart Tave. University Park: Pennsylvania State University Press, 1982.

Barbauld, Anna Laetitia. "Life of Samuel Richardson." In *Correspondence of Samuel Richardson, Author of* Pamela, Clarissa, *and* Sir Charles Grandison, *Selected from the original manuscripts, bequeathed by him to his family, to which are prefixed, a biographical account of that author, and observations on his writings* (1804). New York: AMS Press, 1966. 6 volumes.

Bennett, Agnes Maria. *The Beggar Girl and Her Benefactors*, 3d ed. 5 vols. London: Printed at the Minerva-Press, for A. K. Newman and Co, Leadenhall-Street, 1813.

Blackstone, William. *Commentaries on the Laws of England, in four books*. London: Printed by A. Strahan and W. Woodfall for T. Cadell, 1793–95.

Boswell, James. *Boswell's Life of Johnson* (1791). Edited by George Birkbeck Hill, D.C.L., revised and enlarged edition by L. F. Powell. 6 vols. London: Oxford Clarendon Press, 1971.

Bray, Thomas. *A Memorial Concerning the Erecting in the City of London or the Suburbs thereof of an Orphanotrophy or Hospital for the Reception of Poor Cast Off Children or Foundlings*. London, 1728.

Brome, Richard. *A Jovial Crew* (1641). Edited by Ann Haaker. Lincoln: University of Nebraska Press, 1968.

Bibliography

Brownlow, John. *The History and Design of the Foundling Hospital with a Memoir of the Founder.* London: Printed by W. & H. S. Warr, 63, High Holborn, 1858.

Burn, Richard. *Ecclesiastical Law*, 5th ed. London, 1763.

Burney, Frances. *The Diary and Letters of Frances Burney, Madame d'Arblay.* Edited by Sarah Chauncey Woolsey. Boston: Robert Brothers, 1880.

———. *Evelina, or a Young Lady's Entrance into the World. In a Series of Letters.* Edited by Susan Kubika Howard. Broadview, 2000.

———. *Memoirs of Doctor Burney, arranged from his own Manuscripts, from Family Papers, and from Personal Recollections, by his daughter, Madame d'Arblay.* London: Edward Moxon, 1832.

Cadogan, William. *An Essay upon Nursing, and the Management of Children, from Their Birth to Three Years of Age.* London, 1748.

Cibber, Colley. *Love's Last Shift.* In *Restoration Drama: An Anthology*, edited by David Womersley, 553–93. Oxford: Blackwell Publishers, 2000.

Colman, George. *The English Merchant, A Comedy as it is Acted at the Theatre-Royal in Drury-Lane*, 2d ed. London: Printed for T. Becket and P. A. De Hondt, near Surry-Street, in the Strand; and by R. Baldwin, in Pater-noster-Row, 1767.

Defoe, Daniel. *Augusta Triumphans, or, The Way to Make London the Most Flourishing City in the Universe First, by Establishing an University . . . Concluding with an Effectual Method to Prevent Street Robberies, and a Letter to Coll. Robinson on Account of the Orphan's Tax.* London: Printed for J. Roberts and sold by E. Nutt, A. Dodd, N. Blandford, and J. Stagg, 1728.

———. *The Fortunes and Misfortunes of the Famous Moll Flanders* (1722). Edited by Pat Rogers. London: Everyman, 1993.

———. *The Generous Protector, or a Friendly Proposal to Prevent Murder and Other Enormous Abuses, By Erecting an Hospital for Foundlings and Bastard-Children.* London: Printed for A. Dodd without Temple-bar, 1731.

———. *The History and Remarkable Life of the Truly Honorable Col. Jacque, Commonly Call'd Col. Jack, Who Was Born a Gentleman, put 'Prentice to a Pick-Pocket, was Six and Twenty Years a Thief, and then Kidnapp'd to Virginia. Came back a Merchant, married four Wives, and five of them prov'd Whores; went into the Wars, behav'd bravely, got Preferment, was made Colonel of a Regiment, came over, and fled with the Chevalier, and is now abroad compleating a Life of Wonders, and resolves to dye a General* (1722). Edited by Samuel Holt Monk. London: Oxford University Press, 1965.

———. *Roxana, or The Fortunate Mistress* (1724). Edited by Robert Clark. London: Everyman, 1998.

———. *Street-robberies, Consider'd: The reason of Their Being so Frequent, with Probable Means to Prevent 'em. To Which is Added, Three Short Treatises; I. A Warning for Travellers . . . II. Observations on House-Breakers . . . III. A Caveat for Shop-Keepers. . . .* London, 1728.

Dennis, John. "Remarks on *The Conscious Lovers*" (1723). In *Restoration and Eighteenth-Century Comedy*, edited by Scott McMillin, 529–34. New York: Norton, 1997.

Dryden, John. *Amphitryon; or the Two Sosias* (1790). In *The Broadview Anthology of Restoration and Eighteenth-Century Drama*, edited by Robert Markley and Jeannie Dalporto, 1735–81. Orchard Park, NY: Broadview Press, 2001.

BIBLIOGRAPHY

———. *An Evening's Love or the Mock-Astrologer* (1668), in *John Dryden: Four Comedies*, edited by L. A. Beaurline and Fredson Bowers, 179–276. Chicago: University of Chicago Press, 1967.

Edgeworth, Maria. *Belinda* (1804). Edited by Kathryn J. Kirkpatrick. Oxford: Oxford University Press, 1994.

Farquhar, George. *The Recruiting Officer* (1707). In *Restoration Drama: An Anthology*, edited by David Womersley, 735–76. Oxford: Blackwell, 2000.

Fielding, Henry. *The Author's Farce* (1730). Edited by Charles R. Wood. Lincoln: University of Nebraska Press, 1966.

———. *The Covent Garden Journal*. London: J. J. Stockdale: 1810. Volume 1.

———. *The History of Tom Jones A Foundling* (1749). Edited by Fredson Bowers, with an introduction and commentary by Martin C. Battestin. 2 vols. Middletown, CT: Wesleyan University Press, 1975.

———. *The Jacobite's Journal and Related Writings*. Edited by W. B. Coley. Middletown, CT: Wesleyan University Press, 1975.

———. *Joseph Andrews* (1742); *Shamela* (1744). Boston: Houghton Mifflin Company, 1961.

———. *The Life of Mr. Jonathan Wild The Great* (1743). New York: The New American Academic Library, 1962.

———. *Tom Jones* (1749). Edited by John Bender and Simon Stern. Oxford: Oxford University Press, 1996.

———. *Tom Jones*. A and E Home Video. British Broadcasting Corporation, 1998.

Fielding, Sarah. *The History of the Countess of Dellwyn*. In Two Volumes. London: Printed for A. Millar, 1759.

Hays, Mary. *Memoirs of Emma Courtney* (1796). Edited by Eleanor Ty. New York: Oxford University Press, 2001.

———. *The Victim of Prejudice* (1799). Edited by Eleanor Ty. Orchard Park, NY: Broadview Press, 1998.

Haywood, Eliza. *The Fortunate Foundlings: Being the Genuine History of Colonel M—rs, and his Sister, Madam du P—y, the Issue of the Hon. Ch—es M—rs, Son of the late Duke of R—l—d*. London: Printed and Published by T. Gardner at Cowley Head, opposite St. Clement's Church in the Strand, M, DCC, XLIV.

———. *The History of Miss Betsy Thoughtless* (1751). New York: Pandora Press, 1986.

Heliodorus. *An Ethiopian Romance*. Translated with an introduction by Moses Hadas. Philadelphia: University of Pennsylvania Press, 1957.

Holcroft, Thomas. *The Deserted Daughter: A comedy. As it is acted at the Theatre Royal, Covent-Garden*. London: Printed for G. G. and J. Robinson, 1795.

———. *The Adventures of Hugh Trevor* (1794–97). Edited by Seamus Deane. London: Oxford University Press, 1973.

———. *The Road to Ruin* (1792). Edited by Ruth I. Aldrich. Lincoln: University of Nebraska Press, 1968.

Johnson, Samuel. A Dictionary of the English Language (1755). London: Times Books, 1983.

———. *Life of Savage* (1738). Edited by Clarence Tracy. Oxford: Clarendon Press, 1972.

Lennox, Charlotte. *The Female Quixote or the Adventures of Arabella* (1752). Edited by Margaret Dalziel. London: Oxford University Press, 1970.

Bibliography

Maclauchlan, Daniel. *An Essay upon improving and adding to the strength of Great Britain and Ireland by fornication, justifying the same from scripture and reason. By a young clergyman.* Dublin, 1735.

Malthus, Thomas R. *An Essay on the Principle of Population* (1798). London: Penguin, 1970.

Mandeville, Bernard. *The Fable of the Bees: or, Private Vices, Public Benefits* (1728). Edited by Douglas Garman. London: Wishart & Company, 1934.

Montagu, Lady Mary Wortley. *Selected Letters.* Edited by Isobel Grundy. New York: Penguin Books, 1997.

Moore, Edward. *The Foundling, A Comedy, and The Gamester, a Tragedy* (1740). Edited by Anthony Amberg. Newark: University of Delaware Press, 1996.

Opie, Amelia. *Adeline Mowbray* (1802). London, Boston, and Henley: Pandora Press, 1986.

The Order of Keeping a Court Leet and Court Baron. London, 1650.

Pelaguius, Porcupinus. *The Scandalizade, A Panegyri-Satiri-Comic-Dramatic Poem.* London, 1750.

Petty, William. *An Essay Concerning the Multiplication of Mankind: Together with Another Essay in Political Arithmetick, Concerning the Growth of the City of London: With the Measures, Periods, Causes, and Consequences Thereof...* London: Printed for Mark Pardoe, at the Black Raven over against Bedford-house in the Strand, 1686.

———. *Two Essays in Political Arithmetick, Concerning the People, Housing, Hospitals, &c. of London and Paris.* London: Printed for Henry Mortlocke, at the Phonix in St. Paul's Church-Yard, and J. Lloyd, in the Middle Exchange next Salisbury-House in the Strand, 1687.

Pickering, Danby. *Statutes at Large*, vol. 7. Cambridge, 1763.

Pope, Alexander. *The Dunciad* (1728–43). In *Poetry and Prose of Alexander Pope*, edited by Aubrey Williams, 280–378. Boston: Houghton Mifflin Company, 1969.

The Proceedings at the Sessions for London and Middlesex, Holden at the Old Bailey, Beginning on Wednesday, the Sixteenth of July, 1679.

Ramsay, Allan. *An address of thanks from the Society of Rakes, to the pious author of "An essay upon improving and adding to the strength of Great Britain and Ireland by fornication." To which is added, an epistle to the said author, by . . .* Edinburgh: Printed and sold at Allan Ramsay's shop, 1735.

Richardson, Samuel. *Clarissa or The History of a Young Lady* (1747–48). Edited by Angus Ross. Viking, 1986.

———. *The History of Sir Charles Grandison* (1753–54). Edited by Jocelyn Harris. 3 vols. London: Oxford University Press, 1972.

———. *Selected Letters.* Edited by John Carroll. Oxford: Oxford University Press, 1964.

Robinson, Mary. *The Natural Daughter* (1799). In *A Letter to the Women of England and The Natural Daughter*, edited by Sharon M. Setzer. Toronto: Broadview Press, 2003, 89–296.

Ryan, William Burke. *Infanticide: Its Law, Prevalence, Prevention, and History.* London, 1862.

Savage, Richard. *An Author to Be Lett* (1729). Edited by James Sutherland. Los Angeles: William Andrews Clark Memorial Library, 1960.

BIBLIOGRAPHY

———. "The Bastard" (1728). In *The Poetical Works of Richard Savage*, edited by Clarence Tracy. Cambridge: Cambridge University Press, 1962, 87–92.

Shakespeare, William. *Shakespeare: The Complete Works*. Edited by G. B. Harrison. New York: Harcourt, Brace, 1968.

Shaw, Bernard. *Mrs. Warren's Profession* (1893). London: Taylor and Francis, 2002.

Shebbeare, John. *The Marriage Act* (1754). New York: Garland Publishing, 1974.

Smith, Charlotte. *Emmeline, The Orphan of the Castle* (1788). Edited by Anne Henry Ehrenpreis. London: Oxford University Press, 1971.

Smollett, Tobias. *The Adventures of Peregrine Pickle, in which are included Memoirs of a Lady of Quality* (1751). Edited by James L. Clifford. London: Oxford University Press, 1964.

———. *The Expedition of Humphry Clinker* (1771). Edited by O. M. Brack, Jr. Athens: University of Georgia Press, 1991.

Steele, Richard. *The Conscious Lovers* (1722). In *Restoration and Eighteenth-Century Comedy: Authoritative Texts of the Plays, Contexts, Criticism*, 2d ed, edited by Scott McMillin, 321–84. New York: London, 1997.

———. *The Lying Lover: or, The Ladies Friendship. A comedy* (1703). London: Printed for Henry Lintot, 1747.

———. *The Tender Husband: Or, The Accomplished Fools* (1705). In *Richard Steele*, edited by G. A. Aitken, 189–264. New York: Greenwood Press, 1968.

Sterne, Laurence. *The Life and Opinions of Tristram Shandy, Gentleman* (1759–1767). New York: Penguin, 1978.

Swift, Jonathan. *A Modest Proposal* (1729). In *The Norton Anthology of English Literature*, vol. 1, edited by M. H. Abrams, 2181–87. New York: W. W. Norton, 1993.

Swinburne, Henry. *A Briefe Treatise of Testaments and Last Willes*. London, 1728.

Terence, *The Comedies*. Trans. with an introduction by Betty Radice. New York: Penguin Books, 1993.

Terence's Comedies: Made English. With his life; and some remarks at the end. By several hands. London: Printed for A. Swall and T. Childe, at the Unicorn, at the west-end of St. Paul's Church-yard, 1694.

Terence's Comedies: Made English, by Mr. Laurence Echard, and others. Revised and corrected by Dr. Echard, and Sir R. L'Estrange, 6th ed.. London: Printed by S. Palmer, M.DCC.XXIV. Hall in Saxony: Printed by John Frider Krottendorff; and are to be sold by the same, 1726.

Von Kotzebue, August. *Lovers' Vows, A play, In five acts. Performing at the Theatre Royal, Covent-Garden. From the German of Kotzebue. By Mrs. Inchbald*. London: Printed for G. G. and J. Robinson [etc.], 1798.

———. *Lovers' Vows, or, the Child of Love. A Play, in Five Acts. Translated from the German of Augustus von Kotzebue: with a brief biography of the author, By Stephen Porter*. London: Printed for J. Parsons, 1798.

Webster, John. *The Devil's Law-Case* (1619). Edited by Frances A. Shirley. Lincoln: University of Nebraska Press, 1972.

Wycherley, William. *The Country Wife* (1675). In *Restoration Drama*, edited by David Womersley, 171–222. Oxford: Blackwell, 2000.

———. *The Plain Dealer* (1677). In *Restoration Drama*, edited by David Womersley, 223–86. Malden, MA: Blackwell, 2000.

Bibliography

Secondary Sources

Adair, Richard. *Courtship, Illegitimacy and Marriage in Early Modern England.* Manchester: Manchester University Press, 1996.

Albert, Theordore G. *1. The Law vs. Clarissa Harlowe. 2. Pastoral Argument of The Sound and the Fury. 3. Melville's Savages.* Dissertation, Rutgers University, 1976.

Alkon, Paul K. *Defoe and Fictional Time.* Athens: University of Georgia Press, 1979.

Alryyes, Ala A. *Original Subjects: The Child, the Novel, and the Nation.* Cambridge, MA: Harvard University Press, 2001.

Alter, Robert. *Fielding and the Nature of the Novel.* Cambridge, MA: Harvard University Press, 1968.

Amberg, Anthony. "Introduction." In Edward Moore, *The Foundling, A Comedy, and The Gamester, a Tragedy,* 45–134. Edited by Anthony Amberg. Newark: University of Delaware Press, 1996.

Amory, Hugh. "Law and the Structure of Fielding's Novels." Ph.D. diss., Columbia University, 1964.

Andrew, Donna T. *Philanthropy and Police: London Charity in the Eighteenth Century.* Princeton, NJ: Princeton University Press, 1990.

Armstrong, Nancy. *Desire and Domestic Fiction: A Political History of the Novel.* New York: Oxford University Press, 1987.

Aravamudan, Srinivas. *Tropicopolitans: Colonialism and Agency, 1688–1804.* Durham, NC: Duke University Press, 1999.

Backsheider, Paula. *Daniel Defoe: Ambition and Innovation.* Lexington: University Press of Kentucky, 1986.

———. *Daniel Defoe: His Life.* Baltimore: Johns Hopkins University Press, 1989.

Backus, Margot Gayle. *The Gothic Family Romance: Heterosexuality, Child Sacrifice, and the Anglo-Irish Colonial Order.* Durham, NC: Duke University Press, 1999.

Bakhtin, Mikhail. *The Dialogic Imagination.* Edited by Michael Holquist, translated by Caryl Emerson and Michael Holquist. Austin: University of Texas Press, 1981.

Barker-Benfield, G. J. *The Culture of Sensibility: Sex and Society in Eighteenth-Century Britain.* Chicago: University of Chicago Press, 1992.

Barrell, John. *The Political Theory of Painting from Reynolds to Hazlitt: "The Body of the Public."* New Haven, CT: Yale University Press, 1986.

Battestin, Martin C., with Ruthe R. Battestin. *Henry Fielding, a Life.* New York: Routledge, 1989.

Beasley, Jerry C. "Richardson's Girls: The Daughters of Patriarchy in *Pamela, Clarissa,* and *Sir Charles Grandison.*" In *New Essays on Samuel Richardson,* edited by Albert J. Rivero, 35–52. New York: St. Martin's Press, 1997.

———. "Smollett's Art: The Novel as 'Picture.'" In *The First English Novelists: Essays in Understanding,* edited by J. M. Armistead, 143–84. Knoxville: University of Tennessee Press, 1985.

———. *Tobias Smollett, Novelist.* Athens: University of Georgia Press, 1998.

Belsey, Catherine. *Critical Practice.* London: Methuen, 1983.

Bender, John. *Imagining the Penitentiary: Fiction and the Architecture of the Mind.* Chicago: University of Chicago Press, 1987.

BIBLIOGRAPHY

Benedict, Barbara M. *Curiosity: A Cultural History of Early Modern Inquiry.* Chicago: University of Chicago Press, 2001.

Bhattacharya, Nandini. *Reading the Splendid Body: Gender and Consumerism in Eighteenth-Century British Writing on India.* Newark: University of Delaware Press, 1998.

Binion, Rudolph. "'More Men Than Corn': Malthus versus the Enlightenment, 1798." *Eighteenth-Century Studies* 32, no. 4 (Summer 1999): 564–73.

Bonfield, Lloyd. "'Affective Families,' 'Open Elites' and Strict Family Settlements in Early Modern England." *Economic History Review* 49 (1986): 341–54.

———. "Developments in European Family Law." In *The History of European Family, Volume One, Family Life in Early Modern Times, 1500–1789,* edited by David I. Kertzer and Marzio Barbagli, 87–124. New Haven, CT: Yale University Press, 2001.

———. "European Family Law." In *The History of European Family, Volume Two, Family Life in the Long Nineteenth Century, 1789–1713,* edited by David I. Kertzer and Marzio Barbagli, 109–54. New Haven, CT: Yale University Press, 2001.

Booth, Wayne. *The Rhetoric of Fiction.* Chicago: University of Chicago Press, 1961.

Boswell, John. *The Kindness of Strangers: The Abandonment of Children in Western Europe from Late Antiquity to the Renaissance.* New York: Pantheon, 1988.

Bowers, Toni O'Shaughnessy. "Critical Complicities: *Savage* Mothers, Johnson's Mother, and the Containment of Maternal Difference." *The Age of Johnson: A Scholarly Annual* 5 (1992): 115–46.

———. *The Politics of Motherhood: British Writing and Culture, 1680–1760.* Cambridge: Cambridge University Press, 1996.

Bradley, Leslie. "An Inquiry into Seasonality in Baptisms, Marriages, and Burials. Part 2: Baptism Seasonality." In *Population Studies from Parish Registers,* edited by Michael Drake, 41–54. Great Britain: Open University, 1984.

Braudy, Leo. *Narrative Form in History and Fiction.* Princeton, NJ: Princeton University Press, 1970.

———. "Penetration and Impenetrability in *Clarissa,*" In *New Approaches to Eighteenth-Century Literature,* edited by ed. Phillip Harth, 177–206. New York: Columbia University Press, 1974.

Brown, Homer Obed. "*Tom Jones:* The Bastard of History." *Boundary 2* 7 (1979): 201–233.

Brown, Laura. *Ends of Empire: Women and Ideology in Early Eighteenth-Century English Literature.* Ithaca, NY: Cornell University Press, 1993.

Brown, Martha G. "Fanny Burney's 'Feminism': Gender or Genre?" Reprinted in Frances Burney, *Evelina,* edited by Stewart J. Cooke, 394–400. New York: W. W. Norton, 1998.

Butler, Marilyn. *Maria Edgeworth: A Literary Biography.* Oxford: Clarendon Press, 1972.

Campbell, Jill. "'The Exact Picture of his Mother': Recognizing Joseph Andrews." *ELH* 55, no. 3 (Autumn 1988): 643–64.

Canfield, J. Douglas. "Shifting Tropes of Ideology in English Serious Drama, Late Stuart to Early Georgian." In *Cultural Readings of Restoration and Eighteenth-Century English Theater,* edited by J. Douglas Canfield and Deborah C. Payne, 195–228 . Athens: University of Georgia Press.

Bibliography

Caskey, John Homer. *The Life and Works of Edward Moore.* New Haven, CT: Yale University Press, 1923.

Castle, Terry. *Clarissa's Ciphers: Meaning and Disruption in Richardson's "Clarissa".* Ithaca, NY: Cornell University Press, 1982.

———. *Masquerade and Civilization: The Carnivalesque in Eighteenth-Century English Culture and Fiction.* Stanford, CA: Stanford University Press, 1986.

———. "'Matters Not Fit to Be Mentioned': Fielding's *The Female Husband.*" Chapter 5 in *The Female Thermometer: Eighteenth-Century Culture and the Invention of the Uncanny,* 67–81. New York: Oxford University Press, 1995.

Cave, Terence. *Recognitions: A Study in Poetics.* Oxford: Clarendon Press, 1988.

Chaber, Lois A. "Matriarchal Mirror: Women and Capital in Moll Flanders." *PMLA* 97.2 (1982): 212–26.

———. "'This Affecting Subject': An 'Interested' Reading of Childbearing in Two Novels by Samuel Richardson." *Eighteenth-Century Fiction* 8, no. 2 (1996): 193–250.

Chandler, James. "Moving Accidents: The Emergence of Sentimental Probability." In *The Age of Cultural Revolutions, Britain and France, 1750–1820,* edited by Colin Jones and Dror Wahrman. Berkeley: University of California Press, 2002.

Chaplin, Susan. *Speaking of Dread: Law, Sensibility, and the Sublime in Eighteenth-Century Women's Fiction.* Aldershot: Ashgate, 2004.

Clark, Gilliam. *Correspondence of the Foundling Hospital Inspectors in Berkshire, 1757–68.* Berkshire Record Society, Vol. I, 1994.

Coale, Ansley J. "The Decline of Fertility in Europe since the Eighteenth Century as a Chapter in Demographic History." In *The Decline of Fertility in Europe,* edited by A. S. Coale, 1–30. Princeton, NJ: Princeton University Press, 1986.

Colley, Linda. *Britons: Forging the Nation 1707–1837.* New Haven, CT: Yale University Press, 1992.

Collins, R. G. "The Hidden Bastard: A Question of Illegitimacy in Smollett's *Peregrine Pickle.*" *PMLA* 94 (1979): 91–105.

Connely, Willard. *Sir Richard Steele.* New York: Charles Scribner's Sons, 1934.

Cook, Elizabeth Heckendorn. *Epistolary Bodies: Gender and Genre in the Eighteenth-Century Republic of Letters.* Stanford, CA: Stanford University Press, 1996.

Copeland, Edward. "Money." In *The Cambridge Companion to Jane Austen,* edited by Edward Copeland and Juliet McMaster, 131–48. Cambridge: Cambridge University Press, 1997.

Cutting-Gray, Joanne. *Woman as "Nobody" in the Novels of Fanny Burney.* Gainesville: University Press of Florida, 1992.

Damme, Catherine. "Infanticide: The Worth of an Infant Under Law." *Medical History* 22 (1978): 1–24.

Damrosh, Leopold, Jr. *God's Plots and Man's Stories: Studies in the Fictional Imagination from Milton to Fielding.* Chicago: University of Chicago Press, 1985.

Darby, Barbara. *Frances Burney Dramatist: Gender, Performance, and the Late-Eighteenth-Century Stage.* Lexington: University Press of Kentucky, 1997.

Davin, Anna. "Imperialism and Motherhood." *History Workshop* 5 (1978): 9–65.

Davis, Lennard J. *Factual Fictions: The Origins of the English Novel.* New York: Columbia University Press, 1983.

BIBLIOGRAPHY

Dickeman, Mildred. "Demographic Consequences of Infanticide in Man." *Annual Review of Ecology and Ecosystematics* 6 (1975): 107–37.

Dickinson, J. R., and J. A. Sharpe. "Infanticide in Early Modern England: The Court of Great Sessions at Chester, 1650–1800." In *Infanticide: Historical Perspectives on Child Murder and Concealment, 1550–2000*, edited by Mark Jackson, 35–51. Aldershot: Ashgate, 2002.

Dolan, Frances E. *Dangerous Familiars: Representations of Domestic Crime in England, 1550–1700*. Ithaca, NY: Cornell University Press, 1994.

Doody, Margaret Anne. "Beyond *Evelina:* The Individual Novel and the Community of Literature." *Eighteenth-Century Fiction* 3 (1991): 359–71. Reprinted in Frances Burney, *Evelina*, edited by Stewart J. Cooke, 474–86. New York: W. W. Norton, 1998.

———. *Frances Burney: The Life in the Works*. New Brunswick, NJ: Rutgers University Press, 1988.

———. "Jane Austen's Reading." In *The Jane Austen Companion*, edited by J. David Grey, 347–63. New York: Macmillan, 1986.

———. *A Natural Passion: A Study of the Novels of Samuel Richardson*. Oxford: Clarendon Press, 1974.

———. "Saying 'No,' Saying 'Yes': The Novels of Samuel Richardson." In *The First English Novelists: Essays in Understanding*, edited by J. M. Armistead, 67–108. Knoxville: University of Tennessee Press, 1985.

———. *The True Story of the Novel*. New Brunswick, NJ: Rutgers University Press, 1996.

Douglas, Aileen. *Uneasy Sensations: Smollett and the Body*. Chicago: University of Chicago Press, 1995.

Dupaquier, J., A. Fauve-Chamoux, and E. Grebenik, eds.) *Malthus Past and Present: International Conference on Historical Demography*. New York: Academic Press, 1983.

Durston, Gregory. *Moll Flanders: An Analysis of an Eighteenth Century Criminal Biography*. Chichester: Barry Rose Law Publishing Ltd, 1997.

Dwyer, June. *Jane Austen*. New York: Continuum, 1989.

Eagleton, Terry. *The Rape of Clarissa: Writing, Sexuality and Class Struggle in Samuel Richardson*. Oxford: Basil Blackwell, 1983.

Eaves, T. C. Duncan, and Ben D. Kimpel. *Samuel Richardson, A Biography*. Oxford: Clarendon Press, 1971.

———. "The Composition of Clarissa and Its Revision before Publication." *PMLA* 83 (May 1968): 416–28.

Ehmer, Josef. "Marriage." In *Family Life in the Long Nineteenth Century, 1789–1913*, edited by Daniel I. Kertzer and Marzio Barbagli, 282–321. New Haven, CT: Yale University Press, 2002.

Erickson, Robert A. *The Language of the Heart, 1600–1750*. Philadelphia: University of Pennsylvania Press, 1997.

———. "Moll's Fate: 'Mother Midnight' and *Moll Flanders*.," *Studies in Philology* 76, no. 1 (1979): 75–100.

———. *Mother Midnight: Birth, Sex, and Fate in Eighteenth-Century Fiction (Defoe, Richardson, and Sterne)*. New York: AMS Press, 1986.

Bibliography

Estrin, Barbara L. *The Raven and the Lark: Lost Children in Literature of the English Renaissance*. Lewisburg, PA: Bucknell University Press, 1985.
Faller, Lincoln B. *Crime and Defoe: A New Kind of Writing*. Cambridge: Cambridge University Press, 1993.
Fildes, Valerie. "Maternal Feelings Re-assessed: Child Abandonment and Neglect in London and Westminster, 1550–1800." In *Women as Mothers in Pre-Industrial England*, edited by Valerie Fildes, 139–78. New York: Routledge, 1992.
Findlay, Alison. *Illegitimate Power: Bastards in Renaissance Drama*. Manchester: Manchester University Press, 1995.
Fizer, Irene. "The Name of the Daughter: Identity and Incest in *Evelina*." In *Refiguring the Father: New Feminist Readings of Patriarchy*, edited by Beth Kowaleski-Wallace and Patricia Yaeger, 78–107. Carbondale: Southern Illinois University Press, 1989.
Flynn, Carol Houlihan. *The Body in Swift and Defoe*. Cambridge: Cambridge University Press, 1990.
Fogel, Robert W. *The Relevance of Malthus for the Study of Mortality Today: Long-run Influences on Health, Mortality, Labor Force Participation, and Population Growth*. Cambridge, MA: National Bureau of Economic Research, 1994.
Folkenflik, Robert. "Introduction." In *The English Hero, 1660–1800*, edited by Robert Folkenflik, 9–21. Newark: University of Delaware Press, 1982.
Foucault, Michel. *Madness and Civilization: A History of Insanity in the Age of Reason*. New York: Vintage Books, 1988.
Fraiman, Susan. "Getting Waylaid in *Evelina*." Reprinted in Frances Burney, *Evelina*, edited by Stewart J. Cooke, 454–74. New York: Norton, 1998.
Francus, Marilyn. "Monstrous Mothers, Monstrous Societies: Infanticide and the Rule of Law in Restoration and Eighteenth-Century England." *Eighteenth-Century Life* 21, no. 2 (May 1997): 133–56.
Freeman, Lisa A. *Character's Theater: Gender and Identity on the Eighteenth-Century English Stage*. Philadelphia: University of Pennsylvania Press, 2002.
Freud, Sigmund. *The Standard Edition of the Complete Psychological Works of Sigmund Freud*, vol. 9. Edited by James Strachey. New York: W. W. Norton, 2000.
Frye, Northrop. *Anatomy of Criticism*. Princeton, NJ: Princeton University Press, 1990.
Fuchs, Rachel G. "Charity and Welfare." In *Family Life in the Long Nineteenth Century, 1789–1913*, edited by Daniel I. Kertzer and Marzio Barbagli, 155–94. New Haven, CT: Yale University Press, 2002.
Gallagher, Catherine. *Nobody's Story: The Vanishing Acts of Women Writers in the Marketplace, 1670–1820*. Berkeley: University of California Press, 1994.
Geyer-Kordesch, Johanna. "Infanticide and the Erotic Plot: a Feminist Reading of Eighteenth-Century Crime." In *Infanticide: Historical Perspectives on Child Murder and Concealment, 1550–2000*, edited by Mark Jackson, 93–127. Aldershot: Ashgate, 2002.
Gillis, Christina Marsden. *The Paradox of Privacy: Epistolary Form in Clarissa*. Gainesville: University Press of Florida, 1979.
Gillis, John R. *For Better, For Worse: British Marriages, 1600 to the Present*. New York: Oxford University Press, 1985.

BIBLIOGRAPHY

Goodman, Dena. "Public Sphere and Private Life: Toward a Synthesis of Current Historiographical Approaches to the Old Regime." *History and Theory* 31, no. 1 (1992): 1–20.

Goux, Jean-Joseph. *Oedipus, Philosopher.* Translated by Catherine Porter. Stanford, CA: Stanford University Press, 1993.

Greenfield, Susan G. *Mothering Daughters: Novels and the Politics of the Family Romance. Frances Burney to Jane Austen.* Detroit: Wayne State University Press, 2002.

Gwilliam, Tassie. *Samuel Richardson's Fictions of Gender.* Stanford, CA: Stanford University Press, 1996.

Habakkuk, John. *Marriage, Debt, and the Estates System: English Landownership 1650–1950.* Oxford: Clarendon Press, 1994.

Habermas, Jürgen. *The Structural Transformation of the Public Sphere: An Inquiry into a Category of Bourgeois Society.* Translated by Thomas Burger. Cambridge, MA: MIT Press, 1989.

Hammond, Brean S. *Professional Imaginative Writing in England, 1670–1740.* Oxford: Clarendon Press, 1997.

Harris, Jocelyn. *Jane Austen's Art of Memory.* Cambridge: Cambridge University Press, 1989.

Hayami, Akira. "Illegitimacy in Japan." In *Bastardy and Its Comparative History,* edited by Peter Laslett, Karla Oosterveen, and Richard M. Smith, 397–402. Cambridge, MA: Harvard University Press, 1980.

Hemlow, Joyce. "The Composition of *Evelina.*" Reprinted in Frances Burney, *Evelina,* edited by Stewart J. Cooke, 372–94. New York: W. W. Norton, 1998.

Hill Christopher. "Clarissa Harlowe and Her Times." *Essays in Criticism* 5 (1955): 315–40.

Hoffer, Peter, and N. E. H. Hull. *Murdering Mothers: Infanticide in England and New England, 1558–1803.* New York: NYU Press, 1981.

Hollander, Samuel. *The Economics of Thomas Robert Malthus.* Toronto: University of Toronto Press, 1997.

Holmes, Richard. *Dr. Johnson and Mr. Savage.* New York: Pantheon Books, 1994.

Hopkins, Lisa. "Mr. Darcy's Body: Privileging the Female Gaze." In *Jane Austen in Hollywood,* edited by Linda Troost and Sayre Greenfield, 111–21. Lexington: University Press of Kentucky, 1998.

Hudson, P., and W. R. Lee, eds. *Women's Work and the Family Economy in Historical Perspective.* Manchester: Manchester University Press, 1990.

Hume, Robert D. "The Aims and Limits of Historical Scholarship." *The Review of English Studies* 53, no. 211 (2002): 399–422.

———. *Reconstructing Contexts: The Aims and Principles of Archaeo-Historicism.* New York: Oxford University Press, 1999.

Hunt Lynn. *The Family Romance of the French Revolution.* Berkeley: University of California Press, 1992.

Hunter, J. Paul. *Before Novels: The Cultural Contexts of Eighteenth-Century English Fiction.* New York: W. W. Norton, 1990.

———. "Fielding and the Disappearance of Heroes." In *The English Hero, 1660–1800,* edited by Robert Folkenflik, 116–42. Newark: University of Delaware Press, 1982.

Bibliography

Jackson, Mark. *New-Born Child Murder: Women, Illegitimacy and the Courts in Eighteenth-Century England.* Manchester: Manchester University Press, 1997.

———. "The Trial of Harriet Vooght: Continuity and change in the history of infanticide." In *Infanticide: Historical Perspectives on Child Murder and Concealment, 1550–2000,* edited by Mark Jackson, 1–17. Aldershot: Ashgate, 2002.

Johnson, Claudia L. "Austen Cults and Cultures." In *The Cambridge Companion to Jane Austen,* edited by Edward Copeland and Juliet McMaster, 211–26. Cambridge: Cambridge University Press, 1997.

———. *Jane Austen: Women, Politics, and the Novel.* Chicago: University of Chicago Press, 1988.

Kellum, Barbara. "Infanticide in England in the Later Middle Ages." *History of Childhood Quarterly* 1, no. 3 (1974): 367–88.

Kelsall, Malcolm. "Terence and Steele." In *The Eighteenth-Century British Stage,* edited by Kenneth Richards and Peter Thomson, 11–27. London: Methuen, 1972.

Kenny, Shirley Strum. "Richard Steele and the 'Pattern of Genteel Comedy.'" *Modern Philology* 70 (1972): 22–37.

Kibbie, Ann Louise. "Monstrous Generation: The Birth of Capital in Defoe's *Moll Flanders* and *Roxana.*" *PMLA* 110, no. 5 (October 1995): 1023–34.

Kinkead-Weekes, Mark. "Clarissa Restored?" *The Review of English Studies* 10, no. 38 (May 1959): 156–71.

Kirkham, Margaret. *Jane Austen: Feminism and Fiction.* Brighton: Harvester Press, 1983.

Kowaleski-Wallace, Elizabeth. *Hannah More, Maria Edgeworth, and Patriarchal Complicity.* New York: Oxford University Press, 1991.

Lamb, Jonathan. *Preserving the Self in the South Seas, 1680–1840.* Chicago: University of Chicago Press, 2001.

Langer, William. "Checks on Population Growth: 1750–1850." *Scientific American* 4 (1975): 93–99.

———. "Infanticide: A Historical Survey." *History of Childhood Quarterly* 1, no. 3 (1974): 353–66.

Laqueur, Thomas. "Bodies, Details, and the Humanitarian Narrative." In *The New Cultural History,* edited by Lynn Hunt, 176–204. Berkeley: University of California Press, 1989).

Laslett, Peter. "The bastardy-prone sub-society." In *Bastardy and Its Comparative History,* edited by Peter Laslett, Karla Oosterveen, and Richard M. Smith, 217–39. Cambridge, MA: Harvard University Press, 1980.

———. *Family Life and Illicit Love in Earlier Generations.* Cambridge: Cambridge University Press, 1977.

———. "Introduction: Comparing Illegitimacy Over Time and Between Cultures." In *Bastardy and Its Comparative History,* edited by Peter Laslett, Karla Oosterveen, and Richard M. Smith, 1–65. Cambridge, MA: Harvard University Press, 1980.

Laslett, Peter, Karla Oosterveen, and Richard M. Smith, eds. *Bastardy and Its Comparative History.* Cambridge, MA: Harvard University Press, 1980.

BIBLIOGRAPHY

Levine, David, and Keith Wrightson. "The Social Context of Illegitimacy in Early Modern England." In *Bastardy and Its Comparative History*, edited by Peter Laslett, Karla Oosterveen, and Richard M. Smith, 158–75. Cambridge, MA: Harvard University Press, 1980.

Lipking, Lawrence. *Samuel Johnson: The Life of an Author*. Cambridge, MA: Harvard University Press, 1998.

Loftis, John. "The Genesis of Steele's 'The Conscious Lovers.'" In *Essays Critical and Historical, Dedicated to Lily B. Campbell*, 173–82. New York: Russell and Russell, 1950.

———. *Steele at Drury Lane*. Berkeley: University of California Press, 1952.

London, April. *Women and Property in the Eighteenth-Century English Novel*. Cambridge: Cambridge University Press, 1999.

Lynch, Deidre Shauna. *The Economy of Character: Novels, Market Culture, and the Business of Inner Meaning*. Chicago: University of Chicago Press, 1998.

MacArthur, Elizabeth J. "Embodying the Public Sphere: Censorship and the Reading Subject in Beaumarchais's *Mariage de Figaro*." *Representations* 61 (1998): 57–77.

Macfarlane, Alan. "Illegitimacy and Illegitimates in English History." In *Bastardy and Its Comparative History*, edited by Peter Laslett, Karla Oosterveen, and Richard M. Smith, 71–85. Cambridge, MA: Harvard University Press, 1980.

MacLean, Marie. *The Name of the Mother: Writing Illegitimacy*. New York: Routledge, 1994.

Markley, Robert. "Recent Studies in Restoration and Eighteenth-Century Literature." *Studies in English Literature, 1500–1900* 37, no. 3 (Summer 1997): 637–72.

———. Email communication. Oct. 2, 2003.

Masciola, Amy L. "'The Unfortunate Maid Exemplified': Elizabeth Canning and Representations of Infanticide in Eighteenth-Century England." In *Infanticide: Historical Perspectives on Child Murder and Concealment, 1550–2000*, edited by Mark Jackson, 52–72. Aldershot: Ashgate, 2002.

May, Allison N. "'She at first denied it': Infanticide Trials at the Old Bailey." In *Criminal Justice in the Old World and the New: Essays in Honour of J. M. Beattie*, edited by Greg T. Smith, Allyson N. May, Simon Devereaux, 19–49. Toronto: Centre of Criminology, University of Toronto, 1998.

Mayer, Robert. *History and the Early English Novel: Matters of Fact from Bacon to Defoe*. Cambridge: Cambridge University Press, 1997.

McClure, Ruth K. "The Captain and the Children: Captain Thomas Coram, 1668–1751, and the London Foundling Hospital, 1739–1799." Ph.D. diss., Columbia University, 1975.

———. *Coram's Children: The London Foundling Hospital in the Eighteenth Century*. New Haven, CT: Yale University Press, 1981.

———. "Johnson's Criticism of the Foundling Hospital and Its Consequences." *The Review of English Studies* 27 (February 1976): 17–26.

McDonagh, Josephine. *Child Murder and British Culture, 1720–1900*. Cambridge: Cambridge University Press, 2003.

McDowell, Paula. *The Women of Grub Street: Press, Politics, and Gender in the London Literary Marketplace, 1678–1730*. Oxford: Clarendon Press, 1998.

Bibliography

McKeon, Michael. *The Origins of the English Novel, 1600–1740.* Baltimore: Johns Hopkins University Press, 1987.

McKillop, Alan Dugald. *Samuel Richardson: Printer and Novelist.* North Haven, CT: The Shoe String Press, 1960.

Meyer Cheryl L. and Michelle Oberman, with Kelly White, Michelle Rone, Priya Batra, and Tara C. Proano. *Mothers Who Kill Their Children: Understanding the Acts of Moms from Susan Smith to the "Prom Mom".* New York: NYU Press, 2001.

Michie, Allen. *Richardson and Fielding: The Dynamics of a Critical Rivalry.* Lewisburg, PA: Bucknell University Press, 1999.

Milhous, Judith, and Robert D. Hume. *Producible Interpretation: Eight English Plays, 1675–1707.* Carbondale: Southern Illinois University Press, 1985.

Miller, Nancy K. *The Heroine's Text: Readings in the French and English Novel, 1722–1782.* New York: Columbia University Press, 1980.

Mills, Dennis R. "The Christening Custom at Melbourn, Cambridgeshire." In *Population Studies from Parish Registers*, edited by Michael Drake, 16–40. Great Britain: Open University, 1984.

Morse, David. *The Age of Virtue: British Culture from the Restoration to Romanticism.* New York: St. Martin's Press, 2000.

Mudrick, Marvin. *Jane Austen: Irony as Defense and Discovery.* Princeton, NJ: Princeton University Press, 1952.

Neill, Edward. *The Politics of Jane Austen.* New York: Macmillan Press, 1999.

Nichols, R. N., and F. A. Wray. *The History of the Foundling Hospital.* Oxford: Oxford University Press, 1935.

Notestein, Frank. "Economic Problems of Population Change." In *Proceedings of the Eighth International Conference of Agricultural Economists*, 13–31. London: Oxford University Press, 1953.

Novak, Maximilian E. "Conscious Irony in *Moll Flanders*." *College English* 26, no. 3 (1964): 198–204.

———. *Defoe and the Nature of Man.* New York: Oxford University Press, 1963.

———. *Daniel Defoe: Master of Fictions; His Life and Ideas.* Oxford: Oxford University Press, 2001.

———. *Eighteenth-Century English Literature.* Frome, Somerset: The Macmillan Press, 1983.

———. "Some Notes Toward a History of Fictional Forms: From Aphra Behn to Daniel Defoe." *Novel: A Forum on Fiction* 6, no. 2 (Winter 1973): 120–33.

Nussbaum, Felicity A. "'Savage' Mothers: Narratives of Maternity in the Mid-Eighteenth Century." *Eighteenth-Century Life* 16 (February 1992): 163–84.

Ogden, Daniel. *Greek Bastardy in Classical and Hellenistic Periods.* Oxford: Clarendon Press, 1996.

Orr, Bridget. *Empire on the English Stage, 1660–1714.* Cambridge: Cambridge University Press, 2001.

Parker, Joe Alyson. *The Authors' Inheritance: Henry Fielding, Jane Austen, and the Establishment of the Novel.* DeKalb: Northern Illinois University Press, 1998.

Paulson, Ronald. *The Beautiful, Novel, and Strange: Aesthetic and Heterodoxy.* Baltimore: Johns Hopkins University Press, 1996.

———. *Hogarth: His Life, Art, and Times.* 2 vols. New Haven, CT: Yale University Press, 1971.

BIBLIOGRAPHY

———. "The Pilgrimage and the Family: Structure in the Novels of Fielding and Smollett." In *Tobias Smollett: Bicentennial Essays Presented to Lewis M. Knapp*, edited by G. S. Rousseau and P.-G. Bouce, 57–78. New York: Oxford University Press, 1971.

———. *Satire and the Novel in Eighteenth-Century England.* New Haven, CT: Yale University Press, 1967.

Paulson, Ronald. *Hogarth: His Life, Art, and Times.* New Haven, CT: Yale University Press, 1971, 2 vols.

Paulson, Ronald, and Thomas Lockwood, eds. *Henry Fielding: The Critical Heritage.* London: Routledge and Kegan Paul, 1969.

Perkin, Harold. *The Origins of Modern British Society, 1780–1800.* London: Routledge and Kegan Paul, 1972.

Perry, Ruth. "Colonizing the Breast: Sexuality and Maternity in Eighteenth-Century England." *Journal of the History of Sexuality* 2, no. 2 (1991): 204–234.

Pocock, J. G. A. *Virtue, Commerce, and History: Essays on Political Thought and History, Chiefly in the Eighteenth Century.* Cambridge: Cambridge University Press, 1985.

Pollak, Ellen. "Moll Flanders, Incest, and the Structure of Exchange." *The Eighteenth Century: Theory and Interpretation* 30.1 (1989):3–21.

Preston Thomas R. "Introduction," In Tobias Smollett, *The Expedition of Humphry Clinker,* edited by O. M. Brack, Jr.. Athens: University of Georgia Press, 1991.

Rabin, Dana. "Bodies of Evidence, States of Mind: Infanticide, Emotion and Sensibility in Eighteenth-Century England." In *Infanticide: Historical Perspectives on Child Murder and Concealment, 1550–2000,* edited by Mark Jackson, 73–92. Aldershot: Ashgate, 2002.

Racaut, Luc. "Accusations of Infanticide on the Eve of the French Wars of Religion." In *Infanticide: Historical Perspectives on Child Murder and Concealment, 1550–2000,* edited by Mark Jackson, 18–34. Aldershot: Ashgate, 2002.

Ramsey, Rachel. "'A mad intemperance . . . of building': The Literary Construction of Early Modern London." Ph.D. diss., West Virginia University, 2001.

———. Email communication. Oct. 16, 2002.

Rawson, Claude J. *Henry Fielding and the Augustan Ideal under Stress: "Nature's Dance of Death" and Other Studies.* London: Routledge and Kegan Paul, 1972.

Richetti, John J. *Defoe's Narratives: Situations and Structures.* Oxford: Clarendon University Press, 1975.

———. *The English Novel in History, 1700–1780.* New York: Routledge, 1998.

———. "Popular Narrative in the Early Eighteenth Century: Formats and Formulas." In *The First English Novelists: Essays in Understanding,* edited by J. M. Armistead, 3–40. Knoxville: University of Tennessee Press, 1985.

———. "The Portrayal of Women in Restoration and Eighteenth-Century English Literature." In *What Manner of Woman,* edited by Marlene Spriger, 65–97. New York: NYU Press, 1977.

———. "Richardson's Revisions in the Third Edition of *Clarissa:* For Better or Worse?" In *Approaches to Teaching Novels of Samuel Richardson,* edited by Lisa Zunshine and Jocelyn Harris. New York: Modern Language Association, forthcoming.

Bibliography

Rivero, Albert J. "Representing Clementina: 'Unnatural' Romance and the Ending of *Sir Charles Grandison*." In *New Essays on Samuel Richardson*, edited by Albert J. Rivero, 209–225. New York: St. Martin's Press, 1996.

Robert, Marthe. *Origins of the Novel*. Translated by Sacha Rabinovitch. Bloomington: Indiana University Press, 1980.

Rogers, Pat. "Introduction," In Daniel Defoe, *The Fortunes and Misfortunes of the Famous Moll Flanders*, edited by Pat Rogers, xv–xxxii. London: Everyman, 1993.

———. "Notes." In Daniel Defoe, *The Fortunes and Misfortunes of the Famous Moll Flanders*, edited by Pat Rogers, 273–87. London: Everyman, 1993.

Rosen, George. "A Slaughter of Innocents: Aspects of Child Health in the Eighteenth-Century City." *Studies in Eighteenth-Century Culture* 5 (1976): 293–316.

Ross, Ian Campbell. "'More to Avoid the Expense than the Shame': Infanticide in the Modest Proposer's Ireland." *Swift's Studies: The Annual of the Ehrenpreis Center* 1 (1986): 75–76.

Sabor, Peter. "'Staring in Astonishment': Portraits and Prints in Persuasion." In *Jane Austen's Business: Her World and Her Profession*, edited by Juliet McMaster and Bruce Stovel, 17–29. London: Macmillan, 1996.

Sampson, H. Grant. "Terence, Comic Patterns, and the Augustan Stage." In *All the World . . . : Drama Past and Present*, edited by Karelisa V. Hartigan, 85–92. Lanham, MD: University Press of America, 1983.

Schattschneider, Laura. "The Infant's Petitions: An English Poetics of Foundling Reception, 1741–1837." *Studies in Eighteenth-Century Culture* 33 (2004):71–99.

Schmidgen, Wolfram. "Illegitimacy and Social Observation: The Bastard in Eighteenth-Century Novel." *ELH* 69, no. 1 (2002): 133–66.

Schor, Hilary M. *Dickens and the Daughter of the House*. Cambridge: Cambridge University Press, 1999.

———. "Notes of a Libertine Daughter: *Clarissa*, Feminism, and the Rise of the Novel." *Stanford Humanities Review* 8, no. 1 (2000): 94–117.

Schwartz, Lita Linzer, and Nathalie K. Isser. *Endangered Children: Neonaticide, Infanticide, and Filicide*. Boca Raton, FL: CRC Press, 2000.

Seber, Barbara K. *General Consent in Jane Austen*. Montreal: McGill-Queen's University Press, 2000.

Setzer, Sharon. "Introduction." In *A Letter to the Women of England and The Natural Daughter*. Toronto: Broadview Press, 2003, 9–32.

Sharpe, J. A. *Crime in Early Modern England*. New York, Longman, 1999.

Sheridan, Frances. *The Memoirs of Miss Sidney Biddulph* (1761). Edited by Patricia Koster and Jean Coates Cleary. Oxford: Oxford University Press, 1999.

Shorter, Edward. "Illegitimacy, Sexual Revolution, and Social Change in Modern Europe." *Journal of Interdisciplinary History* 2, no. 2 (1971): 237–72.

Siskin, Clifford. *The Work of Writing: Literature and Social Change in Britain, 1700–1830*. Baltimore: Johns Hopkins University Press, 1998.

Solkin, David H. *Painting for Money: The Visual Arts and the Public Sphere in Eighteenth-Century England*. New Haven, CT: Yale University Press, 1993.

Sorensen, Janet. *The Grammar of Empire in Eighteenth-Century British Writing*. Cambridge: Cambridge University Press, 2000.

BIBLIOGRAPHY

Spacks, Patricia Meyer. *Desire and Truth: Functions of Plot in Eighteenth-Century English Novels.* Chicago: University of Chicago Press, 1990.

Starr, George A. *Defoe and Casuistry.* Princeton, NJ: Princeton University Press, 1971.

———. *Defoe: Spiritual Autobiography.* Princeton, NJ: Princeton University Press, 1965.

Staves, Susan. *Married Women's Separate Property in England, 1660–1833.* Cambridge, MA: Harvard University Press, 1990.

———. "Resentment or Resignation? Dividing the Spoils among Daughters and Younger Sons." In *Early Modern Conceptions of Property*, edited by John Brewer and Susan Staves, 194–218. London and New York: Routledge, 1995.

Stone, Lawrence. *The Family, Sex and Marriage in England, 1500–1800.* London: Methuen, 1985.

———. *The Road to Divorce: England, 1530–1987.* Oxford: Oxford University Press, 1990.

Straub, Kristina. *Divided Fictions: Fanny Burney and Feminine Strategy.* Lexington: University Press of Kentucky, 1987.

Symonds, Deborah A. *Weep Not for Me: Women, Ballads, and Infanticide in Early Modern Scotland.* University Park: Pennsylvania State University Press, 1997.

Teichman, Jenny. *Illegitimacy: An Examination of Bastardy.* Ithaca, NY: Cornell University Press, 1982.

Thompson, Helen. "Evelina's Two Publics." *The Eighteenth Century: Theory and Interpretation* 39, no. 2 (1998): 147–67.

Thompson, James. *Between Self and World: The Novels of Jane Austen.* University Park: Pennsylvania State University Press, 1988.

———. *Models of Virtue: Eighteenth-Century Political Economy and the Novel.* Durham, NC: Duke University Press, 1998.

———. "Sure I have seen that face before": Representation and Value in Eighteenth-Century Drama." In *Cultural Readings of Restoration and Eighteenth-Century English Theater*, edited by J. Douglas Canfield and Deborah C. Payne, 281–308. Athens: University of Georgia Press.

Thorn, Jennifer. "Introduction: Stories of Child-Murder, Stories of Print." In *Writing British Infanticide: Child Murder and Narrative, 1664–1876*, edited by Jennifer Thorn, 13–41. Newark: University of Delaware Press, 2003.

Thornton, James L., "Introduction." In *Humphry Clinker: An Authoritative Text, Contemporary Responses, Criticism*, edited by James L. Thornton, 7–30. New York and London: Norton, 1983.

Todd, Janet. *Feminist Literary History.* New York: Routledge, 1988.

Travitsky, Betty S. "Child Murder in English Renaissance Life and Drama." *Medieval and Renaissance Drama in England* 6 (1993): 63–84.

Trumbach, Randolph. *Sex and Gender Revolution. Volume One: Heterosexuality and the Third Gender in Enlightenment London.* Chicago: University of Chicago Press, 1998.

Twinam, Ann. *Public Lives, Private Secrets: Gender, Honor, Sexuality, and Illegitimacy in Colonial Spanish America.* Stanford, CA: Stanford University Press, 2001.

Udden, Anna. "Veils of Irony: The Development of Narrative Technique in Women's Novels of the 1790s." Ph.D. diss., University of Uppsala, 2000.

Bibliography

Van Boheemen Christine. *The Novel as Family Romance: Language, Gender, and Authority from Fielding to Joyce.* Ithaca, NY: Cornell University Press, 1987.
Van Marter, Shirley. "Richardson's Revisions of *Clarissa* in the Third and Fourth Editions." *Studies in Bibliography* 28 (1975): 119–52.
Vermillion, Mary. "Capricious Testators and Marriageable Women: Last Wills in Eighteenth-Century Novels." Ph.D. diss., University of Iowa, 1993.
Vermeule, Blakey. *The Party of Humanity: Writing Moral Psychology in Eighteenth-Century Britain.* Baltimore: Johns Hopkins University Press, 2000.
Viazzo, Pier Paolo. "Mortality, Fertility, and Family." In *The History of European Family, Volume One, Family Life in Early Modern Times, 1500–1789,* edited by David I. Kertzer and Marzio Barbagli, 157–87. New Haven, CT: Yale University Press, 2001.
Vom Saal, Frederick S. "The Role of Social, Religious, and Medical Practices in the Neglect, Abuse, Abandonment, and Killing of Infants." In *Infanticide and Parental Care,* edited by Stefano Parmigiani and Frederick S. Saal, 43–71. Langhorne, PA: Harwood Academic Publishers, 1994.Walker, Nigel. *Crime and Insanity in England: Vol. I, The Historical Perspective.* Edinburgh: Edinburgh University Press, 1968.
Ware, Michele S. "'True Legitimacy': The Myth of the Foundling in *Bleak House.*" *Studies in the Novel* 22, no. 1 (Spring 1990):1–9.
Warner, William B. *Licensing Entertainment: The Elevation of Novel Reading in Britain, 1684–1750.* Berkeley: University of California Press, 1998.
———. *Reading Clarissa: The Struggles of Interpretation.* New Haven, CT: Yale University Press, 1979.
Watt, Ian. *The Rise of the Novel.* Berkeley: University of California Press, 1957.
Watt, Jeffrey R. "The Impact of the Reformation and Counter-Reformation." In *The History of European Family, Volume One, Family Life in Early Modern Times, 1500–1789,* edited by David I. Kertzer and Marzio Barbagli, 124–54. New Haven, CT: Yale University Press, 2001.
Weinbrot, Howard. *Britannia's Issue: The Rise of British Literature from Dryden to Ossian.* Cambridge: Cambridge University Press, 1993.
Williams, Raymond. *The Long Revolution.* London: Chatto and Windus, 1961.
Wilson, Edmund. "A Long Talk about Jane Austen." *The New Yorker* 20 (June 24, 1944.
Womersley, David, ed. *Restoration Drama: An Anthology.* Oxford: Blackwell, 2000.
Wordsworth, Jonathan. "Introduction." In August.to Von Kotzebue, *Lover's Vows.* Adapted by Elizabeth Inchbald [1798]. Oxford: Woodstock Books, 1990.
Wright, Andrew. *Henry Fielding: Mask and Feast.* Berkeley: University of California Press, 1975.
Wrightson, Keith. "Infanticide in Earlier Seventeenth-Century England." *Local Population Studies* 15 (1975): 10–21.
———. "Infanticide in European History." *Criminal Justice History* 3, no. 1 (1982): 1–20.
———. "The Nadir of English Illegitimacy in the Seventeenth Century." In *Bastardy and Its Comparative History,* edited by Peter Laslett, Karla Oosterveen, and Richard M. Smith, 176–91. Cambridge, MA: Harvard University Press, 1980.

BIBLIOGRAPHY

Yeazell, Ruth Bernard. *Fictions of Modesty: Women and Courtship in the English Novel.* Chicago: University of Chicago Press, 1991.

Zimmerman, Everett. *The Boundaries of Fiction: History and the Eighteenth-Century British Novel.* Ithaca, NY: Cornell University Press, 1996.

———. *Defoe and the Novel.* Berkeley: University of California Press, 1975.

Zomchick, John P. *Family and the Law in Eighteenth-Century Fiction: The Public Conscience in the Private Sphere.* Cambridge: Cambridge University Press, 1993.

Index

abandonment of children, 178n18, 192n20; of legitimate children vs. illegitimate children, 107, 174n15, 178n20; in urban vs. rural areas, 178n20; in antiquity and Renaissance, 6; in eighteenth-century England, 29; and French Revolution, 15; and the theme of incest, 185n61. *See also* exposure of unwanted infants; child murder; infanticide

Adair, Richard, 174n15, 180n6, 184n34, 192n20, 194n59

Addison, Joseph, 31, 41, 45, 46–48, 50, 51

adoption: informal social networks of, 29

Agnew, Jean-Christophe, 83

Albert, Theodore, 81, 186n3

Alkon, Paul, 185n49

Allen, Ralph, 191n32

Alryyes, Ala A., 15–16, 185n53

Alter, Robert, 189n2

Amberg, Anthony, 71, 186n9

Andrew, Donna, 112, 113, 177n17, 191n10

Armstrong, Nancy, 114, 193n44

Austen, Jane: *Emma*, 9, 21, 152–67; *Mansfield Park*, 9; *Sense and Sensibility*, 9, 59, 155–56, 163, 165

Backsheider, Paula, 180n2

Bage, Robert: *Hermsprong; or, Man As He Is Not*, 8, 127

Bakhtin, Mikhail, 29

Barbauld, Anna Laetitia, 70

Barker-Benfield, G. J., 175n52

Barrell, John, 186n2

bastard characters: and progressive ideology, 15, 20, 21, 34, 92, 100, 162–64, 166; and literary self-marketing, 89; as literary "blank slates," 95; as religious visionaries, 89–90; as talented actors, 91, 190n19; and stereotypes of excess, 87, 88–89; compared to orphan characters, 15; contrasted to foundling characters, 7, 93–95, 108, 198n32; evolution of their fictional representation, 19–20, 86–87, 164–67; and the fictional chronicles of political upheavals, 94–95, 191n29, 191n30; in *Colonel Jack* (Defoe), 58–59; in *Moll Flanders* (Defoe), 57–63; in *Clarissa* (Richardson), 79–83; in *Tom Jones* (Fielding), 86–100; in "The Bastard" (Savage), 87–89; in *King Lear* and *Cymbeline* (Shakespeare), 88; in *King John* (Shakespeare), 94; in *Humphry Clinker* (Smollett), 89–90; in *Peregrine Pickle* (Smollett), 90–92; in *The Fortunate Foundlings* (Haywood), 94; in *Life and Death of Jack Straw* (Anon.), 94; in *Claudius Tiberius Nero* (Anon.), 94; in *History of Sir Charles Grandison* (Richardson), 120–24; in *Evelina* (Burney), 133, 143, 147; in

INDEX

Emmeline (Smith), 148–49; in *The Beggar Girl and Her Benefactors* (Bennett), 149; in *Sense and Sensibility* (Austen), 155–56; in *Emma* (Austen), 159, 162–65, 166–67; spectrum of in the eighteenth-century fiction, 87–92; and the novels named after them, 93; and the discourse of "innocence," 129, 132, 141–45; twentieth-century revisions of, 169–72
Bastardella, La (La Signora Agujari), 141
bastardy: definition of, 2, 189n4; laws concerning, 2, 42; multiple meanings of the term, 6; hypothesis of "bastardy-prone sub-society," 156; Catholic vs. Protestant treatment of, 181n9, 184n35. *See also* illegitimacy; family
Battestin, Martin, 191n32
Baudelaire, Charles, 89
Beasley, Jerry, 189n15, 194n68, 194n69
Becon, Thomas, 181n10
Bedford (4th Duke of), John Russell, 54, 113
Behn, Aphra, 136
Bender, John, 180n2
Benedict, Barbara, 184n38
"benefit-of-linen" defense, 119–20. *See also* infanticide
Bennett, Agnes Maria: *The Beggar Girl and Her Benefactors*, 7, 8, 9, 13, 59, 99–100, 137, 157, 162, 163
Berlant, Lauren, 15–16
Bhattacharya, Nandini, 179n42
Binion, Rudolph, 183n29
Blackstone, William: *Commentaries on the Laws of England*, 2, 60, 131
Bonfield, Lloyd, 174n25, 194n59
Booth, Wayne, 156
Boswell, John, 6, 29, 178n19
Bowers, Toni O'Shaughnessy, 28, 57, 178n23, 189n10
Bradshaigh, Lady, 70
Braudy, Leo, 187n19, 191n28
Bray, Thomas, 5, 29, 41, 47, 50, 51
Brocklesby, Richard, 113
Brome, Richard, *A Jovial Crew*, 18, 175n54
Brontë, Emily, *Wuthering Heights*, 167
Brown, Homer Obed, 190n27, 199n3
Brown, Laura, 174n31, 176n4
Brownlow, John, 45, 113
Brown, Martha, 145, 146, 150, 175n32
Burney, Charles, 21, 113; and his plan for turning the Foundling Hospital into a public school of music, 128–31, 142, 148
Burney, Frances, 59, 111; and her father's plan for turning the Foundling Hospital into a public school of music, 128–31; *Cecilia*, 197n6; *Evelina*, 3, 7, 8, 15, 100, 127–51, 154, 157, 163, 193n43; *Memoirs of Doctor Burney*, 128–30, 148; *The Woman-Hater*, 196n31
Burn, Richard, *Ecclesiastical Law*, 180n6
Butler, Marilyn, 161

Cadogan, William, 113
Campbell, Jill, 190n19
Canfield, J. Douglas, 33
Caskey, John Homer, 186n7, 186n8
Castle, Terry, 87, 189n7
Cave, Terence, 179n46
Chaber, Lois A., 119–20, 123, 185n55
Chandler, James, 188n32
Chaplin, Susan, 182n23
charity, and religion, 193n50. *See also* female philanthropy; London Foundling Hospital
Charles XII (of Sweden), 94
child murder: sermons condemning, 42; laws designed to prevent, 42; and the image of infanticidal mother, 56–57, 178n23, 182n23. *See also* abandonment of children; exposure of unwanted infants; infanticide
children, illegitimate: demonizing of, 141–42, 164, 170–71; and the discourse of "innocence," 124, 129, 141–44. *See also* illegitimacy; bastardy
Cibber, Colley, 33, 69; *Love's Last Shift*, 24

INDEX

Clark, Gillian, 54
Claudius Tiberius Nero (Anon.), 94
Clifford, James, 196n27
Colley, Linda, 191n10
Collier, Jeremy: *A Short View of the Immorality and Profaneness of the English Stage*, 25, 27, 176n11
Collins, R. G., 90
Colman, George (the Elder): *The English Merchant*, 7, 66, 84–85
Connely, Willard, 31
Coram, Thomas, 4, 41, 48, 98–99, 103, 110, 112, 113
"courtship pregnancy," 170; in BBC's *Tom Jones*, 169–70
Cradock, Charlotte, 17
Crisp, Samuel, 141
Cutting-Gray, Joanne, 131

Dacier, André: his critique of recognition plots, 37
Darby, Barbara, 196n31
Davis, Lennard, 190n27
Day, Thomas, 161
Defoe, Daniel: *Augusta Triumphans*, 183n28; *Colonel Jack*, 8, 16, 58–59, 93; *The Generous Projector*, 41, 45, 47–48; *Moll Flanders*, 8, 16, 39, 40–63, 66, 85, 93; *Roxana*, 8; *Robinson Crusoe*, 16; *Tour thro' Great Britain*, 51
De Nevral, Gerard, 89
Dennis, John, 23, 31; his critique of *The Conscious Lovers*, 36–37
Derrida, Jacques, 89
Dickens, Charles, *Bleak House*, 167
Dickinson, J. R., 181n11, 182n20, 183n33
Dodd, Juliana, 111, 113, 128
Dolan, Frances, 178n23
Doody, Margaret Anne, 14–15, 131, 145, 146, 150, 175n32, 187n20, 188n25, 196n31
Douglas, Aileen, 90–91
Durston, Gregory, 180n2, 184n38
Dryden, John: *An Evening's Love*, 26, 30; *Amphitryon*, 176n8, *Oedipus* (with Nathanel Lee), 66, 76

Eagleton, Terry, 188n27
Eaves, T. C., and Ben D. Kimpel, 186n10, 188n23
Echard, Laurence, 25, 26, 29–30, 177n12
Edgeworth, Maria, 59; *Belinda*, 7, 93, 153, 161–62
Ehmer, Josef, 173n3, 178n20, 198n27
Erickson, Robert A., 184n38, 184n42
exposure of unwanted infants: in Terence's *Andria*, 28; in ancient Rome, 28–29; in England, 28; and the late-seventeenth-century tradition of representing "Roman customs and manners," 26, 177n16; references to in *Clarissa* (Richardson), 72. *See also* abandonment of children; infanticide; child murder

Faller, Lincoln, 185n58
family: responses to illegitimacy, 1; relationship between the legitimate and illegitimate siblings, 2; as threatened by illegitimate pretenders to its property, 123–24, 166–67
Farquhar, George: *The Recruiting Officer*, 24
Fatherless Fanny (Anon.), 7, 153, 158, 159, 162, 163
female bastards: and the eighteenth-century marriage market,14, 34, 134–35; possibility of economic independence of, 165; in fiction, 9, 59; and "polite" fictional discourse, 140–41; obligatory transformation into foundlings in eighteenth-century fiction, 35, 40–41, 59, 83–84, 153, 157–58, 166–67; ambiguous representations of in *Moll Flanders*, 57-63; in *Tom Jones* (Fielding), 86, 96–97, 157; in *Peregrine Pickle* (Smollett), 117, 139–40; and treatment of Clarissa by her family, 78–79; in *The Fortunate Foundlings* (Haywood), 136–37; in *The Beggar Girl and Her Benefactors*

INDEX

(Bennett), 13, 149; in *Emma* (Austen), 153–61; in *Sense and Sensibility* (Austen), 155–56; in *The Victim of Prejudice* (Hays), 155, 156; in *Bleak House* (Dickens), 167; in *Mrs. Warren's Profession* (Shaw), 165–66

female foundlings in fiction: 7, 33; and increase in the number of female protagonists in eighteenth-century fiction, 12, 174n31; and social class, 133–40, 143–46; relationship between their class and gender, 139; the plot of "divided bastardy," 142–47, 148–51; the tradition of correlating the chastity of daughters with the chastity of their mothers, 13, 96–97, 155, 156; the discourse of "fate," 61–61, 76–77; the discourse of "innocence," 142–43, 150, 186n65; the theme of incest, 84, 146; their tendency to receive advantageous marriage proposals prior to finding their biological parents, 34, 146–47; their tendency to have fathers who support lost political causes, 84–85; in the novel of antiquity, 145–46, 151; in Renaissance drama, 12; and *Moll Flanders* (Defoe), 57–63; and *Clarissa* (Richardson), 74–77; and *The Foundling* (Moore), 84–85; and *The English Merchant* (Colman), 84–85; and *Evelina* (Burney), 145–48; and *Emmeline* (Smith), 148–49, 150–51; and *The Beggar Girl and Her Benefactors* (Bennett), 149–51

female philanthropy, 110–15; in *Peregrine Pickle* (Smollett), 116–18; in *History of Sir Charles Grandison* (Richardson), 124–25, 194n71. *See also* infanticide prevention campaign; London Foundling Hospital

Fielding, Henry, 113; *The Champion*, 191n34, *The Covent Garden Journal*, 191n9, 194n72; *Jonathan Wild*, 4, 8; *Joseph Andrews*, 92, 136, 166, 190n20; *Tom Jones*, 8, 16, 17, 86–100, 127, 154, 157; *Tom Jones* (BBC's 1998 production), 169–72; and Moore, 68–69, 71, 186n15, 187n17

Fielding, Sarah: *The History of the Countess of Dellwyn*, 9

Fildes, Valerie, 174n15, 192n20

filius nullius (the son of nobody), rhetoric of: in legal discourse, 2; in *Evelina* (Burney), 131; in *Tom Jones* (Fielding), 127; in *The Rehearsal* (Villiers), 127; in *Hermsprong* (Bage), 127; in *The Deserted Daughter* (Holcroft), 133; in *The Fortunate Foundlings* (Haywood), 133; in *Emma* (Austen), 157. *See also* illegitimacy; bastardy; bastard characters

Findlay, Alison, 12

Fizer, Irene, 132, 196n29

Flynn, Carol, 184n49

Folkenflik, Robert, 176n2

Foucault, Michel, 105

foundling narrative: conventions of, 14, 16, 36–38; in *Moll Flanders*, 42, 59–60; in *Clarissa* (Richardson), 74–77; in *Tom Jones* (Fielding), 94, 190n24; in *Evelina* (Burney), 145–47; parody of in *An Ethiopian Romance* (Heliodorus), 38, 59; in *Oedipus Rex* (Sophocles), 39; in *Emma* (Austen), 154–55, 159; as a compensatory fantasy for a culture troubled by its treatment of bastards, 147, 154–55, 164

foundlings: in fiction 1, 6–7, 190n20; symbolic meaning of, 14–17; gender of in fiction, 7–14; tokens used to establish their identity in fictional narratives, 35, 195n13; and the fictional chronicles of political upheavals, 94–95, 191n30; in everyday discourse, 6; inmates of the London Foundling Hospital; definition of as opposed to bastards, 6–7. *See also* female foundlings; bastard characters

Francus, Marilyn, 178n23, 180n5, 183n32, 184n52

Freeman, Lisa, 23, 24, 174–75n31,

INDEX

188n34
Fuchs, Rachel, 193n49, 193n50

Gallagher, Catherine, 131
Garrick, David, 69, 70
Gillis, John, 173n3
Goethe, Johann Wolfgang von, *Faust*, 196n24
Goodman, Dena, 115
Goux, Jean-Joseph: *Oedipus, Philosopher*, 39
Gray, Thomas, 140
Greenfield, Susan, 131, 156, 159, 175n32, 198n22

Habakkuk, John, 4, 134, 194n63, 196n154
Habermas, Jürgen, 46, 104, 114–15
Hamilton, Jenny, 71, 187n15
Handel, George, 113
Hanway, Jonas, 113, 128, 160
Hardwicke Act, 9. *See also* Marriage Act
Harris, Jocelyn, 197n5
Hayami, Akira, 175n46
Hayman, Francis: *The Finding of the Infant Moses in the Bullrushes*, 106–7
Hays, Mary: *Memoirs of Emma Courtney*, 9; *The Victim of Prejudice*, 21, 155, 156, 163
Haywood, Eliza: *The Fortunate Foundlings*, 9, 94, 100, 133, 136–37, 156; *Lasselia*, 8
Heliodorus: *An Ethiopian Romance*, 12–13, 14, 38, 59, 61, 94, 145, 151
Highmore, Joseph, 113
Hill, Aaron, 69, 70
Hill, Astraea and Minerva, 92–93, 95, 98
Hill, Christopher, 81, 186n2
Hoffer, Peter, and N. E. Hull, 180n5, 182n19, 193n52, 193n56
Hogarth, William: *Study for the Foundlings*, 43–45; *The March to Finchley*, 101–3, 113, 126
Holcroft, Thomas: *The Deserted Daughter*, 7, 133; *Hugh Trevor*, 8; *The Road to Ruin*, 8

"House of Orphans," 48, 50; as envisioned in Defoe's *Moll Flanders*, 50–51, 55, 62; and the control of female reproductive behavior, 55, 184n50
Hume, Robert, 176n8, 176n11, 179n28
Hunt, Lynn, 15, 175n35
Hunter, Paul, 185n54, 190n24, 191n29

illegitimacy: upsurge of in the eighteenth century, 1; rates of, 173n3, 173n7, 178–79n27, 192n20, 198n27; definitions of, 2, 27, 180n48; in Victorian England, 181n8; in countries other than England, 173n9, 174n27, 175n46, 181n9; everyday responses to, 1; casual monitoring of, 141–42; punishment for, 180n6; and infant mortality, 174n16; among aristocracy, 3–4, 123, 132, 134–35, 138, 166, 173n10, 173n14; among agricultural laborers, 3; among middling classes, 2–3, 18–19, 131, 132, 133–40, 166; and the politics of succession, 173n14, 190n27; social institutions dealing with, 41, 52; as reflected in parish registers, 49; and baptism, 181n10; informal networks for dealing with, 52; and gender, 6–14, 155; and Marriage Act of 1753, 9–10; and the practice of "keeping" mistresses, 82, 120–25, 190n22; and the socioeconomic history of England, 18–19, 164–67; and the Industrial Revolution, 164; and property, 164–67; in the Old Testament, 13; in Renaissance drama, 12, 18; in novels of antiquity, 12; in ancient Greece and Rome, 27; eighteenth-century representations of, 6, 87–92; Freudian and Lacanian interpretations of, 16; and "polite" comedy, 25; and the eighteenth-century novel, 62–63, 65, 85, 89–92; and eighteenth-century drama, 62–63; genre-related differences in treatment of, 83–85; and twentieth-century

223

INDEX

representations of the eighteenth century, 169–72. *See also* bastardy; bastard characters; children, illegitimate; female bastards; female foundlings in fiction; foundlings; foundling narrative; property; inheritance; London Foundling Hospital

Inchbald, Elizabeth: *Nature and Art*, 8, 185n52; *Lovers' Vows*, 7–8, 177n16

infanticide: use of the term, 180n4; debates about the rates of, 177–78n18; "killer-nurses," 4, 28; and baptism, 42, 43, 182n13, 182n15, 182n16; and Christian social morality, 42; and social class, 120, 193n53, 194n24; methods of, 42–43; women accused of, 48–49, 193n53; men accused of, 183n33; triple case of in Colchester, 51–52; cases of in the courts of law, 45, 120, 180n5; trial transcripts, 185n54; legal response to in countries other than England, 181n7, 182n16, 182n26, 183n29; in Catholic vs. Protestant countries, 182n26; and "benefit-of-linen" defense, 119; and insanity defense, 185n54; as a Malthusian population check, 182n29; motivation for, 46; as a touchstone of English national self-definition, 47; as depicted in the press, 47–48; as depicted in broadsides, pamphlets, and ballads, 49, 183n32; and the novel, 56–57; "polite" way of speaking of, 47–50, 57, 62; in *Moll Flanders* (Defoe), 56, 184n52, 185n54; in *History of Sir Charles Grandison* (Richardson), 118–20. *See also* abandonment of children; child murder; infanticide prevention campaign

infanticide prevention campaign: traditional infanticide prevention measures, 42–43; and their perceived failure, 43–46; as initiated by the "people of England," 46–48; its rhetoric of "national interest" and "public good," 41, 47–48, 183n29; its relationship to informal networks of wet nurses, 54; and British national pride, 47; women's participation in, 103, 110–15, 118, 126; and *Moll Flanders* (Defoe), 40, 50–57, 62; and *Tom Jones* (Fielding), 99–100; and *The History of Sir Charles Grandison* (Richardson), 118–26. *See also* London Foundling Hospital

infant mortality, 174n15

inheritance, 2, 3, 164–65, 198n29; *inter vivos* settlements, 121; strict settlements, 122–23; *fee simple*, 122; breaking the entail, 122; in *The Conscious Lovers* (Steele), 34–35; in *Moll Flanders* (Defoe), 60; in *Clarissa* (Richardson), 64–65, 78–83, 198n28; in *The Foundling* (Moore), 186n7; in *Tom Jones* (Fielding), 99; in *The History of Sir Charles Grandison* (Richardson), 121–23; in *The Beggar Girl and Her Benefactors* (Bennett), 149, 150; in *Mrs. Warren's Profession* (Shaw), 165. *See also* property

Jackson, Mark, 180n4, 180n5, 181n7, 182n19, 193n52, 193n56
Jacobite Rebellion of 1745, 94–95, 190n27
Johnson, Claudia, 155–56, 197n5, 198n18
Johnson, Samuel: *Dictionary of the English Language*, 2; *Life of Savage*, 32, 179n38; and the London Foundling Hospital, 106, 128, 194n1
Joyful News to Batchelors and Maids (Anon.), 110

Kelsall, Malcolm, 177n13
Kenny, Shirley Strum, 176n7, 179n33
Knox, Bernard, 39
Kowaleski-Wallace, Elizabeth, 162

Lamb, Jonathan, 183n29
Langer, William, 174n18, 178n26, 182n18
Laqueur, Thomas, 178n23

INDEX

Laslett, Peter, 173n3, 174n15, 178n27, 194n59, 197n12

law: "Bill to remove the legal disabilities of children born out of wedlock" (1978), 19; National Council for the Unmarried Mother and Her Child, 175n53; Act of 1575, 42; Act of 1609, 42; "Fornication" Act of 1650, 42, 45; 1624 Jacobean Stature, 42, 180n5, 181n7; Lord Ellenborough's Act of 1803, 42; 1828 Offences against the Person Act, 181n7; Hardwicke's Marriage Act of 1753, 9–10; Poor Laws, 45–46, 181n8

legitimation of bastards in the works of fiction: in BBC's *Tom Jones*, 169–72

Lennox, Charlotte: *The Female Quixote*, 61

Life and Death of Jack Straw (Anon.), 94

Life of Mr. Richard Savage (Anon.), 32

Lipking, Lawrence, 179n37

Locke, John: *Second Treatise of Government*, 60

Loftis, John, 32

London, April, 81, 174n31

London Foundling Hospital, 2, 5, 19, 20, 45, 83, 98–99, 101–10, 124; petitions for establishing, 48; admission rules, 107; its reliance on established networks of wet nurses, 54; hymns sung by its charges, 5, 109, 135; as a sightseeing attraction, 107–8, 147; Charles Burney's plan for turning it into a public school of music, 128–31; its pointed openness to public scrutiny, 105–6, 109; the fears that it would encourage "irresponsibility and licentiousness," 55, 109–10, 111–12; women's participation in its establishment and governance, 103–4, 192n41; its views of the education of its young charges, 56, 109; social mobility of its charges, 56, 108–9, 160; religious education of its charges, 194n1; pictorial representations of, 51; its art exhibition, 105–8; its manipulation of the cultural categories of "bastard" and "foundling," 106–8, 148; as a "reality check" for late-eighteenth-century fiction writers, 160–62; and *Tom Jones* (Fielding), 99–100; and *The History of Sir Charles Grandison* (Richardson), 123–26; and *Evelina* (Burney), 131, 148; and *Emma* (Austen), 159–61, 162; in *Belinda* (Edgeworth), 161–62; and its appeal to the British sense of patriotism, 105; and the fears of depopulation, 191n10; its real-estate ventures, 159–60, 198n19

Lying-In Hospitals, 110, 112

Lynch, Deidre Shauna, 36

Lyttelton, George, 71, 186n15, 187n17

MacArthur, Elizabeth, 193n47

MacFarlane, Alan, 181n10, 184n39

MacLean, Marie, 89, 198n32

Magdalen House, 105, 112, 113, 115, 116, 123, 124, 125

Malthus, Thomas, *An Essay on the Principle of Population*, 183n29

Mandeville, Bernard, *The Fable of the Bees*, 5, 47, 56

Manley, Delariviere, 136

Marina (*Pericles*), 12

Markley, Robert, 38

Marriage Act of 1753, 9–10, 174n25. See also Hardwicke Act

Marshall, David, 83

Masciola, Amy, 184n50

May, Allison, 180n5, 183n31

Mayer, Robert, 180n2

McClure, Ruth, 3, 109, 111, 112, 134, 192n16, 192n17, 192n32

McDonagh, Josephine, 183n27

McDowell, Paula, 180n3, 193n47

McKeon, Michael, 15, 92, 100, 160

McKillop, Alan Dugald, 70, 186n13, 187n17, 188n22

Mead, Richard, 113

"Memoirs of a Lady of Quality" (in Smollett's *Peregrine Pickle*), 139–40

Michie, Allen, 190n23

INDEX

Milhous, Judith, 176n8
Miller, Nancy, 185n60, 186n64, 187n20
Montagu, Lady Mary Wortley, 74, 119, 140
Moore, Edward: *The Foundling*, 7, 15, 63, 65, 67–69, 73–74, 93, 99–100, 157; *The Gamester*, 69, 70; *The Trial of Selim the Persian*, 71
Morse, David, 186n65
motherhood, deviant, 56–57, 178n23, 182n23, 184n52, 185n55, 193n49; virtuous, 189n10, 194n71
Mudrick, Marvin, 163, 197n15

Nichols, R. N., and Wray, F.,A., 183n29, 184n48, 191n1, 191n2
Novak, Maximilian, 180n2, 185n53, 185n55, 189n15
Nussbaum, Felicity, 114, 189n10

Ogden, Daniel, 27–28, 175n46
Oldfield, Anne, 179n43
Opie, Amelia: *Adeline Mowbray*, 9
orphans: as traditionally viewed in the same category as bastards and foundlings, 15; and eighteenth-century nationalist narratives, 16
Orr, Bridget, 177n14
Ousley, Elizabeth, 14, 25, 31–34, 88. *See also* Savage; Steele

Paris Foundling Hospital (L'Hôpital des Enfants-Trouvés): evoked in *Moll Flanders*, 50; praised by Bray, 51, 112; viewed as a model for and a rival of the London Foundling Hospital, 51, 184n36
Parker, Joe Alison, 95, 176n55
Paulson, Ronald, 187n20, 190n27, 191n3
Perdita (*The Winter's Tale*), 12
Perry, Ruth, 114
Petty, William, 28, 51
Pickering, Danby, *Statutes at Large*, 181n7
Pocock, J. G. A., 17–18, 60
Pollak, Ellen, 185n55
Pope, Alexander, 92

Poyntz, Anna Maria, 110, 113
pregnancy, unwanted: concealment of 4, 42, 181n11; viewed as a responsibility of one parent vs. two parents, 49; "courtship pregnancy," 170. *See also* illegitimacy
property: transfer of, 3, 34; and illegitimacy, 17–20; its relationship with the foundling narrative, 35, 37–38; as a catalyst of social personality, 17–18; in *Moll Flanders* (Defoe), 60; in *The Conscious Lovers* (Steele), 34–35; in *Clarissa* (Richardson), 64–65, 77–78; in *The History of Sir Charles Grandison* (Richardson), 121–23; in *Evelina* (Burney), 146–47; in *Sense and Sensibility* (Austen), 156; in *Emma* (Austen), 165. *See also* inheritance

Rabin, Dana, 185n54, 193n52
Ramsey, Rachel, 109, 191n10, 192n12, 192n10, 196n1
Rawson, Claude, 91
Richardson, Samuel: *Clarissa*, 6, 8, 63, 64–85, 118, 121, 137–38, 142; *History of Sir Charles Grandison*, 6, 8, 19, 21, 83, 104, 118–26, 128, 163–64; *Pamela*, 9, 69, 75, 136; *Selected Letters*, 97, 186n11; and Fielding's *Tom Jones*, 17, 97; and the London Foundling Hospital, 83, 113, 123; and Moore, 69–71, 187n17; and Moore's *The Foundling*, 67, 71–75; and Smollett's "Memoirs of the Lady of Quality," 140
Richetti, John, 20, 57, 183n32, 185n56, 187n20
Rivero, Albert J., 188n25
Robert, Marthe, 16, 175n32
Robinson, Mary: *The Natural Daughter*, 6, 10–12
Rogers, Pat, 51
Rousseau, *Emile*, 161, 194n71
Ryan, William Burke, 43

Sabor, Peter, 197n5
Sampson, H. Grant, 177n13

226

INDEX

Sartre, Jean-Paul, 89, 167
Savage, Richard, 5, 14; and Elizabeth Ousley, 31–33; "Bastard," 21, 87–89; *Love in a Veil*, 31; *An Author To be Lett*, 32; and his pursuance of the Countess of Macclesfield, 31; and his relationship with Lord Tyrconnel, 32, 179n38
Scandalizade, The (Anon.), 110
Schattschneider, Laura, 180n47
Schmidgen, Wolfram, 15, 190n19
Schor, Hilary, 188n28, 198n33
Schwarz, Lita, and Nathalie Isser, 181n8
Shakespeare, William: *King Lear*, 88; *Cymbeline*, 88; *King John*, 94, 175n54
Sharpe, J. A., 181n11, 182n20, 183n33
Shaw, Bernard, *Mrs. Warren's Profession*, 165–66
Shebbeare, John: *The Marriage Act*, 9–10, 128
Sheridan, Frances: *The Memoirs of Miss Sidney Biddulph*, 8, 182n23
Shorter, Edward, 173n2
Siskin, Clifford, 154, 197n8
Sloane, Hans, 113
Smith, Charlotte, 59; *Emmeline*, 7, 8, 61, 100, 137, 163
Smollett, Tobias: *Humphrey Clinker*, 8, 89–90, 191n10; *Peregrine Pickle*, 8, 59, 79, 90–91, 100, 104, 115–18, 139–40, 163
Solkin, David, 105, 184n37, 191n10, 192n11
Sophocles: *Oedipus Rex*, 16, 39, 174n23
Spacks, Patricia Meyer, 195n15
Spence, Joseph, 69
Staves, Susan, 114–15, 173n11, 194n65
Steele, Richard: *The Conscious Lovers*, 6, 7; 23–39, 40, 61, 62, 65, 83, 93, 128, 166; and the tradition of "she-tragedy," 176n4; *The Funeral*, 37; *The Lying Lover*, 37; *The Tender Husband*, 37, 154; and his natural daughter, Elizabeth Ousley, 14, 25; his concept of "new comedy," 30–31, 33
Sterne, Laurence: *Tristram Shandy*, 1, 8, 39

Stone, Lawrence, 173n7
Straub, Kristina, 131
Swift, Jonathan, 92; *A Modest Proposal*, 47, 183n27
Symonds, Deborah, 178n23, 183n32

Teichman, Jenny, 175n46, 175n53, 189n4
Terence, 26, 35; and Restoration comedy, 30; and "new comedy," 30–31; *Andria*, 25, 26–27, 29, 65, 66–67, 128
Thompson, James, 33, 185n62, 190n24, 196n37, 197n6
Thorn, Jennifer, 178n23
Todd, Janet, 197n5
tokens: figuring in fictional foundling narratives, 36, 154; used in the London Foundling Hospital, 180n47
Travitsky, Betty, 178n23
Tristan, Flora, 89
Trumbach, Randolph, 4, 173n3
Twinam, Ann, 173n1

Van Boheemen, Christine, 16
Van Marter, Shirley, 187n21
Vansittart, Martha, 110, 111, 113
Vermeule, Blakey, 179n37
Viazzo, Pier Paolo, 174n27, 179n27
Villiers, George, 2nd Duke of Buckingham: *The Rehearsal*, 127
von Kotzebue, August: *Love Child*, 8, 177n16

Wale, Samuel: *A Perspective View of the Foundling Hospital with Emblematic Figures I*, 51
Walpole, Horace, 68, 72, 111, 113
Warner, William B., 71, 75, 136, 180n2, 184n43, 188n25
Warwick, Hannah, 48, 120
Watt, Ian, 190n27
Weinbrot, Howard, 177n14
wet nursing: as depicted in *Moll Flanders*, 51–55; as depicted in *The Beggar Girl and Her Benefactors*, 195n13; as constituting an earlier proto-professional organization of

women, 54; and the eighteenth-century non-formal economy, 184n34
Whitworth, Charles, 129
Williams, Raymond, 176n3
Wollstonecraft, Mary, 12
Wrightson, Keith, 29, 42, 180n6, 199n1

Wycherley, William (*The Plain Dealer*), 2; *The Country Wife*, 173n5

Yeazell, Ruth Bernard, 196n39

Zimmerman, Everett, 190n25
Zomchick, John, 81–82, 188n26

www.ingramcontent.com/pod-product-compliance
Lightning Source LLC
Chambersburg PA
CBHW030135240426
43672CB00005B/137